1994

The Total Marketing and Sales Plan

The Total Marketing and Sales Plan

Patrick D. O'Hara, PhD

John Wiley & Sons, Inc.

New York □ Chichester □ Brisbane □ Toronto □ Singapore

Library of Congress Cataloging-in-Publication Data
O'Hara, Patrick D.
    The total marketing and sales plan / by Patrick D.
O'Hara.
        p.   cm.
    Includes index.
    ISBN 0-471-57114-8 (book/disk set)
    1. Marketing.   2. Sales promotion.   I. Title.
  HF5415.044   1992   91-45830
658.8'02—dc20

Printed in the United States of America
10 9 8 7 6 5 4 3 2 1

Preface

This book is a sequel to the previous book "The Total Business Plan," which was written to explain the concept of writing general business plans for specific purposes.

The business plan is a brief document explaining the business, its mission, uniqueness, organization, and financial opportunity. The Marketing Plan is a highly researched supporting document to the business plan. It explains in great detail how the business is going to market and sell its product(s) or service(s). It is the collection and summary of inputs from other departments that critically affect the marketing effort, such as engineering and sales. In order to develop the plan it must first be determined if the proposed product is needed (desired) by the market; if, how, and in what quantities it can be sold; and if and how it can be produced in sufficient quantities at a cost that permits competitive pricing, and, above all, a profit. The Sales Plan is a major supporting document for the Marketing Plan.

Provided herein are full conceptual explanations of the marketing and sales planning processes, such as market planning, strategizing, research processes and sources, and pricing strategies. Also included are questionnaires and checklists for facilitating the market and sales planning process. Suggested marketing plan outlines and each sections' reasoning are included, with full knowledge that each plan is unique in its presentation and must be the creation of the marketing and sales teams specifically for the unique marketing and sales situation they are proposing. Again, I have made it as simple yet as thorough as I have found necessary in my own experience. And, I hope you find it helpful in your total planning process.

I sincerely want to thank my wife, Betty, for her special patience and encouragement in the writing of this book, since it was so close on the heels of the previous book and took additional time from our already limited hours together. And, again, a special thanks to Mr. Michael Hamilton and his "right hand assistant" Elena Paperny at John Wiley & Sons for their encouragement, advice, and assistance in getting this book to print.

Patrick D. O'Hara
Fremont, CA

v

Contents

Introduction

One of the greatest needs of managers of businesses is to understand and develop marketing programs for their products and services. Business success is based on the ability to build a growing body of satisfied customers. Modern marketing programs are built around the "marketing concept" and performance. This directs managers to focus their efforts on identifying, satisfying, and following up the customers' needs—*all at a profit*.

Marketing must be willing to provide the information and resources necessary for other units to fulfill their responsibilities in the organizational framework. In addition, marketing must rely on and appreciate direction from top management. After all, the marketing effort can hardly be effective if its goals and strategies do not mesh with the course charted by the chief executive and his closest advisers.

But, in the final analysis, marketing must lead the way. As Peter Drucker wrote in *Management: Tasks, Responsibilities and Practices*, "A business is not defined by the company's name, statutes, or articles of incorporation. It is defined by the want the customer satisfies when he buys a product or service. To satisfy the customer is the mission and purpose of every business."

What Is Marketing?

For many years, professionals and laypeople have equated marketing with sales. However, the field of marketing encompasses far more than just the act of selling. In fact, selling is but one of many areas that make up the discipline of marketing. But, keep in mind that selling is not marketing; it is a distinct discipline unit itself. The two disciplines should not be confused.

Marketing is a very broad concept. As defined by the American Management Association (AMA), it is "the process of planning and executing the conception, pricing, promotion, and distribution of ideas, goods, and services to create exchanges that satisfy individual or organization objectives." In lay terms, marketing involves everything that it takes to get a product off the drawing board and into the hands of the ultimate customer.

The concept of exchange is integral to marketing. Marketers use exchange as a means to satisfy needs and wants. Exchange is the process of trading something of value (e.g., money, time, or goods) to someone who voluntarily offers you something of value in return (e.g., ideas, goods, or services) that you want.

There are other methods of satisfying needs or wants that individuals or corporations can use if they desire. One method is to make something that satisfies their need or want; another is to steal what they need or want. However, when we discuss marketing, exchange is the heart of the process of satisfying needs and wants.

How Marketing and Sales Differ

We tend to use the term marketing interchangeably with the term sales and think of it as an activity of profit-making ventures. But it is not only businesses—for-profit organizations, that is—who market and must do so even to survive, let alone prosper. Most organizations, including nonprofit groups and even certain government agencies such as the U.S. Postal Service and the U.S. Federal Supply Service, now have marketing departments, whether so-called or not. Nor are the words marketing and customer always the terms used in describing the objectives of marketing—what it seeks to achieve or create—except perhaps allegorically. For example, marketing by military organizations (who often commission major advertising agencies to create campaigns for them) is called recruiting—attracting enlistees to the service. Marketing by associations means signing up new members, called membership drives. In organizations supported by grants or donations, marketing means gaining grantors and donors through fund drives. In politics it is called campaigning, winning both donors and voters to causes and candidates.

Marketing is itself a major industry in the United States. Although it is an integral and internal function of most organizations (most have at least one individual and larger organizations an entire department charged with the function), all require at least some assistance and services from suppliers, and many "contract out" for all or nearly all of their marketing needs. There are, therefore, many thousands of enterprises based solely on the provision of marketing supplies and services, supporting the marketing efforts of others, and often taking over the entire function for others. This includes many consultants, service firms, manufacturers, and suppliers who market to marketers. Marketing organizations make extensive use of computers, computer software, printing, mailing, and commercial advertising; sundry services, equipment, and manufacturing of items used as premiums; and supplies and services connected directly and indirectly with all the aforementioned. Also, there are several periodicals—from simple newsletters to expensive, slick magazines—dedicated to marketing.

To make a meaningful contribution to their companies' abilities to grow in unstable business environments, nonmarketing decision makers must have a broad, though not necessarily deep, knowledge of marketing techniques and trends. For example, they should know what the marketing manager means when discussing market "share," "niche," "segments," etc. They should know precisely who their customers are and, generally, how those customers are changing through modifications in the demographic picture—geographic, lifestyle, etc.

Surprisingly, however, many nonmarketing managers at all levels have a confused notion about what marketing really is. A common misconception is that marketing is synonymous with advertising. Not so. Advertising is only one part of the "marketing mix."

While it's true that in many smaller companies functions of both marketing and sales are combined or managed by one executive (vice president of marketing and sales), the two have distinct missions and goals. Both marketing and sales are concerned with customers but in different ways. *Marketing's purpose is to identify customers and serve their needs more effectively than the competition. Sales is concerned with getting the customer to buy, and its objective is to achieve increased volume.* Determining whether the product is appropriate and serves the needs of the target market is outside the function of the sales effort. Marketing, on the other hand, has a profit objective that it seeks to serve by ensuring that the company offers the right product to the right customer. *Sales is action oriented*, making optimum use of prevailing conditions in the marketplace. *Marketing is research and planning oriented*—seeking to understand how changes in the marketplace are affecting its customer base, and what changes in product or market target may be indicated to achieve desired profit objectives.

Finally, sales and marketing differ in how they view the competition. To sales, the competition's challenge is one of seeking superiority in selling and merchandising tactics. Sales also has an intelligence-gathering role in that it feeds back information about the competition to marketing and top management. But the strategy for achieving profit objectives through sales of products or services belongs to marketing. The marketing department uses market positioning, product innovation, pricing, research, and analysis to carve out the desired niche among a class of customers that will yield the highest possible rate of return on investment. Minimizing the competition's effect on the company's profit objectives is a by-product of the marketing strategy, a correlative consequence rather than a primary objective.

Marketing and Its Direct Relationship to Success

Probably no business or career activity is as closely related to the success of both organizations and individuals in organizations as is marketing. If the organization fails to manage its marketing successfully, superlative management in all other departments will avail the organization and the individuals little in the way of success.

More and more American executives are concluding that they can no longer "conduct business as usual." From the plush suites and boardrooms of America's largest corporations to the modestly furnished offices of small-company presidents, management teams are gathering to discuss new realities in the marketplace.

To be sure, the decision makers of most companies are not ready to press the panic button. But they are putting their employees on a high state of alert. The new-found concern with developments in the marketplace can be attributed to three basic factors:

1. Demographic and other structural shifts (the global marketplace concept).
2. The scramble by competitors to meet changing needs through new or revamped products and services.
3. Advancements in technology that speed both obsolescence of existing products and the means by which goods and services are created and transferred to the customer.

Since the marketing function bears primary responsibility for positioning the company in its efforts to deal with these challenges, it has assumed a top priority status in the eyes of chief executives, even to those who have a marketing director or a vice president specifically charged to oversee the organization's marketing strategy. This is not to say that top management treats finance, human resources, sales, technical support, and production as stepchildren in the corporate family. It does suggest that marketing decisions eventually have the greatest impact on the bottom line.

Consider, for example, the potential impact of one of the most critical decisions likely to confront a top executive—the launching of a new product. Before giving the green light, the CEO, in consultation with key managers and department heads, must assess the likely ramifications of the decision on each company function. Here are a few key questions that will figure into such assessments:

□ **Research and Development.** Is this the best possible product or service we can design at this time, given our resource base and longer-term objectives? Is it as good or better than the competition? Do we have the technical expertise to make modifications, if required? Do we have the means and capability to meet the servicing and technical support requirements of customers?

□ **Production.** Is production scheduling adequate to meet projected sales? Will we need to build new manufacturing facilities? Do we have the necessary equipment and maintenance procedures? Where will we find new sources of raw materials? How do we increase productivity of our plant workers?

□ **Finance.** Do we have the funds to support the marketing of a new product? Will we have to turn to external sources for the capital? How will the budget for other products be affected? What changes will we have to make in credit and collection procedures? At what point ahead in time can we expect to turn a profit from the new product? What contingency plans do we have in case our forecasts are off target?

□ **Personnel/Human Resources.** To what extent can we use existing staff to support the new product introduction? What jobs will we have to fill from outside recruiting? Is our personnel department equipped to handle a major new recruitment initiative? What will be our manpower needs should sales of the new product exceed our expectations? How will the creation of new jobs affect our salary structure, job descriptions, performance appraisal policy, etc.? What changes should we make in our sales and/or service and technical support compensation policies to garner support for the new product from our customer contact forces?

To help ensure the success of the new product—or, for that matter, any other crucial marketing decision—the top executive must create and sustain an atmosphere of cooperation between marketing and the other company functions. While it is natural, and sometimes even desirable, for department heads to promote the value of their spheres of influence, conflicts and political infighting will result if the CEO allows self-interest to govern. The better course is to stress to all concerned the key role of marketing in efforts to accomplish the short- and long-term success of the business.

Astute business managers have come around to the view that today's unstable business environment demands that they move beyond their limited areas of interest and expertise and assume a greater role in charting the future course of their companies. The new breed of manager is all too aware of the fact that, despite his or her personal contribution, the company may not survive unless it is equipped to anticipate and deal with change. The industry shakeouts of recent years in computers, video games, airlines, trucking, and banking, for example, and others yet to come, have underscored the point that today's booming business may be filing for bankruptcy tomorrow.

Increasingly, executives from all disciplines are turning nervously to the marketing department as the core of the company's plans for dealing with change. Consider, for example, the following scenarios:

□ The financial manager for a once-thriving shoe manufacturer is no longer content to merely "count beans." He goes about his daily tasks of managing cash flow, tightening collection practices because of slow-paying retailers, and appraising the company's budget. However, he is most concerned with declining profits. This manager knows that cost-cutting measures, while helpful, are not the solution. The real problem is that sales are lagging well behind forecasts. Why? And what will it take to turn things around? The financial manager, like other industry executives, had read that cheap foreign imports are flooding the market. He would like to see the firm's marketing department expand and conduct more market research. He believes that only by knowing the nature of the competition, and the marketing options and opportunities available, can the company know who should be buying its products.

□ The top engineer and research development manager for a growing computer company is proud of the fact that industry analysts rate the firm's latest entry in the crowded home computer field as "state-of-the-art." Despite the critical acclaim, the manager is not sure that the new model is catching on with consumers. Results for the first six months have not met top management's expectations. This person fears that the company may prematurely scuttle the product in favor of a new project now in the works. Why, he/she wonders, are consumers not getting the message? Are the company's advertising and promotion practices archaic? Are distribution policies faulty? Is the new model overpriced? Was the product introduced too late to meet seasonal consumer demand (in time for Christmas shopping or the start of the fall school semester, for example)? Though this manager likes the technical and innovative atmosphere promoted by the company through top management, he/she believes the company lacks an appreciation for marketing that could prevent it from maturing into a stable and well-balanced enterprise.

Appropriate to the above situation, marketing managers are not sure what to make of all the attention bestowed on them by their colleagues and associates. In one sense, they are pleased with occupying the center of the corporate stage and want the support of the entire executive team in helping to formulate realistic goals and strategies that will move their companies forward. In another sense, they may view with chagrin the encroachment on their territory by managers with theories, ideas, and possibly even policies based purely on subjective opinions and hypotheses. Nonetheless, it is a fact that the business challenges of the next decade make the marketing function too important to be left solely to marketing executives. The analog to this is that top executives who are responsible for the overall health of the company must know enough about the marketing function to make effective, composite decisions.

At the heart of the marketing function is the so-called "marketing concept" that holds "the customer is king." Companies that advocate this proposition are considered "marketing oriented." In their view, the key to profits lies in creating, marketing, and selling of products that satisfy customer needs.

The marketing concept rests on this importance of customers to a firm and states that all company policies and activities should be aimed at satisfying customer needs, and profitable sales volume is a better company goal than maximum sales volume.

To use the marketing concept, a business should:

1. Determine the needs of their customers (Market Research)
2. Analyze their competitive advantages (Market Strategy)
3. Select specific markets to serve (Target Marketing)
4. Determine how to satisfy those needs (Market Mix)

The marketing concept evolved from a production-oriented economy that prevailed during and after World War II. To overcome preexisting shortages and keep pace with demand for all kinds of consumer and industrial products, such as appliances, cars, television sets, rubber, and chemicals, companies geared up for mass production. In other words, satisfaction of consumer demand, however nondiscriminating, was the overriding concern. Few companies in the late 1940s and early 1950s took the trouble to find out what was happening in the marketplace or what the consumer truly needed or wanted. As a result, the market for many consumer and industrial goods became saturated. What's more, companies were finding that a product's life cycle—the time between its introduction, growth in sales, and decline—had dropped sharply from two decades to one decade, and today it is much less.

To stay in business, executives began building into their organizations the capability to develop new products more in line with the changing needs of the marketplace. The marketing concept was a strategy that stressed product development planning based on systematic studies of customer behavior, market testing before full-scale introductions, and continuous planning to meet the roadblocks and opportunities created by a fickle business environment.

The 1960s emerged as a period of increased domestic competition among companies and more selective buying behavior by consumers. To meet these challenges, companies began to develop sophisticated advertising and promotion techniques. Automobile manufacturers, for instance, had to convince consumers that what they wanted was a Chevrolet or a Ford, not simply "a car."

Economic and political uncertainty—characterized by on-again and off-again rounds of inflation and recession, and the upheaval in the Middle East that resulted in the traumatic energy shortages—created a new marketing environment in the decade of the 1970s. The wholesale shifts in political, economic, and social trends upset the marketing concept's infatuation with the customer. The business community, rocked by its failure to anticipate the enormous impact of outside influences, embraced strategic and long-term planning as the key to its salvation. Companies learned that they could still be marketing oriented but, in most cases, would have to sacrifice short-term profit for long-term growth.

The specter of foreign competition that surfaced abruptly when fuel-concious Americans gave up their love affair with luxury cars and embraced Toyotas, Datsuns, and Hondas, became the major problem for domestic companies in the late 1970s and early 1980s. The fact that Japanese and other foreign companies could produce goods of better quality, that met the customer's perceived needs and desires more cheaply than their U.S. counterparts, set off a wave of criticism leveled at the marketing concept. The charge was that, for far too long, American companies put too much emphasis on luring the consumer and not enough emphasis on product innovation, thereby sacrificing quality. According to one critic, "the marketing concept has diverted our attention from the product and its manufacture; instead we have focused our strategy on responses to market wants and have become preoccupied with advertising, selling and promotion techniques. In the process, product value has suffered."

Advocates of the marketing concept concede that, since consumers don't always know what they want, they represent an unreliable source of new product ideas. Yet, they argue, to downplay consumer wants and expectations is to invite disaster. It is one thing to create an innovative product, it is quite another to find the people who will buy it.

Marketing and Strategic Planning

Far from outliving its usefulness, strategic planning is still the guiding philosophy of conducting business today. However, strategic planning has also undergone a change. During the 1970s, when inflation kept profits up, marketing was not a priority. Corporate strategies centered on acquisitions, cash management, or overseas expansion.

The recession of the early 1980s changed all that. As consumer spending dropped and interest rates soared, companies found the competition for sales intense. What's more, the gradual release of data from the 1980 Census confirmed that deep changes were occurring in the marketplace. For example, the U.S. was no longer a nation consisting of family-of-four households with homogeneous buying habits. The population was far more diverse and required new marketing approaches and techniques. Besides demographic change, companies had to rethink their strategies to cope with increased foreign and domestic competition, deregulation, and the rapid pace of technological innovation. It is therefore not surprising that markets and marketing strategies have now assumed the central role in shaping strategic plans.

Central to the formulation of any business strategy is the answer to the question, "Who are our customers?" Often, demography—the statistical study of population trends—provides the answer. Data produced by the U.S. Census Bureau is more meaningful for market research because of advances in computer technology, and offer insight into income, occupation, education, and lifestyle factors of various age groups. This information allows executive strategic planners to find new ways of positioning their products and services. While it is the job of a market researcher to gather, tabulate, and analyze demographic data, all executives should be familiar with the latest trends. Here is a sample:

☐ **The new, but short-lived, baby boom.** The number of children born each year is growing almost to the levels of the baby boom years of the 1950s. This is because the baby boomers of the '50s are now adults and potential parents. Once these young adults pass their childrearing age, they will be replaced by those of the baby bust generation of the 1960s and 1970s. This will result in a new baby bust in the 1990s.

☐ **The changing nature of the family.** Couples are getting married later, are getting divorced more often, and are having fewer children. The typical American family now has only 3.25 people, as opposed to 3.58 people in 1970. During the 1990s, the projected family size will be 3.0 people. In addition, only 19 percent of families are married couples with children in which only the husband is employed, down from 30 percent in 1970. What's more, half of all women with preschool children are working outside the home.

☐ **The aging population.** There are currently more people over age 65 than there are teenagers, and life expectancy is rising. But the number of people over 65 grew more slowly between 1980 and 1990 than it did between 1970 and 1980. The next big jump in the number of older Americans will not occur until the early part of the next century, when the baby boomers of the 1950s reach 65.

While trends by themselves are interesting, they are almost without real value unless they are used to assess profit-making opportunities. Businesses must transform their products or services to meet changing customer behavior, tastes, and lifestyles. For example, the supermarket of the 1980s became a vastly different type of retail store than it once was. The increased number of wage-earning women spurred the need for one-stop shopping. Thus, the new supermarket sells everything from eggs to television sets. A new Giant Foods, Inc., store is part gourmet store, grocery, and pharmacy. It also has fresh pasta, discounted cosmetics, imported fragrances, and automatic teller machines. Supermarkets with beauty salons and restaurants also are becoming more common.

G.D. Searle's NutraSweet™ low-calorie sweetener is a classic example of product innovation that scored a success because it answered a customer need. A diet-conscious public had long sought an alternative to saccharin, which not only left a bad aftertaste, but was also labeled by the government as a cancer risk. Searle's aspartame-based NutraSweet was immediately attractive to the soft drink industry because it was clean tasting and did not pose a health risk. Sales of Searle's low-calorie sweetener in 1983 topped all expectations.

Still another company that was able to cash in on customer demand for low-calorie foods is Stouffers. The company's share of the $500 million frozen entree market jumped from 33 percent to 46 percent. Almost half its sales were credited to its Lean Cuisine line. The product met consumers' cravings for a low-calorie, filling, and tasty meal.

One top executive in the highly competitive fast food industry observed, "You have to out-execute the competition, and that's why marketing is more important than ever before." This comment sums up a fact of business life not only in fast foods, but in scores of industries where the inability to keep pace with the competition has doomed many companies. To a large extent, this message has not been heeded. A company that has long experienced success by marketing a particular product in a particular manner will be inclined to maintain its winning formula. It is only after the competition has made significant inroads in market share that the company may begin to look at alternative strategies, such as product innovation, increased advertising, lower prices, and new channels of distribution. Another type of company that can be badly hurt is the imitator. This firm copies the strategies of its competitors. Its philosophy is "Let the other guy take all the risks." The danger with this approach is that when the imitator reacts, the competition has already milked the market and is moving on to new products or services.

Marketing Measures Competition

In some industries, companies are pulling out all stops to battle the competition. Most are looking for ways to differentiate themselves from the competition, either by appealing to new consumer tastes, stressing quality, or broadening their product and service offerings. A good example is the fast food industry. McDonald's Corp. leads a pack of some 2,500 restaurant chain companies. To go up against this kind of competition, a chain must carve a niche for itself in the market and work out a strategy to fend off its rivals. McDonald's relies heavily on its financial muscle to keep the heat on through high advertising expenditures, especially behind its new products, Chicken McNuggets being a case in point. Burger King, the number two hamburger chain, was able to ring up double-digit sales increases by pushing the high caliber of its burgers to quality-conscious consumers. Wendy's strategy is to expand its menu and back it up with increased spending on equipment, advertising, and testing. It added a new baked potato with toppings and has tested a "gourmet" hamburger. Chicken George Chicken, Inc., a Baltimore-based chicken chain, has more than quadrupled sales by appealing to black consumers. Other chains have successfully sliced a share of the market by pushing Mexican foods, pizza, salad bars, for example.

In other industries, lack of marketing know-how has crippled the ability of companies to survive, let alone prosper. The computer industry shakeout is probably the most glaring example of how innovative firms allowed themselves to be shoved aside by a late-coming industry giant. Osborne Computer

Corp., for one, experienced a meteoric rise to the top by pioneering the world's first portable computer. Sales were hitting an annual level of $70 million. The roof suddenly caved in on Osborne because of poor management and its inability to handle the competition. Other companies, such as Kaypro, cracked the market with lower-priced models, and IBM's personal computer, launched in 1981, took off with state-of-the-art technology that consumers would find incompatible with Osborne's portable.

Osborne was not alone. Texas Instruments bowed out of the home computer market after suffering spectacular losses in 1983. Apple Computer, long the industry leader, allowed IBM to play catch-up to the point that each commanded about 25 percent of the personal computer market. IBM's introduction of the PCjr computer was expected to shake up the home computer market and cut into the market shares of Commodore, Atari, Coleco, Tandy, and Apple. Industry observers noted that IBM garnered much free publicity by shrewdly allowing the media to speculate on the date of the PCjr introduction. They also point out that though the PCjr would not actually be available until 1984, IBM, by announcing the new model in November 1983, purportedly sought to freeze the Christmas sales of its competition.

The computer industry shakeout that followed presents a clear-cut example of how the lack of marketing expertise, coupled with the inability to plan and formulate strategies to deal with change, severely hurt the capacity of many firms to compete. In some cases, companies had no strategy at all. They simply jumped into the market, compiled orders, and shipped. Others had strategies that either showed a complete lack of marketing sophistication or were misdirected. Here, in brief, is a review of some of the microcomputer industry's marketing miscues:

□ **Failure to target advertising to carefully-defined market segments.** Some manufacturers engaged in costly but ineffective mass advertising. In other words, they tried to sell their products to any potential buyer instead of zeroing in on a particular segment—small business or the corporate workstation market. On the other hand, IBM, the most financially able firm to mass advertise, segmented its markets and directed advertising to those segments.

□ **Faulty distribution policies.** Many companies didn't realize that certain distributors reach particular buyers better than others. Too often the manufacturer was simply content to let its dealers select the market.

□ **Overemphasis on price as a competitive weapon.** A price strategy could be attractive to some customers—standalone users, for example—but hurt the product's image with quality-minded business customers. The better strategy for many firms would have been to differentiate their product—by offering free software, for example—and tack on a competitive price.

□ **Inability to carve out a defensible niche.** By going after a broad market, companies invited intense competition. By narrowing the focus of their market—say, to small business or private medical practices—a company could automatically limit its competition. In addition, the manufacturer must communicate its targeted market to its dealers.

Marketing strategy encompasses identifying customer groups (Target Markets), which a business can serve better than its competitors, and tailoring its product offerings, prices, distribution, promotional efforts, and services (Market Mix) toward that particular market segment. Ideally, the strategy should try to address customer needs that currently are not being met in the marketplace and that represent adequate potential size and profitability. A good strategy implies that a business cannot be all things to all people and must analyze its market and its own capabilities so as to focus on a target market it can best serve.

Marketing and Product Innovation

As noted earlier, product life cycles for both consumer and industrial products have shortened considerably since the years immediately following World War II. This is an outgrowth, in part, of the ever-shifting trends in consumer tastes and lifestyles and, in part, of advancements in technology that have speeded the product development process. Because products tend to reach the maturity stage of the product life cycle and then begin to decline much sooner than in previous decades, companies must constantly put new ideas on the drawing board and hasten development in the manufacturing process if they hope to stay competitive. As Konosuke Matsushita, founder of Matsushita Electric Industrial Company, remarked in *Fortune* magazine, "Technology is changing too fast. An invention ought to be good for two to three years. Today, the same day you put a new product on the market it's out of date. We are so eager to compete that we spoil a new product by coming out with an even newer one." To underscore his point, Matsushita noted that during a one-month period in the summer of 1983, his company and Sony put out new products at a one-per-workday clip.

Another technological trend now taking shape that will, in all likelihood, have a profound impact on managers responsible for plotting company strategy, is the so-called automated factory. Just as the computer revolutionized office operations, so will the computer—and its cousin, the robot—dramatically alter plant operations. Experts agree that robotics, computer-aided design, and computer-aided manufacturing (CAD/CAM), will further shorten product life-cycles. The "flexible factories" of tomorrow will be capable of turning an idea into a finished product more quickly and more cheaply than is possible today. No longer will production be a barrier in the way of new product introduction schedules. Sales managers will rejoice over the fact that these new computer-based plants will be far more able to produce customized products to meet the particular specifications of individual groups of customers. Simultaneously, however, marketing will be under tremendous new pressures to move quickly to anticipate market demand. In the not-too-distant future, all managers will need to react more quickly to change than they do today. This means that chief executives will request, if not demand, a team approach to new product development involving the full cooperation of research and engineering, production, distribution, marketing, technical (customer) support, and sales.

In the face of the growing superior technological expertise of the competition, executive planners are putting less faith in pricing and advertising as viable strategies and more in production innovation, including support services (such as warranties, repair, and accessories). A price cut or an increase in ad expenditures, though appropriate in certain circumstances, is a meek response to a competitor who has just introduced a superior line, especially given the consuming public's growing preoccupation with quality. Recent surveys provide ample evidence that product development is fast becoming the heart of corporate strategy. Late in 1983, the National Science Foundation released a study showing that private industry expected to increase funding of research and development by 11 percent in 1984. Industry analysts attributed the increase to the need of many companies to keep up with rapidly advancing technology, and the growing impact of foreign competition. The report noted that five of the six industries surveyed had planned double-digit increases in R&D (research and development) expenditures over the 1982–84 period, varying from an annual average of 17 percent for machinery to 12 percent for chemicals and allied products.

A survey conducted by the advertising agency, Dancer Fitzgerald Sample, tracked new products in food and drug stores. It found that 1,483 new items had been introduced in the first 10 months of 1983. That figure represented an increase of 23 percent over the corresponding period in 1982, and a 44 percent boost over the 1980 period.

But marketers and other corporate strategists know only too well that the odds of coming out with a winner are not in their favor. Two of every three new offerings can be expected to fail, the same figure as in the 1960s. About $50 million is needed to launch a major nationally targeted item. What, then, is the key to success? A 1983 survey of 138 companies compiled by the Association of National Advertisers provides some clues. It reported that over half the responding marketers recommended a greater investment of time, money, and personnel for seeking out new markets. This explains the emergence of marketing research as an increasingly significant business endeavor. One-third of the respondents suggested that a greater effort be made in product development and testing. Thus, by comparison, marketing emerged as the priority. The survey also noted that new products can fall flat when a firm lacks a formal new products strategy and when R&D is not permitted to participate in strategy sessions.

Marketing and Product Development

Interdepartmental cooperation is a desirable goal in all areas of business operations, but it is central to new product development functions. When problems do arise, they generally spring from a lack of communication between marketing and research and development (R&D). Much has to do with differences in the nature of the people involved, their backgrounds, training, and career goals. Usually the difficulties are created by the orientation of top management. The chief executive and his closest advisers set the tone for the organization. If the firm is technically oriented, R&D will likely play a prominent role in product development. This will inevitably lead to conflict with marketing. The roles reverse in marketing-oriented companies. Whatever the orientation of the company, management must strike a balance between the diverse views of both departments, and direct the effort toward achievement of company goals. For this reason, clear communication of objectives is crucial. Confusion reigns when top management can't decide on a course.

Some degree of tension between marketing and R&D is conducive to a creative and competitive environment. However, conflict that leads to persistent animosity and ill will can be highly destructive to the company. To promote cooperation, management should take steps to see that there is frequent contact, both formal and informal, between the two departments.

Market Research

To manage the marketing functions successfully, good information about the market is necessary. Frequently, a small market research program, based on a questionnaire given to present customers and/or prospective customers, can show problems and areas of dissatisfaction that can be easily remedied, or new products or services that could be offered successfully.

Market research also should encompass identifying trends that may affect sales and profitability levels. Population shifts, legal developments, and the local economic situation should be monitored to enable early identification of problems and opportunities. Competitor activity also should be monitored. Competitors may be entering or leaving the market, for example. It is also very useful to know what your competitors' strategies are (how they compete, for example).

Target Marketing

Businesses have limited resources to spend on marketing activities. Concentrating their marketing efforts on one or a few key market segments is the basis of target marketing. The major ways to segment a market are:

☐ Geographical segmentation—specializing in serving the needs of customers in a particular geographical area (for example, a neighborhood convenience store may send advertisements only to people living within one-half mile of the store).

☐ Customer segmentation—identifying and promoting to those groups of people most likely to buy the product. In other words, selling to the heavy users before trying to develop new users.

Managing the Market Mix

There are four key marketing decision areas in a marketing program. They are:

1. Products and Services
2. Promotion
3. Distribution
4. Pricing

The marketing mix is used to describe how managers combine these four areas into an overall marketing program.

□ *Products and services.* Effective product strategies for a business may include concentrating on a narrow product line, developing a highly specialized product or service, or providing a product-service package containing an unusual amount of service.

□ *Promotion.* This marketing decision area includes advertising, salesmanship, and other promotional activities. In general, high quality salesmanship is essential for small businesses because of their limited ability to advertise heavily. Good yellow-page advertising is essential for small retailers. Direct mail is an effective, low-cost medium of advertising available to small businesses.

□ *Price.* Determining price levels and pricing policies (including credit policy) is the major factor affecting total revenue. Generally, higher prices mean lower volume and vice versa; still, small businesses can often command higher prices because of the personalized service they can offer.

□ *Distribution.* The manufacturer and wholesaler must decide how to distribute their products. Working through established distributors or manufacturers' agents generally is most feasible for small manufacturers. Small retailers should consider cost and traffic flow as two major factors in location site selection, especially since advertising and rent can be reciprocal. In other words, low-cost, low-traffic location means you must spend more on advertising to build traffic.

The nature of the product/service also is important in locational decisions. If purchases are made largely on impulse (such as flavored popcorn), then high traffic and visibility are critical. On the other hand, location is less a concern for products/services that customers are willing to go out of their way to find (such as restaurant supplies). The recent availability of highly segmented mailing lists (purchased from list brokers, magazines, or other companies) has enabled businesses to operate anywhere—and serve national or international markets.

Measuring Marketing Performance

After marketing program decisions are made, managers need to evaluate how well decisions have turned out. Standards of performance need to be set up so results can be evaluated against them. Sound data on industry norms and past performance provides the basis for comparing against present performance.

Managers should audit their company's performance at least quarterly. The key questions to ask are:

1. Is the company doing all it can to be customer oriented?
2. Do the employees make sure the customer's needs are truly satisfied and leave them with the feeling that they would enjoy coming back?
3. Is it easy for the customer to find what he or she wants, and at a competitive price?

In the remainder of this book we will expand on the points made thus far.

2

The Marketing Plan Concept

Not long ago two Harvard Business School students, Mike Wigley and Jerry De La Vega, were talking about how to promote record sales. Their idea was to enable people to order any record they wanted right from their living rooms. Twelve months later the idea caught fire. Joined by a third classmate from Harvard, David Ishag, these entrepreneurs used a cable television network that airs rock'n'roll videos 24 hours a day to advertise their business, Hot Rock, Inc. By the seventeenth day Hot Rock, Inc., had received 50,000 inquiries, and some weeks later sales growth was running at 10–14 percent a month with first-year projected sales at $6.7 million.

Meanwhile, Stouffers Lean Cuisine, a line of frozen food, suddenly boosted its market share by more than 30 percent in the $500 million frozen-entree food market, catching the entire industry by surprise.

In 1978 the Clorox Company had reached $1 billion in sales but profits were unimpressive, and shortly after that half the $1 billion revenue disappeared when a key division was sold. Yet only six years later Clorox again hit $1 billion in sales, but this time profits were double those of 1978.

What do these three vastly different types of companies in totally different industries have in common other than success? The answer is a marketing plan. In each case a marketing plan played a major role in enabling the company to reach the success that surprised competitors and business associates alike.

Products don't sell themselves. Companies have to reach out to potential buyers. They must make their goods and services accessible. They must communicate a very persuasive message, too, that the goods and services will benefit these customers.

Small businesses can find and sell customers by the seat-of-the-pants. It is far better, though, to start with a plan: a formulation of the approaches and actions needed to achieve some challenging sales objectives. Most successful concerns develop a coherent market plan that pulls together all the relevant market considerations and identifies the strategies and actions required to achieve high but realistic sales goals.

A marketing plan is essential for every business operation and for efficient and effective marketing of any product or service, even for marketing within a company. Seeking success for any project without the use of a marketing plan is like trying to navigate a ship through incredibly stormy waters while under torpedo attack and with neither a map nor a clear idea of where you are going. It requires time to develop a marketing plan, but it is time well spent and will save you time overall. The marketing plan will allow you to visualize clearly both where you are going and what you want to accomplish along the way. At the same time, a marketing plan details the very important steps required to get you from where you are to where you want to be. An added benefit is that in compiling and developing the marketing plan, you will have thought through how long it will take to accomplish each step and what resources in money, time, and effort will be needed to do this. Without a marketing plan, you will never know when or if you have reached your objectives.

Marketing Decision-Making Background

Every business organization, whether for-profit, nonprofit, or a government agency, has a culture. Terrance Deal and Allen Kennedy, in *Corporate Culture*, described this culture as an environment that prescribes procedures for carrying out the business of doing business.

The pervasive role of marketing largely dictates the strengths and weaknesses of a firm's culture. To be effective, marketing must be a two-way function: it communicates to management the needs and reactions of customers and society, and it promotes to current and prospective purchasers the goods and services of the organization. To paraphrase Peter Drucker in *The Practice of Management*, marketing is the unique function of a business. An organization in which marketing is absent or incidental is operating on the "dark side." It is not being run as a true business.

Some companies have been accused of lacking a marketing perspective. For instance, according to some critics Chrysler and Texas Instruments were once very weak marketers. Marketing people had little say in the planning and operations of either company; engineers were believed to dominate both. In short, the firms were out of touch with their customers. Following are the basic principles to maintain informed and relevant customer contact.

☐ **Marketers must have systematic and formalized input when vital strategic plans, policies, and operations are developed.** This does not necessarily mean that the president or CEO must have marketing experience or be biased toward the field, but top marketing executives should report to a top corporate-level executive. Marketing should not be subservient to such areas as production, finance, and personnel. When Chrysler was reorganized, an executive position aimed at long-term market planning was created. Marketing is now an integral corporate function at Chrysler.

☐ **Top executives must take an active interest in, and even at times become part of, the marketing process.** In analyzing successful organizations, one characteristic stands out. Top management appreciates the opportunities, challenges, and potential contributions of marketing.

When professional service firms are having a difficult time marketing their services, the major causes are often that their personnel do not fully understand the role and scope of marketing and the marketing responsibilities are given to a junior executive who has little status or formal authority. To motivate managers to push marketing ideas, a distinguished and respected executive in the firm should formally assume the marketing tasks. Managers at the lower level will then see that top management is serious about marketing.

□ **Marketing must be marketed within the organization.** Ironically, some outstanding marketing people who do an excellent job of marketing their firm's multitude of products or services externally, fail miserably when trying to apply the same ideas and tools internally. They often conflict with accountants, production managers, engineers, and others. Perhaps these marketers lose credibility because they fail to identify the needs, concerns, and objectives of their company peers. They neglect marketing research or fail to make use of an effective management information system (MIS). Marketing personnel are thus handicapped in communicating and promoting the wishes of the marketplace to other company managers.

□ **Marketing research and a management information system (MIS) used by marketers must be vital functions to the firm.** For its firm to be classified as a good marketing organization, management should do extensive research on the behavior of consumers, channel members, competitors, suppliers, and other "publics" that interact with the firm. Opportunities and challenges should then be noted via an effective MIS. A sound marketing research function should not be viewed as a one-shot project: it is done on a timely and continuous basis to anticipate and prevent potential problems. An ailing organization is often one that has ignored marketing research—or used it only to overcome such catastrophes as declining sales, lower profits, or loss of market share. In such a firm, the MIS is devoted almost entirely to bookkeeping, accounting, and/or financial concerns. Therefore, it does not serve the entire organization.

□ **Marketers must skillfully balance consumer demands with organization objectives.** Marketing people are sometimes so busy advocating customer satisfaction at all costs that they forget organization objectives. In the short run there can be conflict between satisfying consumer expectations and fulfilling profit goals. High market share and sales volume objectives, despite the costs, may indeed hurt bottom-line profits. Marketers must be careful to balance the environmental challenges of competition, government, channel members, customers, and even their peers within the organization.

Decentralized decision making is sometimes mandatory, but marketing executives still must make decisions within the guidelines, policies/procedures, and strategic plans set by top management.

□ **Managers must think beyond promotional bias.** Some executives with marketing problems automatically think that the solution is to increase advertising or personal selling efforts. This "quick fix" tactic is perceived as a means to a strong marketing program, especially in industrial manufacturers, nonprofit organizations, and professional service firms to which marketing is new. They ignore the other aspects of marketing that should be addressed first: reorganization, marketing research, planning, and pricing.

□ **Long-term strategic objectives and considerations must be carefully evaluated and appreciated.** A good company does not allow short-run concerns to outweigh its long-term plan. Poor quarterly reports or unexpected downturns in sales should not adversely affect a sound strategic plan. A firm with a solid marketing function learns how to balance short-term performance standards with long-term expectations. Sound contingency planning, which assumes different strategies for various scenarios, enables marketers to chart a steady course in the changing and rough seas of the marketplace. An equitable reward system, strategic objectives and priorities, corporate planning teams for different business units, and a stable environment give managers confidence that the firm is committed to them over the long haul. A clear sense of direction and purpose breeds loyalty.

□ **The organization must learn how to anticipate and *listen* to the marketplace.** Safeway Stores, a large supermarket chain, has gone, and is still going, through a major transformation. Through management changes, innovation, store design changes, marketing research, and newer merchandising ideas, Safeway is learning how to monitor the marketplace more effectively. Management is becoming a better listener by finding out what consumers want and then developing desirable products and services. In this way, Safeway management will be able to improve their predictions of future consumer trends.

□ **The organization must be able to respond quickly in the marketplace.** Rapid market changes and surprises are realities to all companies, even when they have a good track record of predictions. No matter how successful their schemes have been in the past, corporations must still encourage feedback from their marketing, sales, and customer support people and be ready to act fast in the tumultuous marketplace. For instance, Campbell's Soup recently reorganized its four divisions into 50 major groups. Each group manager has responsibility for marketing, manufacturing, and profit/loss for his or her unit. This structure enables group managers to act expeditiously in the marketplace.

□ **Top management should expect marketing personnel to be leaders in innovation and new ideas.** Executives should have many opportunities to interact with internal and external marketing groups to understand and enhance the innovation process.

Theodore Levitt, in a well-known article entitled "Marketing Myopia," noted that top management can be responsible for the decay and decline of a company. Shortsighted managers become myopically loyal to obsolete products or manufacturing processes. Their focus is the product instead of the benefits to and the needs and satisfactions of the consumer. Eventually consumers find substitutes that provide greater satisfaction, sometimes even at a lower price.

Also, it is difficult to pinpoint consumer trends and to quantify successful marketing decisions; a marketing credibility problem often surfaces with chief executives. For example, how can one measure the productivity of a marketing researcher who may have astutely noticed something in focus interviews that results in a highly profitable product five to ten years later?

□ **Marketing must be part of the strategic planning process.** Marketing people are sometimes overlooked in the strategic planning process. Also, organizational problems may take precedence over consumer problems. Acquisition of a certain company, for example, may look financially appealing, but the acquired company can become an albatross if marketing realities are ignored. New competition, changing distribution channels, product/technology obsolescence, poor synergism with product lines, and diminishing market potential are possible problems.

□ **Marketers must be given authority to make decisions and act like entrepreneurs.** In *The Decentralized Company*, Robert Levinson, former owner of Steelcraft Manufacturing, noted that corporate managers have become mechanical robots. To overcome this stagnation, marketing people need freedom to adjust to rapid changes in the market. They need a creative climate that provides ample opportunities to take the initiative and make decisions that reflect the wishes of local markets and special market segments. Most marketers are not afraid to be held accountable if they are wrong. Taking good calculated risks is exciting, and having real authority inspires their ingenuity at playing the game.

□ **The organization should strive to be a marketing leader in its industry.** Management should constantly "think" and "talk" marketing. IBM, Taylor Wine, Levi Strauss, Southwestern Airlines, Philip Morris, and Coca-Cola all have outmarketed their competition. They all applied basic marketing ideas, such as market segmentation, brand (product) management, product planning, and product positioning, to industries that were slow to appreciate creative marketing strategy and tactics. Philip Morris, for example, used its packaged-goods techniques and "tobacco marketing approach" to develop and sell Miller Lite Beer. In doing so, it revolutionized the marketing approach to the brewery industry.

□ **Management must search for the organization's niche.** When developing marketing strategies, marketers should identify and develop the company's strengths in the marketplace. Management must search for differentiation that will offer the firm valuable competitive advantages. A "me too" approach does not give consumers a reason to patronize a business. Good marketers try to enhance their position by seeking such competitive advantages as favorable reputation, quality product, lower prices, exceptional customer service, or unique location, technology, promotion, or packaging. By "listening" to consumers and observing the competition, marketers can identify voids in the market that the company can fill.

□ **Top management must appreciate the wonderful world of marketing synergism.** In looking at new corporate business opportunities, managers must identify their current marketing strengths, technology, and distribution structure. Good opportunities for natural expansion can come about through horizontal or vertical integration. For instance, many consumer food packaging companies, such as General Foods, Procter & Gamble, and General Mills, develop new businesses or acquire firms that fit nicely with their current business goals or services. Not only do the new businesses complement existing business units, but the synergistic impact enables the firm to achieve further economies of scale (e.g., delivery routes, trucks, and a sales force may already be established) and substantially increases revenues at little additional cost. New business units—including those gained by acquisition or merger—may enhance the general prestige of the firm. By carefully developing the synergistic effect, top management can cultivate a balanced and effective symbiosis of the many parts of the corporation.

□ **The organizational structure and ideas of the company must coincide with market realities.** A corollary to synergism is the idea of adjusting to the traditions and realistic norms of the market. When Smith Kline began selling its services in laboratory medical testing, it simply expanded its sales approach for pharmaceuticals. However, even though its representatives were already calling on doctors, Smith Kline found that the selling of lab work was quite different from the selling of pills. Different ideas, organization structure, and commitment were needed. Smith Kline had to modify its selling strategy. It was now trying to take lab business away from other suppliers, some of whom had strong local ties that even helped doctors with patient referrals. Smith Kline was asking these doctors to switch their loyalty to a distant and impersonal lab testing chain.

□ **Marketers must be held accountable through progressive and objective performance standards.** Much has been written about improving productivity in the factory. However, the cost of marketing a product or service is often greater than the cost of production. Thus it is vital for top managers to observe the level of marketing efficiency. Specific marketing people, such as product managers and sales personnel, must be answerable for the generation of direct costs versus revenue. A good marketing organization must be able to plan and implement budgeting and control procedures. In functions such as advertising, marketing research, and planning, whose bottom-line contributions are hard to measure, a solid marketing company tries to develop criteria for evaluating performance.

To implement various control procedures, companies like General Foods, R. J. Reynolds, Johnson & Johnson, and Du Pont have even created the career slot of marketing controller: a manager who appreciates the role and contributions of marketing personnel while controlling wasteful marketing expenditures and overseeing productivity. Rewarding effective marketers gives incentive to others.

□ **Top executives should demand periodic evaluations of the entire marketing operation of their firm.** Marketing is a dynamic field. Successful products, businesses, practices, and strategies can quickly become obsolete. Therefore, management should regularly schedule systematic marketing audits that examine the entire marketing program. These audits help identify the firm's strengths and weaknesses, the changing environment, and future marketing opportunities. The audit should be perceived as both diagnostic and prescriptive.

Audits need not be done yearly if management annually reviews the performance of subunits, such as advertising and product development functions. However, a complete marketing audit may be necessary every three, five, or ten years. Environmental circumstances should dictate the time frame.

☐ **A sound marketing organization distinguishes between bad symptoms (omens) and real problems in its marketing operations.** A weak marketing firm wrongly treats symptoms instead of the disease itself. For instance, an organization may assume that creating new products will automatically overcome declining sales and loss of market share.

Managing the Product Life Cycle

All products pass through life cycles with periods of ups and downs. An ideal sequence of sales might be represented as follows:

Introduction → Rapid Growth → Slow Growth → Leveling Off → Decline

Of course, some products never make it past introduction, others skip a stage or two, and still others continue indefinitely as if renewed from time to time. Whatever the pattern of sales, management must orchestrate the application of marketing tactics throughout the life cycle of a product through the market planning process. In this sense, the product life cycle is at least partially controllable by management. Each stage in the life cycle of a product will require a different balance among marketing tactics. Resources must be allocated to advertising, promotion, personal selling, distribution, and pricing in a way that meets the goals of the firm.

During the product introduction phase, profits are nonexistent and the objective typically is to increase consumers' product awareness and trial purchases (and stimulation of a healthy repurchase rate in the case of frequently purchased products). Advertising will be heavy to inform people. Promotions will be used to motivate dealers and consumers. The sales force will concentrate its efforts on building distribution. The price may be set low to take advantage of experience curve effects and forestall competition. Or it may be set high to reap early rewards.

During periods of rapid growth, adjustments must be made. These should, in turn, be guided by market research, including so-called tracking studies of awareness, attitudes, intentions, trial purchase rates, and repeat purchase rates. Market share may become a critical barometer too. Fine-tuning and shifts in emphasis from one marketing tactic to another invariably take place. Normative managerial models and simulations may be used to aid in decision making here also. Advertising will shift from information presentations to persuasion and may be reduced somewhat from the initially high levels during introduction. Promotions, too, will be reduced and shifted from trial-inducing tactics, such as sampling, to repeat-purchase teasers, such as coupons or cents-off deals. The sales force will work to cement dealer relationships and ensure that deliveries, product quality, and so forth will be fulfilled. Prices may be lowered somewhat to meet the competition.

Slow growth and leveling-off periods demand still other responses. Here the firm must assess its own growth in relation to market growth and consider its market share as well. A change in product design may be required to meet the demanding tastes of people who are slow in trying the product or to compete effectively with a new entrant. Advertising and promotions may have to be changed again to combat wear-out (a decline in ad effectiveness over time) or meet the competition. Prices may have to be lowered still further. Market segmentation takes on a special urgency as a means of survival and furthering the goals of the firm.

As the decline phase approaches, difficult decisions must be faced. Should the firm harvest, disinvest, or reinvest? Again, growth and market share must be weighed against the goals and capabilities of the firm and the nature of the market and competition. An outcome to avoid is the self-fulfilling prophecy by which an "apparent" decline is accelerated by a withdrawal of marketing support, and a potentially viable product is brought to a premature end. If the firm decides to harvest, then most expenditures on marketing will be reduced and the product will be left to die on its own. If the firm chooses instead to reinvest, it may have to do so across the board, with major product design innovations, repositioning, and renewed expenditures on advertising, promotions, selling, and distribution.

A final set of product decisions concerns product-line planning. The firm must decide whether or not to have a product line and, if so, what its composition should be. Consumer needs, the location of market segments, competition, market growth, market share, cannibalization, and profitability are important inputs to the decision process. Creating a well-designed product line entails looking not only at the health of each brand but also at the synergy among brands. The image and profitability of brands may be enhanced by careful design of the entire line, since cross-fertilization often occurs. The role of the product line also changes over time with the leveling-off phase of the product life cycle revealing the product line's maximum contribution. The product portfolio and strategic group frameworks are especially useful in product line decisions. Given the decision to employ product lines, the marketer must view his or her task as allocating marketing expenditures to the support of strategies and tactics that will best meet the firm's goals for profitability, market share, and growth.

It is through these marketing planning ideas and management processes that markets for products and services are managed and brought to their full potential. If management chooses not to fully plan the marketing of their products or services, they are destined merely to accept what "chance" has in store and any "management" becomes superfluous.

3

Characteristics of Marketing Personnel

Marketing attracts people with all types of backgrounds, personalities, and lifestyles. A variety of marketing positions and careers are available in both the business and nonbusiness environments. The field of marketing is so broad that generalizing on the necessary qualifications of marketers is difficult. Despite the lack of an ideal model for staffing the marketing function, a few general guidelines are still feasible.

☐ **Marketing personnel must understand and accept the scope and role of marketing.** To be effective, a marketing organization must have a spokesperson committed to the philosophical core of marketing—the marketing concept. A business will seriously suffer in long term if it does not have a leader who convinces (teaches) management to "listen" to the marketplace. He or she must be able to clearly communicate (sell) the marketing message.

☐ **A marketer's attitudes, communication, interests, and professional development must be open minded (eclectic).** Marketing is a people-oriented profession. Marketers have multidimensional responsibilities and must interact with all types of groups within and outside the organization. A good marketer must therefore be able to acquire knowledge about and empathy for a variety of corporate functions, customer targets, and environmental sectors. He or she must be flexible, since the marketing field is in a constant state of evolution. Management must avoid hiring a marketer who is narrow in scope, a poor communicator, or too dogmatic.

☐ **Proper planning, analysis, and matching of job requirements, job specifications, and available marketing candidates are vital.** Every business must try to develop its own profile of a successful marketer. If the industry or a business is new to marketing and there are no track records from which to create a profile, management must borrow ideas and/or hire talent from a related industry.

□ **Marketers should know the marketing process or the industry—preferably both.** Marketers must know how to find out what their consumers want and then decide how or whether the organization can provide it. This capability requires experience and expertise in market analysis, research, product development, price formulation, distribution planning, channel management, and promotional strategies. In some industries, management is willing to pay a premium for people who have been successful in marketing. In others, experience in the industry itself is considered more important than formal marketing education. People with industry experience may offer key contacts among customers, suppliers, channel members, associations, and even competitors.

□ **Excellent marketers have a thirst for formal marketing education and development.** Through formal and informal marketing education, marketers achieve the continual energy, creativity, and cleansing needed for the marketing function. Successful marketers learn continuously. By studying marketing theory and classic marketing mistakes and successes, professionals learn how to be effective. They should know how to keep up in the field and should welcome opportunities for taking marketing/management development programs and pursuing self-study.

The following lists a few of the characteristics of a successful marketer. Such a person:

□ Is innovative and entrepreneurial in thought and action.
□ Appreciates the financial dimensions of marketing actions.
□ Knows how to promote products and services under various conditions.
□ Is mentally agile, adaptable, and technically competent.
□ Appreciates the multitude of relevant factors that affect pricing decisions.
□ Is able to monitor and predict necessary channel changes.
□ Knows how to plan and implement the strategic and tactical elements, with reasonable accuracy.
□ Attempts to understand and appreciate consumer behavior.
□ Looks constantly for ways to improve the marketing intelligence system within the organization.

Some Responsibilities of Key Marketing Personnel

Product or Brand Manager

During the 1930s, 1940s, and even in the 1950s, it was not unusual to find one individual in a corporation who had both the responsibility and the authority over sales, advertising, sales promotion, public relations, and new product development. From a marketing person's viewpoint, this is the ideal situation. The title usually was director of marketing. This position can still be found in many corporations.

As corporations grew larger and offered a greater selection of products and services, the management structure of marketing began to change. Two

150,636

of the major consumer packaged goods companies, Procter & Gamble and General Foods, feared that some of their brands would be lost in the shuffle and not receive the individual attention needed. The brand or product manager position was developed to ensure that each brand or product received the necessary support from the various functional activities of the business, such as manufacturing, promotion, and sales. Yet, rather than having the responsibility and the authority for these activities, as the director of marketing had in the past, the product or brand manager usually had complete control in only one area—promotion. Product and brand managers were responsible for the sales of their brands, but they did not have control of the sales force. Likewise, they were responsible for the profit but did not have complete authority over the manufacturing function.

For this reason, the product or brand management concept failed in many companies. This type of organization is usually best only in multiproduct companies where it is impossible to separate the various functions, such as sales, promotion, and new-product development. Before a company sets up a product or brand management structure, it should be sure that this is the best of all possible worlds. If it is, then management has to be sure that there are clearly established lines of communication between the product or brand manager and the various line functions.

The product or brand manager should be in a position to present a written plan to top management once a year. After this document is approved, the manager should have the authority to make most day-to-day operating decisions. The manager also should have an appropriate line of communication directly to the field to be sure that all aspects of the plan are known and quickly executed. The management tasks of the product manager should include the following:

1. Preparing the complete marketing plan
2. Establishing measurements and controls
3. Communicating the plan through the entire company
4. Creating and maintaining enthusiasm for the plan
5. Preparing a periodic report to management

Decision areas for which the product manager should have primary responsibility are:

1. Product
2. Packaging
3. Advertising
4. Communications research
5. Sales promotion

The task actions of the product manager should influence the behavior and activities of practically all departments within the company, including engineering, manufacturing, research and development, marketing research, sales and customer service, finance and accounting, data processing, and legal.

The product manager's role with engineering is primarily interpretive. Product managers should communicate the needs of the market to engineering as well as monitor the product or service to be sure that changes in function, quality, and design are favorable. To manufacturing, product managers are the source of information about past and anticipated sales volume, which is used for developing production schedules. They should balance market needs against cost in recommending inventory levels and continually feed back information on product performance in the marketplace.

Besides suggesting market needs and product concepts to research and development, product managers also must evaluate R&D ideas from the viewpoint of market needs. If there isn't close communication between these two departments, the successful new product development rate will be even lower than the pitiful national average of 10–30 percent.

The product manager should continually use market research to measure market needs and the satisfaction of those needs by the company's product or service as well as by the competition.

In dealing with sales and customer service, product managers should serve as a source of information on their product line, convince sales to execute the sales portion of the marketing plan, and help train customer service teams about the functions of the product or service. In contrast, the product manager must consult with and obtain planned input from the sales and customer service managements when establishing sales and service philosophies, delivery, and goals.

Product managers play a major role in obtaining the necessary financial support for the marketing plan from upper management, the finance department, and the accounting department. They should develop thorough knowledge of the profit-and-loss statement, including a concern for net as well as gross profit. They should be on the lookout for arbitrary assignments of administrative or staff charges to the product line. Ideally, product managers should have the right to sign off on all administrative charges. That means that they can reject, for example, an assigned cost of $20,000 from a staff department. Of course, if a product manager rejects the charge, then the service is not provided.

Electronic data processing (EDP), or management information systems (MIS), is becoming a more important marketing tool each year. Every product manager should be familiar with what MIS can and cannot do to provide more accurate and timely marketing information. If product managers have no experience with MIS, they should strongly consider attending educational seminars on the subject.

Product managers should always remember that the company's legal department is friend, not enemy. All advertising and sales promotion activities should be cleared with this department in the development stages to prevent wasted time and expenditures. Remember, you as an individual can be prosecuted for misleading and false advertising claims and be fined, imprisoned, or both (refer to Appendix). It's not worth the gamble, so always check everything with your legal department.

Marketing Manager

The marketing manager is very similar to the product or brand manager except that the marketing manager's efforts are devoted to one or more products within one or more market segments. A marketing manager is normally used when a company has many similar or closely related products that are sold to different segments of the market. The market manager, like the product or brand manager, is responsible for getting the products to the market but also does not normally have direct line authority over all the various functions required to get the job done.

Advertising Manager

The advertising manager is normally responsible for only the advertising function, just as the sales promotion manager is responsible for sales promotion and the public relations director is responsible for public relations.

Marketing Director Requirements

While it is desirable, but not necessary, for a nonmarketing executive to know the requirements for various marketing management positions—market research, product manager, and ad manager, for example—it is essential to have a good idea of the tasks the top marketing executive should be prepared to undertake. Although most nonmarketing executives will not be responsible for the marketing director's performance review, they should be in a position to roughly assess the adequacy of his or her performance. Typically, the marketing director bears responsibility for:

☐ Promoting the marketing unit's standing in the company.
☐ Building a customer-oriented marketing department.
☐ Monitoring the activities of competitors.
☐ Assessing and acting on market research data.
☐ Segmenting markets into practical and growth-oriented groups.
☐ Planning and implementing marketing objectives and strategies.
☐ Ensuring that marketing objectives complement the corporate strategic plan.
☐ Expanding market share.
☐ Promoting additional sales volume and revenue.
☐ Contributing to the company's profitability.
☐ Managing all elements of the marketing mix—advertising, quality, product development, distribution, and pricing, for example.
☐ Managing the marketing staff and providing the requisite leadership talent.
☐ Working constructively with both top management and the department heads of other functions.

The Marketing Director Must Be Prepared and Qualified to Address the Following Market Issues

☐ *Market Entry Timing* can be everything. Moreover, the development of a new market can be very long and very expensive. "Early entry" risks should be an important concern when one or more of the following indicators is lacking:

1. Customers must be ready, have a strong need for a product, and a strong desire to buy at an affordable price.

2. Using the product must create very satisfied customers who will buy again and/or refer others through word of mouth.
3. There must be a reasonable method of economically distributing the product into the market.

If any one of these elements is missing, a very expensive process of market development will be necessary, entailing considerable financial outlay.

For example, since the early 1950s, communications companies have been promoting video telephones that enable the user to see the person to whom they are talking. The Japanese have entered the market in recent years. But despite new technologies, new players, and new promotions, the market simply has not developed. Money cannot yet buy this market.

Late market entry is equally frustrating because, at the time of entry, demand is already satiated, price margins are shrinking, and market position is dominated by others. Unless a venture can provide a dramatic improvement in price or performance, late market entry will be costly and probably nonproductive.

Renault's joint venture with AMC never yielded success because its auto product was neither a price nor a performance breakthrough. The product lacked market distinctiveness. The Ford and Toyota joint venture produced one of America's most reliable, best-built cars—the new Chevy Nova—but unlike its nearly identical Toyota counterpart, the American version lacked the distinctiveness U.S. buyers associate with an American car.

☐ *"Foreign Intrigue"* is a version of the "grass is greener on the other side of the fence" syndrome. A company experiencing success in its domestic marketplace may look at another country as a potential market, only to find foreign intrigue was really economic disappointment.

For example, a European instrument manufacturer was seeking to expand its market and attempted a joint venture with a U.S. sales firm to distribute a digital precision instrument line imported from Italy. An agreement was signed, a warehouse site selected, and financial commitments put in place. However, the European partner failed to understand that its primary U.S. competitor had a steel-hardened grip on the marketplace, with over 85 percent share of the market. The U.S. product was considered the standard in the industry, even though, when compared with the European competitor, it was a technologically obsolete analog device. The venture was failing from poor sales until the product was repositioned to have both an archaic (but accepted in the marketplace) analog readout and a digital interface that could be fed into a computer.

☐ *Forecasting Follies.* Market forecasts can have a tendency to be terribly understated or overstated. The marketing director must be aware that unless conducted by an experienced market researcher, sales projections can lie more profusely than a crooked politician or an iconoclastic economist.

For example, alliances in the robotics industry have watched sales forecasts fall far short of projections year after year. The market for robots has never met expectations, principally because the customer demand is highly specialized and centered around specific, custom needs. Money invested based on these forecasts has seldom seen a return on investment.

The Transition

Many advertising or marketing executives are promoted from field sales and make the mistake of not altering their perspectives to reflect the requirements of their new positions. Salespeople have a tendency to concentrate on sales volume rather than on profit, on the short run rather than on the long run, on individual customers rather than on market segments, and on fieldwork rather than on desk work. Usually they are not attentive to profit differences between products or customer classes. They do not tend to think of product or market expansion strategies over the next three to five years, and they have less interest in developing strategies for the various marketing segments.

When salespeople are transferred to the marketing operation, they have to alter their planning perspective to include profitability of various products and services, long-run trends, threats and opportunities, customer and segment types, and constant market analysis. They should plan their sales volume around profits; study how to translate market changes into new products, new markets, and new market strategies; determine how to offer superior values to the most profitable product lines; and be familiar with all the financial implications of their marketing plans.

You may be interested in knowing what top management usually considers the basic problems with marketing personnel:

1. They fail to provide sufficient information and make sound marketing decisions.
2. They do not understand the broad implications of marketing, especially relative to return on investment, strategic or long-range planning, financial implications, and manufacturing.
3. They spend too much money on advertising, considering that it is not as exact a science as finance and manufacturing.

Conversely, you may enjoy hearing the most commonly voiced complaints of marketing personnel against people in top management:

1. They lack understanding of the marketing function, especially advertising.
2. They fail to explain the company's long-range goals and financial objectives.
3. They consider themselves advertising experts.

Other Responsibilities and Considerations

The marketer's responsibility regarding competition. Every for-profit and nonprofit organization is vulnerable to the competitive forces of society. Even old and seemingly stable industries and companies have experienced turbulent times. No one can predict where an organization or industry will encounter competition. Consequently, progressive executives—especially marketers—must stay abreast of changes that promote competition.

Marketers must study and analyze competitors' product performance and how consumers perceive it. Strong companies initiate regular and formal evaluations of their own products in comparison with those of the competition. Marketers and quality-control personnel (such as engineers, production managers, and lab technicians) should have input into the development and measurement of variables that rank the firm's products.

In addition, marketing people, especially the sales force, customer representatives, marketing researchers, and channel members, should determine how consumers rate product performance. A common mistake is to believe that the company product is much better than that of the competition and that consumers see it in the same way. Even if the product is indeed superior, the consumer may not be aware of this superiority. Here promotional personnel must educate the public by highlighting and differentiating the features that are better.

For example, many customers strongly believe that the Japanese produce better and stronger cars than the American automotive industry. Whether this is true or not, it means that Detroit marketers must overcome any automotive performance problems and simultaneously deal with consumer perception problems.

When feasible, the company should go through a product teardown of competitors' products. Ford Motor Company breaks down competitors' products to identify various components, determine the materials used, observe how the product is produced, and calculate likely costs. Other companies can learn from Ford's five-step sequence:

Step 1: Purchase the product.
Step 2: Tear the product down, including unscrewing or unbolting removable components, undoing rivets, and breaking spot welds.
Step 3: Reverse-engineer the product. Assemble a parts list while analyzing the entire production process.
Step 4: Determine the cost of manufacturing the various parts. Analyze labor requirements and estimate overheads.
Step 5: Establish economies of scale, break-even, and profit projections.

When individual cost elements have been defined, a bottom-up approach can be used to estimate the feasibility of matching or improving on competitors' products.

Marketers should regularly and systematically use many sources for competitive evaluations. Marketing people should gather pertinent information to monitor current competition and anticipate new competition (see "Competitive Profile"). Sources of data might be:

- Trade shows
- Trade associations
- Government publications and databases
- Commercial on-line databases such as Predicasts, Dialogue, and The Source
- Suppliers
- Trade magazines
- Local government officials
- Channel members, retailers, wholesalers
- Related business contacts, advertising agencies, bankers, lawyers, accountants, consultants
- Professional service and social clubs or organizations
- Previous employees of competitors
- The organization's own employees, such as purchasing managers, engineers, field personnel
- Syndicated commercial auditing reports, such as those by A.C. Nielsen, Market Research Corporation of America, National Purchasing Diary Panel

If use of any of these sources appears to invite unethical behavior, the source should be avoided. Some sources will offer general suggestions about future competition. For example, at one time if a firm hired the Boston Consulting Group, it was almost certain that that firm would adopt specific approaches, portfolio management, and certain actions for a strategic management plan. This allowed competitors to anticipate decisions that might have an impact on their plans.

Other sources of competitive information include:

- Customer warranty information
- Patent/copyright filings
- Product announcements
- Annual reports (10 Ks)
- Government papers from grants on specific industry trends
- Brokerage analyses of specific industries
- Advertising campaigns
- Technical product specifications, manuals, brochures, training literature

By developing competitive profiles and analyses from various data sources over time, the effective marketer will discover which sources have the highest reliability and validity.

A formalized framework and check list should be used to enhance analysis of the competition. Marketing people must be sensitive to common marketing-related variables that can influence the company's competitive strengths and weaknesses. The above form lists the critical marketing factors that must be weighed when intercompetitive comparisons are made for specific products within certain market segments. It also provides a format for doing so. Additional factors may be important depending on specific circumstances.

Representatives from every department should be involved in pinpointing key competitive strengths, weaknesses, and resources. Widespread participation contributes to a comprehensive analysis and united front when

Competitive Profile:
Identifying Strengths and Weaknesses in Marketing

Key Marketing Variables	Major Competing Companies					Comments
	A	B	C	D	E	
Market Share						
Sales Force						
Distribution						
Technological Strengths						
Profitability						
Financial Status						
Consumer Loyalty						
Product Quality						
Advertising						
Trade Allowances						
Key Managerial Personnel						
Pricing Policies						
Services/Warranties						
Future Market Strength						

Each company could be rated excellent, good, fair, poor, or very poor for each variable.

marketing strategy is formulated to meet the competition. A person in manufacturing, for instance, might be able to pinpoint major product weaknesses in the competition on which salespeople can capitalize when meeting prospective customers.

Marketers must be trained to listen for complaints about or subtle vulnerabilities in the competition. Field personnel must be encouraged to observe and communicate back to the home office the following competitor problems:

- ☐ Consumer complaints about products, services, pricing, delivery, for example
- ☐ Reseller concerns and dissatisfactions
- ☐ Government investigations about the conduct of business
- ☐ High turnover of personnel
- ☐ Labor strikes
- ☐ Product shortages
- ☐ Class-action lawsuits by licensees or franchisees

- ☐ Supplier-related problems
- ☐ Financial shortcomings
- ☐ Obsolete technology causing inferior quality control
- ☐ Poor productivity results
- ☐ Increasing shareholder complaints

Company marketers who are familiar with these problems can develop a sound marketing program of their own.

Marketing managers should help develop ethical and legal barriers that impede new competition. Without violating government antitrust or anticompetition statutes (refer to Appendix), marketers can legally and ethically discourage competition from becoming industry entrants. For example, to develop a competitive advantage, marketing people can seek strong patents, copyrights, and trademarks, or develop solid brand loyalty among consumers.

Marketing personnel should clearly decide where the company and products will be positioned within the competitive environment. A good example of this positioning challenge is in the soft drink industry. Both Dr. Pepper and Philip Morris (7-Up) had to decide how to compete with the two cola giants, Coca-Cola and Pepsi-Cola. They used various positioning tactics to emphasize how their products differed from colas (such as lemon-lime flavor, no caffeine, and the "uncola" image). Additionally, to minimize direct confrontation and huge start-up cost in distribution, both beverage companies piggybacked on the Coke and Pepsi bottlers, who felt they needed a full line of beverages to sell to consumers.

Management must periodically answer certain key questions to stay competitive. No organization is an island unto itself. It must have a keen awareness of current and future competitive changes. A handy check list of questions can serve as a basic reference scheme for managers. The following are generic questions. More specific questions should be developed for each business/industry.

- ☐ Who are our stiffest competitors? Are they becoming stronger? Weaker?
- ☐ Do we recognize the limits of our own competitive position?
- ☐ In what markets or product categories are we gaining market share? Losing market share?
- ☐ How can we exploit our competitors' vulnerabilities? Which specific firms provide us with additional selling opportunities? What will be the costs and resulting profits if we take share away from them?
- ☐ How can we overcome our own competitive weaknesses? Are any firms exploiting our weaknesses?
- ☐ What competitive defensive and offensive strategies provide the greatest opportunities? Do the targeted consumers know about our competitive strengths?
- ☐ Are new competitive entrants, including foreign ones, on the horizon?
- ☐ Are many competitors leaving the industry?
- ☐ Does our remaining in a certain industry or product category coincide with our strategic plan?

In conclusion, marketing executives need to become fully cognizant of the competition. Many new and challenging forces, such as government deregulation, industry crossovers, foreign competition, acquisitions/mergers, and high technology advancements, have blurred competitive demarcations. It is no longer a simple task to determine where competition lies. A prime example is the consumer financial services market—competition exists among banks, stockbrokers, savings and loan companies, insurance firms, retail chains, personal finance managers, and so on. A formal approach to analyzing the competition is a major obligation for marketers.

Marketing Plan Forecasting

Situational Diagnosis

The purpose of a situational diagnosis is to identify the strengths and weaknesses of a firm and the threats to and opportunities for its future performance. These four factors provide the basis for planning future directions and actions. An adequate understanding of the structure and nature of a firm's operating environment is a prerequisite to undertaking the situational diagnosis step of the planning process. This understanding allows a firm to zero in on those factors that really affect its performance.

One of the factors that shapes a firm's operating environment is the nature of the firm itself and the structure of its business operations. Some key issues and decisions that shape the nature and structure of a firm are:

1. The values a firm holds regarding growth and expansion.
2. The basis on which a firm chooses to compete (for example, price and quality).
3. The types of customers a firm sells to.
4. The products and services a firm produces or provides.
5. The method used to evaluate or define successful performance.

These decisions provide a framework for identifying strengths and weaknesses in terms of what a firm is doing and how well it is doing it. This framework allows a firm to make valid comparisons between itself and other similar firms. More important, the framework provides the basis for defining the relevant operating environment of a firm.

The Nature and Structure of a Firm's Operating Environment

A firm's operating environment is defined by several sets of factors. The first set is the cast of characters with whom a firm interacts. These characters can affect the firm's performance, and include competitors, customers, suppliers, and regulators. The second set of factors is the forces or trends that can affect a firm's competitive position. These forces include demographic trends that can affect the composition of the customer base; technological trends that can affect the availability, relevance, usefulness, and cost-effectiveness of specific products and services; and economic trends that can affect purchasing behavior and the relative influence of suppliers and customers. A third set of factors is the basic competitive structure of the industry in which a firm exists. The relevant factors here are barriers to entry, or the degree of difficulty for new firms to enter the industry, particularly in times of market growth; and barriers to exit, or the degree of difficulty for existing firms to leave the industry, particularly in times of market decline.

With knowledge and understanding of these factors, marketing management can provide the long-term balance necessary in the forecasting process. In that process, sales will provide the raw, current data input and marketing will provide the researched trend and situational analysis data to balance the forecast for more meaningful application to company objectives.

To adequately understand the nature of an operating environment, several questions must be answered:

□ Who are a firm's competitors? What is the degree of competition—that is, how many competing firms are there, and what is their relative size and influence on each other? What is the nature of the competition—that is, on what basis do firms compete, price or quality?

□ Who are a firm's customers or buyers? What is their purchasing behavior—for example, timing and amount—and what factors affect that behavior? What is the relative power of customers or buyers vis-à-vis the firm on issues such as prices, discount and collections policies, and product/service characteristics?

□ Who are a firm's suppliers, including staff with specialized skills? What are their capabilities? What is the relative power of suppliers vis-à-vis a firm on issues such as prices, discount and collections policies, and production/service requirements?

□ What is the potential for the number of competitors to change? How easy or hard is it for new firms to enter the market or for existing firms to leave the market?

□ What is the impact of technology on the demand for the firm's products/services? What are the demographic trends of a firm's customer segments? What is the availability of and potential for substitute products/services?

□ In what areas is a firm subject to legislative or administrative regulation? How significant are these areas on the firm's business operations and on its ability to control costs and generate revenues?

Any firm must know the answers to these basic questions in order to complete and properly evaluate the results of both the internal and external components of the situational diagnosis.

With an adequate understanding of its environment, a firm will be able to focus the analyses on those factors that most significantly affect its ability to be successful, and on those factors that are most subject to change and variability. This allows a firm to develop appropriate business strategies based on both the expected benefits of the strategy and the expected risks associated with the strategy in terms of impact on and reactions from other elements in the environment.

Evaluating Risks

Risk evaluation is one of the more difficult, least precise elements of the situational financial analysis. After all, how well can anyone accurately figure out the contingencies of the future? However, doing nothing to evaluate risks is even more repugnant.

In analyzing a venture, evaluate each of the following risks. If the risk has a relatively broad range—from high to low—you should make an adjustment in the financial analysis to reflect this range. Eight risk areas to consider are:

1. **Market Risk.** Will there continue to be a market in the future? Will the market grow at a rate that will provide opportunities for us to sustain our growth?
2. **Competitive Technology Risk.** Will a competitor develop a technology that will make ours obsolete? Are our gross profit margins sufficient to sustain ourselves in the event of a price war?
3. **Completion or Technical Risk.** Is the venture sufficiently like a predecessor project, technology, or business to ensure that it will work as planned? Might any new technologies throw a monkey wrench into the successful achievement of the venture?
4. **Cooperative Environment Risk.** What is the chance that someone or something (government, weather, labor unions, subcontractors, or transportation, for example) will stop or slow down the venture?
5. **Management Risk.** Do we have sufficient personnel to carry out the venture? If not, can the proper personnel be obtained on a timely and cost-effective basis?
6. **Political Risk.** Are there any governmental regulations, now or pending, that will interfere with success? Will the necessary permits (such as zoning, EPA, SEC, antitrust, or health department) be issued when needed?
7. **Resources Risk.** Will the supply of customers, materials, or products be available substantially longer than the amortization of the financing? Will the firm have the financial, human, and intellectual resources to see the project through to completion?
8. **Capital Risk.** Will inflation, foreign exchange rates, or government policy dramatically change the value of the investment? What is the chance that our capital will be totally or marginally lost in this investment?

Forecasting Market/Sales

Forecasting predicts the future. To a significant extent it is done by analyzing the past. Of course, this does not necessarily mean that whatever happened in the past will continue to happen in the future, but here the process of forecasting must begin. By forecasting you can establish in your marketing plan more accurate goals and objectives and the strategies and tactics for reaching these objectives. In fact, forecasting will help you to do all of the following:

☐ Determine markets for your products
☐ Plan corporate strategy
☐ Develop sales quotas
☐ Determine whether salespeople are needed and how many
☐ Decide on distribution channels
☐ Price products or services
☐ Analyze products and product potential in different markets
☐ Decide on product features
☐ Determine profit and sales potential for products
☐ Determine advertising and sales promotion budgets
☐ Determine the potential benefits of various elements of marketing tactics

Sales forecasting involves decisions made in all sections of your marketing plan. As you will see as you proceed, forecasting involves some guesswork and a great deal of managerial judgment. Nevertheless, even guesswork becomes far more valuable when supported by facts and careful analysis. If you had simply pulled facts out of thin air and constructed your marketing plan on them as a foundation, rather than using a logical methodology and research integrated with good marketing judgment, even your basic assumptions would likely be as wrong as they would be right. Succeeding under these conditions, then, would be largely a matter of luck.

Market and Sales Potential and Sales Forecast Differences

Market potential, sales potential, and sales forecast mean different things in forecasting. Market potential is determined by market research and refers to the total potential sales for a product or service or any group of products considered for a certain geographical area over a specific period. Market potential relates to the total capacity of the market to absorb everything that an entire industry may produce, whether it is airline travel, light bulbs, or business books.

Sales potential is also determined by market research and is the ability of the market to absorb or purchase the output of a single company in that industry, presumably yours. Thus, if you are manufacturing motorcycle helmets, you might talk about a total market potential of $700 million a year, whereas the ability of the market to purchase that output might be only $50 million.

The term sales forecast refers to the actual sales you predict your firm will realize in this market in a single year; it is primarily determined by the sales department in response to customer demand. In turning to the motorcycle helmet example, perhaps your sales forecast will be only $20 million, though the market potential is $700 million for the entire industry and $50 million for your company. Why the difference? Why can't you reach the full market potential in sales? Sales potential may not exceed market potential because of your production capacity. You can produce only $50 million in helmets, not $700 million. There may be many reasons for not trying to achieve 100 percent of the sales potential of which you are capable. One may have to do with limited resources. Perhaps reaching the entire market would require more money (cost per sale) than you have available for your marketing campaign, or the margin of return on your investment may be responsible. To achieve 100 percent of anything requires consideration of the law of diminishing returns, which means that the marginal cost of each additional percentage point becomes greater and greater as you try to achieve your potential. Therefore it may be wiser to stop at 90, 80, or even 70 percent of your sales potential because the significantly higher costs of achieving those final percentage points to get to 100 percent make the goal less desirable. There may be far better uses for your resources because the return on each dollar you invest elsewhere may be greater. Finally, there may be some factor in the marketplace that will prohibit you from achieving 100 percent; for example, a strong competitor or an unexpected change in environment. Perhaps the law that requires cyclists to wear helmets is suddenly repealed.

Finding Market Potential

Sometimes it is possible to find the market potential for a specific product already in published form in research done by someone else for the U.S. Government, a trade association, or an industrial magazine, for example. At other times it is necessary to derive the market potential for your products by using a chain of information or chain ratio that involves connecting many bits of related facts to arrive at the total you are looking for. For example, you want to explore the market potential for bulletproof vests or body armor used by foreign military forces for an export project. Because at the current time only a few countries use this equipment, the number has to be determined by a chain ration method. First, the number of units of body armor used by U.S. military forces is calculated from a government publication such as the Commerce Business Daily. An average number of ground troops most likely to use the units is also published in U.S. government sources. From these facts—that is, the total annual sales of body armor to the U.S. Army and the average size of the ground forces during the same period—a ratio of body armor units per soldier is developed. Next, you consult the Almanac of World Military Power, which lists the strength of any ground forces for all countries. Because body armor is an export military item, the sale of which is controlled by the U.S. government, not every country is a candidate. Therefore only those candidates likely to be approved by the U.S. government would be included in the data summary. These figures are totaled and a worldwide total of candidates for the product is calculated. Next, the ratio of body armor units per soldier developed earlier from U.S. data is used. The result is a total market potential of military body armor for export from the United States to foreign armies. Note that this is not the sales potential for the sale of body armor by any single company for this market, nor is it a forecast of what body armor would be sold. It is the total market potential.

More general market information can be obtained from the Census Surveys of the Department of Commerce. Sometimes your local Chamber of

Commerce may have this information or surveys may have been done by local or state governments. (See Appendix for resource references.) Once you have the population, the next step is to arrive at the per capita expenditure for the product. Again, government surveys may be helpful or perhaps the industry or associations may be able to provide this information. You also might look for trade magazines about the product. Naturally you must be sure that the geographical information furnished corresponds closely with the geographical area you are examining, because the per capita expenditure can differ greatly depending on the region of the country, its culture and climate, and the feelings and interests of its people. If you multiply the population in the 5-mile area by the per capita expenditure for the product, you will end up with a total annual expenditure.

The market potential for any product or class of product or service can be determined by doing a little thinking about the relevant information you need and then linking it to obtain the final answer.

The Index Method of Calculating Market Potential

An alternate way of calculating market potential is by using indices that have already been constructed by someone else from the basic economic data; for example, Sales and Marketing publishes a survey of buying power indices in July and October each year for consumer markets and in April for industrial and commercial markets. The commercial indices developed by combining estimates of population, income, and retail sales result in a positive indicator of consumer demand data according to regions of the U.S. Bureau of the Census by state, by its organized system of metro areas by counties, or even by cities with populations of 40,000 or more. It is important to recognize that this buying power index, or BPI, is not an absolute one. It therefore must be multiplied by national sales figures to obtain the market potential for any local area. Let's say that you sell a certain brand of national television but only in the local area in your own city store. From the manufacturer you learn that 10 million units are sold every year. Now you want to calculate the market potential for your city that, you assume, is the city of Santa Barbara, California. Take the listed BPI of .1916 and multiply it by 10 million. The answer is a market potential of 1,916,000 for the city of Santa Barbara, California.

Bottom-Up and Top-Down Sales Forecasting

There are two basic ways to forecast sales: the bottom-up and top-down methods. The most valid forecasting technique, however, is any combination of the two methods with direct input from the salesforce. This accomplishes two things: it gives the marketing function a view of the market as seen by the salesforce, and any resultant forecast will have greater credibility within the salesforce. Thus, they will more actively support and try to meet the forecast.

With the bottom-up method the sequence is to break up the market into segments and calculate separately the demand for each segment. You simply sum the segments for the total sales forecast. Typical ways of doing this are by salesforce composites, industry surveys, and intention-to-buy surveys.

To accomplish top-down forecasting the sales potential for the entire market is estimated, sales quotas are developed, and a sales forecast is constructed. Typical methods used in top-down surveys are executive judgment, trend projections, a moving average, regression analysis, exponential smoothing, and leading indicators.

Executive Judgment

Executive judgment is known by a variety of names, such as Jury of Executive Opinion, Managerial Judgment, or Gut Feeling. With this method you just ask executives who have the expertise. This could be many individuals or a single person who may be responsible for the program. This method of forecasting is fairly easy to use. A variation of this method is known as Delphi. In this methodology a survey of opinion is taken, and the results are summarized without revealing any of the respondents. It is then distributed to the respondents, and the process is repeated. This process is repeated several times until a correlation of opinion is obtained. This correlation is the forecast.

Salesforce Composite

A salesforce composite can be obtained by assigning each salesperson the duty of forecasting sales potential for a particular territory. These territorial estimates are then summed to arrive at an overall forecast.

Trend Projections

A trend projection in its simplest form is an analysis of what has already happened, extended into the future. Thus recorded observations of sales over the preceding three years may reveal an increase on an average of 10 percent every year. A simple trend projection would assume that sales will increase by 10 percent for the coming year as well. A moving average is a more sophisticated trend projection.

Industry Survey

In the industry survey method, companies that make up the industry for a particular product or service will be surveyed. A survey may include users or manufacturers or both. The industry method clearly has some characteristics of the bottom-up method, rather than the top-down, and some advantages and disadvantages of executive opinion and sales force composites.

Regression-Type Analyses

A regression analysis may be linear or it could have to do with multiple regression. With linear regression, relationships between sales and a single independent variable are developed to forecast sales data. With multiple regression, relationships between sales and several independent variables are used. Computer programs are written to assist the marketer in this respect. Sales predictions are made by estimating the values for independent variables and incorporating them into the multiple regression equation.

Intention-to-Buy Survey

The intention-to-buy survey is done before the introduction of a new product or new service, or for the purchase of any product or service for some period in the future.

Exponential Smoothing

Exponential smoothing is a timed series approach similar to the moving average method of trend analysis. Instead of a constant set of weights for the observations, however, an exponentially increasing set of weights is used to give the more recent values more weight than the older values. This is exponential smoothing in its most basic form. More sophisticated models include adjustments for factors like trend and seasonal patterns. Again, forecasting methods based on exponential smoothing or incorporating it are available in various computer programs.

Leading Indicators

Leading indicators are used in economics to predict recessions and recoveries and, in fact, are the key issues found to have forecasting value by the National Bureau of Economic Research. Typical leading indicators reported by this bureau include the prices of 500 common stocks, new orders of durable goods, index of net business formation, corporate profits after taxes, industrial material prices, and changing consumer installment credit. The problem of sales forecasting with these leading indicators is in relating them to specific products or services.

Forecasting Cost and Other Important Information

Forecasting sales alone is insufficient when developing financial information for your marketing plan. You must also forecast the costs involved, their timing, and when they occur in relation to sales. This is done with a project development schedule, a break-even analysis, a balance sheet, a projected profit and loss statement, and cash flow projections.

Marketing Plan Financial Ratios

The following financial ratios help provide the information by which your project may be compared with competing plans on a financial basis. Thus they will not only enable you to better understand the efficiency of the plan you have constructed but, assuming the ratios are favorable, they will help you to win support for your project.

Measure of Liquidity

Liquidity is the ability to use the money available in your business. In general, the more liquid, the better the state of financial health. However, this is a bit oversimplified. The ratios intended to measure liquidity in your business will tell you whether you have enough cash on hand, plus assets that can be readily turned into cash, to pay debts that may fall due during any given period. They will also tell you how quickly the assets can be turned into cash.

Current Ratio

The current ratio is possibly the best-known measure of financial health. It answers this question: Does your business have sufficient current assets to meet current debts (liabilities) with a margin of safety for possible losses due to uncollectible accounts receivable and other factors? It is computed by using information on your balance sheet. You simply divide current assets by current liabilities.

Whether or not the result is a "good" ratio is evident only when it is compared with past ratios during known periods of good financial strength of the company, or with the ratios of other companies in your industry. Rule of thumb: A ratio of 2 is good.

Acid Test, or "Quick" Ratio

The acid test, or "quick" ratio, is also an outstanding measurement of liquidity. You calculate this ratio as follows: cash plus government securities plus receivables divided by current liabilities. Thus the quick ratio concentrates on fully liquid assets whose values are definite and well known. Therefore, the quick ratio will answer the question: If all your sales revenue disappears tomorrow, can you meet current obligations with your cash or quick funds on hand? Rule of thumb: A ratio of 1 is good.

Average Collection Period

The average collection period is the number of days that sales are tied up in accounts receivable. This number can be calculated by using your profit and loss statement or income statement. First, take your net sales figure and divide it by the number of days in your accounting period, or 365. This equals the average sales per day in the accounting period. Next, take your accounts receivable figure from your balance sheet and divide it by the average sales per day in the accounting period. This gives you the average number of days sales are tied up in receivables. It is also your average collection period.

This figure also tells you the quality of your accounts (how well your sales people are qualifying their customers) and how good a job your credit department is doing in collecting these accounts. Rule of thumb: The average collection period should not exceed one and one-third times the credit terms offered.

Inventory Turnover

Inventory turnover will show you how rapidly your product is moving. It will also show you how much capital you had tied up in inventory to support the level of your company's operations for the period that you are analyzing. To calculate inventory turnover, simply divide the cost of goods sold that you obtain from your income statement by your average inventory. The average inventory is obtained by summing the latest two inventory figures and dividing that sum by two. Rule of thumb: The higher the turnover rate, the better.

Again, the desirable rate depends on your business, your industry, your method of valuing inventories, and many other factors that are unique to your situation.

Measures of Profitability

Measures of profitability are essential in your business if you are to know how much money you are making, whether you are making as much as you can, or whether you are making money at all. There are several different ratios that will help you in determining this. These are the asset earning power, return on owner's equity, net profit on sales, investment turnover, and, finally, return on investment (ROI).

Asset Earning Power

Asset earning power is determined by the ratio of earnings before interest and taxes to total assets. The total operating profit or income figure is obtained from the income statement. The total assets figure is obtained from the balance sheet. The total operating profit is divided by the total assets to obtain the asset earning power ratio, which is actually the earned rate of return on assets (ROA) expressed in decimal form. Multiply this figure by 100 and you get the ROA expressed as a percentage.

Return on Owner's Equity

Return on owner's equity shows the return that you received in exchange for your investment in your business. To compute this ratio you will usually use the average equity for 12 months, if it is available, or the average of figures from two different balance sheets, your latest and the one before. Divide this figure into the figure for net profit. The result is the figure for the rate of return on owner's equity expressed as a decimal. Multiply this figure by 100 to get the percentage of return.

Net Profit on Sales

The net profit on sales ratio measures the difference between what you take in and what you spend doing business. Here you take the figure for net profit and divide it by the figure for net sales. The result is the profit made on each sale expressed in dollars.

The net profit on sales ratio depends mainly on two factors: operating costs and pricing policies. Therefore, if this figure goes down, it could be because you have lowered prices or because costs have been increasing at the same time prices have remained stable.

Again, this ratio should be compared with like figures from other similar businesses, and you should consider trends over a period of time.

Investment Turnover

This ratio is annual net sales to total assets. Calculate it by dividing total assets into net sales. This ratio should be compared and watched for trends.

Return on Investment (ROI)

ROI is a very useful method of measuring profitability. There are several different ways of calculating return on investment. The simplest calculation is to take net profit and divide it by total assets. You can use this rate of return on investment for intercompany and interindustry comparisons, as well as pricing costs, inventory, and investment decisions, and many other measurements of efficiency and profitability.

Here are some additional measures of profitability using ROI:

- □ Rate of earnings on total capital employed equals net income plus interest and taxes divided by total liabilities and capital. This ratio serves as an index for productivity of capital as well as a measure of earning power in operating efficiency.

- □ Rate of earnings on invested capital equals net income plus income taxes divided by proprietary equity and fixed liabilities. This ratio is used as a measure of earning power of the borrowed invested capital.

- □ Rate of earnings on proprietary equity equals net income divided by total capital including surplus reserves. This ratio is used as a measure of the yield on the owner's investment.

- □ Rate of earnings on stock equity equals net income divided by total capital including surplus reserves. This ratio is used as a measure of the attractiveness of common stock as an investment.

- □ Rate of dividends on common stock equity equals common stock dividends divided by common stock equity. This ratio is used to indicate the desirability of common stock as a source of income.

- □ Rate of dividends on common stock equity equals common stock dividend per share divided by market value per share of common stock. This ratio is used as a measure of the current yield on investment in a particular stock.

5

Developing a Sales
and Revenue Plan

The development of a sales and revenue plan for a firm requires estimates of expected sales in product and service units. These estimates become a critical input to planning production or service capacity, the average unit price for each product or service group, and the marketing and sales expenses associated with achieving a given level of sales. These estimates should be based on an analysis of objective information about historical trends and relationships, market developments, and expectations of future developments and relationships.

A major purpose of the analytical and decision-making processes is to develop an objective set of information that can be used to prepare reasonable and valid estimates of sales, prices, and expenses. Goals and prices must be established for total sales by product/service group, customer segment, and geographic area; for prices to be charged for product/service groups; for size and productivity of the sales effort; for objectives and expenditure levels of advertising and promotion efforts; and for costs and productivity of the distribution system.

These goals and policies are based on an analysis of historical trends; an assessment of market developments and possible competitor actions; and the interaction among prices, advertising/promotion efforts, and sales levels. Although the available approaches for developing sales, price, and expense estimates range from using ballpark figures to using statistical forecasting techniques, a recommended approach for most firms is to begin with an estimate of unit sales provided by the sales group, developed from sales force inputs. The most important consideration here is to ensure that the sales estimate makes sense in terms of each dimension in the matrix approach to goal setting. The price and expense estimates can then be correlated with the sales estimate based on historical relationships and the firm's understanding of the marketplace.

Developing Quarterly Sales and Revenue Objectives

Although the estimate of annual sales has been developed through the goal-setting process, quarterly sales objectives should be developed to support an effective management and control process. Quarterly sales objectives serve a couple of useful management purposes. First, since variable expenses are directly tied to production levels that in turn are directly related to sales levels, quarterly sales objectives provide a leading indicator benchmark that should be used to plan and control production levels and costs, particularly in relation to revenues being generated. Second, quarterly sales objectives, as predictors of revenue being generated, are important indicators in planning and managing the cash-flow position of a firm. Because of these affects on production and financial management, the quarterly sales objectives should reflect an objective and accurate assessment of when sales are expected to occur during the year.

For most firms, sales are not evenly distributed throughout the year. Sales are subject to cyclical patterns of purchasing behavior by customer groups such that more that 25 percent of sales occur in some quarters and less than 25 percent in others. However, if the variability is due to cyclical rather than trend factors, the percentage of sales occurring in any given quarter—for instance, January through March—should remain fairly stable from year to year.

In setting quarterly sales objectives, a firm should first review the quarterly distribution of sales in prior years for each product/service group. The results of this analysis of historical patterns may need to be adjusted depending on the following factors:

1. If new or refined products are introduced during the year, they may have an effect on the pattern of both total sales and the sales of individual products. This will be particularly true if the new products are complements to existing products. An example is the effect of power versus manual painting devices on the sale of paints.

    Similarly, if new or refined products replace existing ones, a firm should subtract the historical effect on sales levels and patterns of the products that are being replaced. This will ensure that double-counting effects do not occur.
2. Expected external developments have a significant effect on cyclical patterns of consumer purchasing—for example, the effect of discounted vacation packages and indoor health clubs on the purchases of swimwear and the like.
3. Upgraded or expanded advertising and promotion campaigns also affect purchasing behavior, at least short term. Quarterly sales objectives should, at least, reflect the timing and expected impact of planned advertising and promotion efforts.
4. Planned price changes during the year may have a positive or negative effect on demand and, consequently, on the pattern of sales.

In summary, the anticipated pattern and distribution of sales should reflect both historical patterns and relationships and the impact of new or external developments.

Once the quarterly distribution pattern has been established, a firm can use this information and the annual sales goal to develop forecasts of the number of product/service units to be sold in each quarter. The next step is to use average unit price data to develop quarterly forecasts of revenues. The key variable is the average unit price. Current price information is known; a goal related to individual product unit prices has been established. The consideration is the timing of price adjustments during the year. Obviously, the timing should occur so as to maximize the impact on revenues.

The approach to this analysis reflects two points. First, sales forecasts should be developed for individual products/services; second, sales forecasts should be stated in terms of product or service units, not dollars or revenues. There are three reasons for this approach to the analysis:

1. From a marketing, production, and organization perspective, sales do not occur in dollar terms, they occur in terms of product or service units. Effective planning of marketing, production, and organization and management activity requires a valid estimate of the number of units to be sold.
2. Customer demand and, therefore, sales are primarily a function of the number of units to be consumed and secondarily a function of the prices paid for the units. Any valid forecast of sales should, therefore, be based on an analysis of consumption patterns, not on sales revenue trends.
3. If forecasts are developed based on units, then the impact of any subsequent adjustments in sales on other components of the organization can be more easily computed.

The unit approach or, at least, the level of activity, should be used even if a firm primarily provides services rather than makes products. In service-oriented firms, planning in terms of service units establishes a basis for estimating staff and other organizational requirements.

Developing Estimates of Marketing and Sales Expenses

Marketing and sales expenses are of three types—fixed, variable, and special, one-time expenses. Fixed expenses are those that tend to be stable and do not fluctuate according to changes in sales volume. Such expenses have to do with maintaining a minimum sales force, marketing and advertising effort, and the distribution system. Variable expenses are those that fluctuate in direct proportion to the level of sales volume. Such expenses are the size of sales force, sales salaries and travel expenses, distribution costs, and the like. Special, one-time expenses are those associated with special promotions or advertising efforts, setting up new channels of distribution, and the like. A firm should use this basic structure to develop estimates of overall marketing and sales expenses and to schedule the incurrence of those expenses over the period covered by the marketing plan.

In developing estimates of marketing and sales expenses, a firm should recall that cost analyses have been completed and goals have been developed in the following areas:

1. Size and productivity standards for sales activity.
2. Objectives and expenditure levels for advertising and promotion efforts.
3. Organization and productivity standards for the distribution system.
4. Sales volume by product/service group and geographic area.

Further, quarterly sales objectives have been established for each product/ service group and, thus, can be developed for individual geographic areas. Developing sales objectives for individual geographic areas requires analyzing and considering such factors as the historical allocation of sales among areas, the composition of sales mix within individual areas and sales mix plans for the future, and the growth of customer segments in individual areas.

With this information, a firm should develop quarterly estimates of marketing and sales expenses using specific formats. The process for completing these formats has the following steps:

1. First, variable expenses should be isolated to the finest degree possible— that is, variable expenses related to sales, to advertising and promotion, and to distribution should be identified separately. Variable expenses are those ongoing expenses that a firm is not committed to incurring despite sales volume.
2. For each year in a two- to three-year historical trend, the variable expenses should be totaled and divided by the sales volume for the year to obtain a variable expense to volume ratio. Expenses and sales volume should be compared on whatever basis the expense data can be developed. That is, if expense data is maintained based on individual product groups, then a ratio should be developed for each product group; if expense data is maintained based on geographical areas, then a ratio should be developed for each area; and so forth.
3. Based on the historical trends, a variable expense to volume ratio should be developed for the performance period covered by the plan. Rather than a straight extrapolation of the historical trend, this ratio should reflect revised productivity and cost standards for marketing and sales activities and economies of scale that may be achieved—that is, variable unit costs may decline as the level of activity increases. The total of the variable expenses for the forecast period is easily computed by multiplying the ratio by the forecast level of sales volume.
4. The ratio should be multiplied by the quarterly sales objectives to obtain quarterly estimates of variable marketing and sales expenses.
5. Fixed marketing and sales expenses for the year should be computed. These expenses are those that have an associated obligation or commitment, regardless of sales volume. Typically, these expenses will be equal on a quarter-to-quarter basis.
6. Special expenses, which are established through the goal-setting process, should be scheduled according to the timing of the activities supported by the expenses—for example, the point during the year when special advertising or promotion campaigns will be conducted.

From this information, quarterly and annual totals for marketing and sales expenses can easily be calculated.

Special expenses will not necessarily be incurred in every quarter. Scheduling these expenses depends on the marketing objectives to be accomplished and the required timing to achieve the desired impact.

Pulling Revenue and Expense Objectives Together

The quarterly and annual revenue and expense objectives should, of course, be summed across all product/service groups, geographic areas, and so forth to obtain a total picture of planned volume, revenues, and expenses and to see that the interrelationships at this level still make sense in terms of feasibility and productivity of the marketing and sales effort. At this point, it will be useful for a firm to decide if further economies can be achieved in sales, promotion, and distribution. There may be, for example, opportunities for linking sales, promotion, and distribution activities for related products or services in the firm's total product line.

Linking the Marketing Plan with the Research and Development Plan

Research and development objectives and plans flow from the market analysis and, consequently, are directly linked with the market strategy and the sales and revenue plan. Although research and development activities relate to production technologies as well as to product development, in practice the R&D focus is on product development and refinement.

The research and development plan should have a specific timetable for initiating and completing the various phases in the research and development process. These phases are conceptualization, prototype development, prototype testing and refinement, selective market introduction and testing, final refinement and production, and market introduction. As the R&D process enters the fourth phase, the sales and revenue plan is affected.

As new or refined products/services are introduced to the market on either a selective pilot or a full-scale basis, several things can or will happen:

1. An additional, special marketing and sales effort will be required.
2. Additional revenues will be generated through sales of the new or refined product.
3. Depending on the relatedness of the new product/service to existing products, the sales of established products can be affected in either a positive or negative direction. For example, if a new product complements an existing product—that is, it expands the usefulness of the existing product—the sales impact will be positive. If a new product is a substitute—that is, it is a potential replacement for the existing product—the sales impact will be negative.

The basic point is that the development of quarterly sales objectives and estimates of marketing and sales expenses must reflect more than historical relationships and the annual performance goals established in Step 3 of the

Gantt Chart Describing
the Purchase of an Automobile

Task Name	Duratn (Days)	Start Date	Resources	Oct 3	11	17	24	31	Nov 7
Research Current Models	15	3-Oct							
Read Magazines	10	3-Oct	Dave						
Talk to Friends	5	18-Oct	Dave, Mary						
Visit Dealers	3	25-Oct							
Ford	1	25-Oct	Dave						
Honda & Acura	1	26-Oct	Dave, Mary						
Chevy	1	27-Oct	Dave						
Buy Car!	1	28-Oct	Dave, Mary						
Arrange Financing	2	31-Oct							
Call for Rates	1	31-Oct	Mary						
Submit Credit Apps	1	1-Nov	Mary						
Arrange Insurance	1	2-Nov	Dave, Mary						

planning process (see page 50). They also must reflect the impact of research and development activities.

Again, to provide an adequate basis for planning the impact of research and development activities, the research and development operating plan should provide a timetable related to accomplishing each R&D objective. A useful format for establishing such a timetable is a Gantt chart. (A simple chart for the purchase of an automobile is shown in the above illustration.) This format has a couple of uses related to managing R&D activities. First, it shows the interrelatedness, in terms of scheduling, of the phases in the R&D process. It also suggests when the marketing and sales and production functions can expect additional work loads due to new product introduction. In addition, where there are several concurrent R&D objectives, a Gantt chart provides a structure for planning and allocating R&D resources.

The R&D operating plan can be rounded out by assigning a level of staff effort or an expense estimate for each R&D objective and phase. This provides a basis for management control and replanning if the milestones are not achieved.

Sales and Revenue Plan Finalization

The effect of sales discounts must similarly be incorporated into the final quarterly revenue plan because they are not a financial management issue based on historical trends; they are a matter of market strategy, particularly when new products or new customer segments are involved.

Developing an estimate of the impact of sales discounts on revenues depends on knowing what products/services will be sold to what customer segments and what kinds of sales discounts will be required to gain or maintain the loyalty of specific customer segments. For existing customer segments, this information should be available through the internal diagnosis; for new customer segments, discount policies should reflect the results of the market analysis. A firm should attempt to develop an estimate of the impact of sales discounts on the revenue for each product group. This is simply because sales and revenue objectives have been established based on individual product groups, and the competitive environment, which may define a need for sales discounts, probably will vary among product/service groups.

Finally, the sales and revenue plan should reflect the goals, policies, and operating assumptions of the market strategy. This ensures that operations reflect the strategic direction that has been established for the firm. Further, since consistency among the basic business strategies (market, production, finance, and so forth) has been established previously, the operating plans also should be consistent.

Because the sales and revenue objectives have a significant impact on the other components of the business, a firm may want to establish alternative sets of sales and revenue objectives. The objectives established through the process described here should reflect a firm's best estimate of expected sales. To provide a basis for contingency planning, a firm should develop a higher and lower estimate around the expected level. A typical approach is to establish three sets of sales and revenue estimates—a moderate or expected growth estimate, a worst-case estimate, and a best-case estimate. The range of these estimates depends on the firm's degree of confidence in the accuracy of the initial estimate of expected sales. If confidence is high, the range should be narrower than if confidence is low. As a general rule of thumb, a firm should feel that there is at least a 95 percent probability that actual sales will fall somewhere within the established range.

6

Growth—It Must Be Managed

We hear so frequently of the spectacular sales growth that supported the success of highly publicized glamour-businesses; the growth that, through forecasting, budgeting, and monitoring, allows orderly, step-by-step development of an enterprise. Rarely is heard the equally impressive sales growth that sabotaged the orderly, step-by-step development of many other promising enterprises.

There is a strain in American business culture that makes high, fast growth particularly alluring and dazzling and blinds us to its perils. Big, new sales figures carry an intoxication. They cause one to recall Napoleon's headiness as he sleepwalked to his doom in Russia: "I felt I had been carried up into the midst of the air and could hear the earth turning below me."

Bigger is Better, we think. Growth is unwittingly pursued for its own sake. It is fun. It requires little discipline to grow, and all systems are go.

The issue, of course, is not "to grow or not to grow." The obvious goal of a small business, either a start-up or following a big push, is rising profit propelled by impressive sales growth, always assuming cash liquidity, which must constantly be kept in mind in the planning process.

The emotional rewards of rapid sales growth must not be allowed to rationalize the failure to build a firm through sustained liquidity to *growing* profits.

Significant growth is a severe test of a manager's skill to control and direct his/her firm and to do it based on an appropriate sensitivity to the specific pitfalls and vulnerabilities of rapid growth.

Managing Growth

Because rapid growth is so difficult to manage (because it is so frequently mismanaged), most managers who have experienced the explosive growth trap counsel a very watchful eye. A Harvard Business Review survey of the growth problem concluded: "Most firms do better with conservative growth rates." Most firms do better growing incrementally, one step at a time. Not all firms—most firms! Some firms, of course, must plunge ahead for fear of losing a major one-shot opportunity, or "missing your niche," in the words of business consultant Robert W. Philip. He points out that a firm may "need to move as fast as it can to exclude competition." But here, do not succumb to marketing's siren song of the "market window." This is another pitfall for management to avoid by questioning marketing and gaining responsible commitment.

The point is that rapid expansion is perilous, and managers must manage growth. They must control and direct it, lest it control and direct the company itself.

By all means, grow—and take calculated risks in the process. Grow and grow some more. Just don't let it kill you. Manage that growth.

Anticipate the Pitfalls

What does it mean to manage growth? It means an acute sensitivity to the various pitfalls of expansion. Those are the problem areas that have demoralized or destroyed so many thousands and thousands of high growth firms.

Anticipate the dangers. And keep a close eye out for any actual evidence that the firm may be veering out of control. That requires an intimate understanding of the specific needs and behavior of the firm and a close eye on the firm's financial position *at all times*.

You must carefully consider, before the business takes off, how much growth is anticipated and how that growth is apt to affect the firm. How soon will the growth occur? For how long? What are the critical areas within the firm that will most likely be affected? Consider these factors:

1. Will the increased paper flow necessitate more sophisticated accounting and administrative procedures (office computerization/automation)?
2. What impact will the growth have on the costs?
3. Is the present staff prepared for the burdens of additional responsibility, of growing complexity? What training will be needed? What will it cost in terms of committed time and course costs?
4. Where will the firm be likely to suffer? Will the expansion damage an established product line or the company's main business? Can deliveries continue on schedule? Will customer service suffer? Will product quality be imperiled? How, why, and when?
5. Where is the firm feeling the pinch already? Where are its relative weaknesses? Will they be aggravated by the pressures of expansion? Can the firm withstand the consequences of growth without significant adjustments? Which adjustments should be carried out in the short- and long-term?

To manage growth requires that you consider such questions and many more before, as well as after, the growth is underway.

Planning for Growth

Successful management of growth also requires that you plan growth, at least to the extent of keeping these factors right before you and anticipating and planning changes in the firm appropriate to new circumstances, new needs, and pitfalls of the growth.

If you are not directly building on an established, solid foundation of achievement and expanding into areas where you know the business well enough, what it is about and what it is doing. You must have good reasons for taking the proposed course. What are the risks and how do you suppose you will, or can, cope with them?

Are you dissipating yours and the firm's strengths, or is the firm, in fact, exploiting an innovative opportunity for which it is reasonably prepared? If moving into new territory, are there any crippling surprises that might possibly beset it? Have you talked with other experienced businesspeople about this particular expansion? And, if and when the firm encounters problems with the expansion, will the firm's established business activities be jeopardized through management neglect? Can the expansion be carried through in separate stages, so that the firm can cut its losses on a solid showing of failure? Also, if it is an all-or-nothing project, are there contingencies for failure?

Guarding the Cash

Above all, your highest priority and responsibility must be to anticipate the cash needs before the onset of expected growth as well as well down the road. You must face this priority squarely. For example, the Osborne Computer Corporation, mentioned earlier, was experiencing very high growth when management realized there was no cash in the bank. A "who-can-tell?" attitude won't do, even if it may be partly correct. You must make a best-effort stab at systematically understanding how and where the growth will affect the business and how it may exhaust the firm's cash. Consider, in turn, estimated sales, associated expenditures, and total cash needs.

The following are some thoughts and questions that should be posed during the planning process.

1. **Sales.** Sales projections, based on growth expectations, must be ventured and constantly reviewed and adjusted. Scrutinize these revenues. Ask questions about the sales:
   a. How soon is the growth expected?
   b. What are the implicit assumptions on which the growth is expected? How realistic do those assumptions appear in cold daylight?
   c. Is the growth based on product advantage? An innovation? Technological superiority? How long will those advantages last? What then?
   d. Is the growth based entirely on a sales or marketing campaign? Will sales drop when the campaign is over?

e. To what extent are easy credit terms a part of a promotional campaign? Have you discounted in advance a certain amount of bad debts or considered probable contractual dispute problems that will forestall actual payments?

f. When will these sales be realized in hard cash—when will customers pay you?

2. **Expenditures.** Estimate the increased or new expenditures associated with revenue increases. Capital costs must be estimated. This shouldn't be difficult, since they will normally be expended relatively early. What other expenditures are involved? What ongoing expenditures are likely to increase? What new ones will be incurred?

3. **Cash Needs.** Determine these needs through a cash flow analysis and examination of cash management requirements. This is particularly germane to the rapidly expanding business. The firm must budget for whatever cash needs can be foreseen in the months ahead. What is the magnitude of those cash needs? Will sales receipts really be sufficient to meet them? And what about the "bad luck" or "Murphy's Law" factor and the inevitable contingencies? For example, sales may never take off as planned, but the firm will have incurred relatively huge expenses, such as expanded inventory and debt financing, in anticipation of a surge. Or the economy may flatten out, and the firm's products will be among the nonessentials that first suffer in a downswing. Or extraordinary expenses may arise—a tax assessment from the past or an unanticipated but major repair or capital replacement, for example.

Is the company's cash sufficient for the periodic crises that often besiege growing companies? Can you fall back on your personal wealth if and when necessary? Are there other ready sources of cash when needed?

In short, if a realistic cash analysis, constantly reviewed and updated, shows the possibility of a liquidity crisis, you must engage in some first-rate cash management in advance. You can consider ways of preserving and producing more cash from the firm's working capital. Or you can develop contingency plans for reducing expenses drastically in time of need. You may, for example, determine that many older accounts contribute no profit, while causing a disproportionate amount of expenses, and simply cease doing business with those customers. Sales will fall; but profits and cash will increase. You can develop plans to shrink the product base and cut associated costs quickly.

Finally, if necessary, you must plan to acquire additional funds from outside sources, either lenders or investors, before it is too late. Otherwise, you are unnecessarily rolling the dice.

This is the kind of management that is required to guide the business beyond the pitfalls of expansion. Managers who direct and control growth, eyes wide open, are seldom heard bemoaning their "bad luck." And few, beside themselves, know just how difficult that achievement was and the first-rate management that was responsible for it.

That "first-rate" management normally has included a marketing management team member who fully understands the responsibilities of the position and calmly but firmly directs all efforts to the controlled growth of sales, product expansion, and especially *profits*.

7

Marketing Research

Information is crucial to planning. Current business thinking has it that planning is crucial to organizational success. But how are managers to plan effectively if they lack an understanding of the factors influencing current conditions or those that may prevail five or ten years down the road? Similarly, executives are urged to embrace the entrepreneurial spirit—to be risk takers. But how many managers are willing to gamble with scarce company funds in high-stakes new ventures unless they are totally familiar with the nature of the business, customers, markets, and competitors? Clearly, the single most important element in boosting the odds for successful planning and risk taking is information. Thus, it is a fact that we are in the midst of an "information explosion." The extraordinary growth of the data processing industry was no accident or historical aberration. It developed to meet the business need for more extensive, reliable, and easily accessible information on which decisions are formulated and implemented.

Why should a nonmarketing executive be interested in how market researchers collect and analyze data? These managers have their information needs, but neither the time nor the inclination to become enmeshed in the nitty-gritty work of the researcher. The reason for this attitude can be attributed to a lack of understanding of how the nonmarketing executive can contribute to the market research effort.

First, any knowledgeable manager, especially one with a hand in corporate strategy making, knows that decisions must be based on valid and comprehensive information. Without at least a working familiarity with the techniques of gathering information and the sources from which data are compiled, the task of evaluating the information from which decisions are made becomes an exercise in futility.

Second, nonmarketing executives are often called upon to provide input for the market research effort. Financial managers, for example, may be asked for financial statements, including balance sheets and profit and loss statements. Sales managers will most certainly be asked for sales records covering customers, products, and size of orders. Only by knowing why the information is required, how it is used, and how it fits into the larger scheme of the project, can managers appreciate the need for such data.

Finally, it is most often not necessary, or even desirable, for nonmarketing executives to get involved with complex statistical tabulation or reams of computer printouts. That's the job of the market researcher. What is necessary for those managers is to know the types and sources of market research material so that they can make informed judgments on the adequacy of data used in the decision-making process.

What Is Marketing Research?

Marketing research is concerned with information of relevance to the marketing function specifically, but also to all corporate managers involved in both short- and long-term planning. According to the American Marketing Association, "Marketing research is the systematic gathering, recording, and analyzing of data about problems relating to the marketing of goods and services." This general "textbook" definition of marketing research fails to sort out the particular types of data essential to the planning process. Basically, these include the customers, markets, competitors, and the business environment.

Marketing research is an organized way of finding objective answers to questions every business must answer to succeed. Every business owner/manager must ask:

☐ Who are my customers and potential customers?
☐ What kind of people are they?
☐ Where do they live?
☐ Can and will they buy?
☐ Am I offering the kinds of goods and services they want—at the best place, at the best time, and in the right amounts?
☐ Are my prices consistent with what buyers view as the products' values?
☐ Are my promotional programs working?
☐ What do customers think of my business?
☐ How does my business compare with that of my competitors?

Marketing research, as with any people-oriented study, is not a perfect science; it deals with people and their constantly changing likes and dislikes that can be affected by hundreds of influences, many of which simply can't be identified. Marketing research tries, however, to learn about markets scientifically. That is, simply, to gather facts in an orderly, objective way; to find out how things are, not how you think they are or would like them to be; and to determine what people want to buy, not just what you want to sell them.

Market Research Benefits Decision Making

It's tough, practically impossible, to sell people what they don't want. (Remember the Edsel?) That is pretty obvious. It is just as obvious that nothing could be simpler than selling people what they do want. Big business has to do marketing research to find out what is wanted. The same reasoning holds for small business.

For once, small business holds an edge. The giants must hire experts to go out and discover what's what in the mass market in which they sell. Owner-managers of small businesses are close to their customers; they can learn much more quickly about the likes and dislikes of their specific customers. They can react quickly to changes in their customers' buying habits.

Owners of small businesses often have a "feel" for their customers (their markets) that comes from years of experience. Experience can be a double-edged sword, though, since it comprises a tremendous mass of facts acquired at random over several years. Information about markets gained from long experience may no longer be timely enough to base current selling decisions on. In addition, some "facts" may be vague, misleading impressions, or folk tales of the "everybody knows that . . ." variety.

Marketing research focuses and organizes marketing information. It ensures that such information is timely. It provides what you need to:

□ Reduce business risks.
□ Spot problems and potential problems in your current market.
□ Identify and profit from sales opportunities.
□ Get basic facts about your markets to help you make better decisions and set up plans of action.

Surveys conducted over the last several years have shown that many companies have downplayed the role of market research. Proof of this has been the size of budget allocations for market research. One survey of some 240 companies revealed the average allocation per firm was only 2.2 percent of the operating budget. The major reasons given for the low budget allocation include:

1. Lack of management commitment to, or trust in, market research.
2. Lack of financial resources available for research.
3. Lack of appreciation or understanding of the benefits of market research to the organization.

Other more recent surveys show, yet, that spending for market research is beginning to rise, sometimes to six percent or more of budgetary allocations. A major reason for the increase is that following the recession of 1981–82, chief executives began to recognize the diversity of their customer base and the intensity of competitive market forces. Both factors played havoc with profits and sales during the recession. Now, there is a growing sense that the benefits of market research are well worth the costs. Among the most frequently cited benefits of market research:

□ It reduces the chance of error in decision making by providing managers with the data needed to objectively evaluate all the options in planning a course of action.
□ It enables managers to forecast future trends more accurately by highlighting the relationships between the various "environmental" factors, such as markets, customers, competition, and the economy.

☐ It uncovers often latent business opportunities. For example, it reveals weaknesses that exist in the competition or previously undetected customer needs. Market research can be crucial in determining customer attitudes and behavior and thus eliminate many risks inherent in planning and decision making.

☐ It allows the justification and assumptions upon which both corporate and marketing strategies are formulated.

☐ It assembles and evaluates data on the performance of a firm's products and services.

☐ It pinpoints the risks and opportunities of proposed new ventures.

☐ It helps in the design, supervision, and analysis of market tests.

☐ It contributes to the cost/benefit review of a proposed new product or service.

☐ It aids in the current and potential performance evaluation of various elements of the marketing mix, such as sales, advertising, promotion, pricing, and packaging.

Market Research Process

Owners and managers probably do some market research every day during their routine management activities without being aware of it. They check returned items to see if there is some pattern. When they see an old customer who has stopped coming to their shop, they ask why he hasn't been in lately. They look at a competitor's ad to see what that store is charging for the same product they're selling.

Marketing research simply makes this process more orderly. It provides a framework that lets you objectively judge the meaning of the information you gather about your market. The following list shows the steps in the marketing research process:

1. Define the problem (limit and state clearly)
2. Assess available information
3. Assess additional information. If required
   a. Review internal records and files
   b. Interview employees
   c. Consult secondary sources of information
   d. Interview customers and suppliers
   e. Collect (or have collected) primary data
4. Organize and interpret data
5. Make decision(s)
6. Watch the results of the decision(s)

Defining the Problem

This, the first step of the research process, is so obvious that it is often overlooked. Yet, it is the most important step of the process.

You must be able to see beyond the symptoms of a problem to get at the cause. Seeing the problem as a "sales decline" is not defining a cause, it's listing a symptom.

In defining your problem, list every possible influence that may have caused it. Has there been a change in the areas your customers have traditionally come from? Have their tastes changed? Put all the possible causes down. Then set aside any that you don't think can be measured, since you won't be able to take any action on them.

You must establish an idea of the problem with causes that can be objectively measured and tested. Put your idea of the causes in writing. Look at it frequently while you're gathering your facts to keep on track, but don't let it get in the way of the facts, either. (Incidentally, this technique can be used to investigate potential opportunities as well.)

Assessing Available Information

Having formally defined your problem, you should assess your ability to solve it immediately. You may already have all the information you need to determine if your hypothesis is correct, and solutions to the problem may have become obvious while defining it. Stop there. You'll only be wasting your time and money if you do further marketing research.

What if you aren't sure whether you need additional information at this point? What if you'd feel more comfortable with additional data? Here, you've got to make a subjective judgment to weigh the cost of more information against its usefulness.

You're up against a problem similar to guessing in advance your return on your advertising dollar. You don't know what return you'll get, or even if you'll get a return. The best you can do is to ask yourself how much making a wrong decision will cost to balance that against the cost of gathering more data to make a better informed decision.

Assessing Additional Information

Think low cost and local. Before considering anything fancy like surveys or field experiments, look at your records and files. Look at sales records, complaints, receipts, or any other records that can show you where your customers live or work, or how and what they buy.

One business (Radio Shack) found that addresses on cash receipts allowed the pinpointing of customers in a market area. With this kind of information, they could cross-reference their customers' address and the products they purchased. From this information they were able to check the effectiveness of their advertising placement.

Your customers' addresses alone can tell you a lot about them. You can pretty closely guess your customers' lifestyles by knowing what the neighborhoods they live in are like. Knowing how they live can give you solid hints on what they can be expected to buy.

Credit records are an excellent source of information about your markets, too. Besides the always valuable addresses of real customers, they give you information about customers' jobs, income levels, and marital status. Granting credit, so it shows, is a multifaceted marketing tool, though one with well-known costs and risks.

When you've finished checking through your records, go to that other valuable internal source of customer information—your employees. Employees may be the best source of information about customer likes and dislikes. They hear customers' minor gripes about your store, product, or service—the ones the customers don't think are important enough to take to the owner-manager. They are also aware of the items customers request that you may not stock. Employees also can probably give you pretty good seat-of-the-pants customer profiles from their day-to-day contacts. Additionally, production and clerical people often have excellent information from friends and acquaintances who use your product or services, on how to improve those products or services.

Collecting Primary Outside Marketing Research Data

Once you've exhausted the best sources of information about your market, your internal data, where do you go? Well, the next steps in the process are to do primary and secondary research on the outside.

There are two broad categories of market data: primary and secondary. Primary data refers to original material collected for the specific purpose of the market research project. Mail surveys, telephone interviews, and focus group discussions are some sources of primary data. Secondary data is information gathered for a nonspecific purpose by someone other than the market researcher, from sources within or outside the company. Company sales records, Census Bureau material, and directories of industry characteristics are examples of secondary data.

A discussion of research information typically begins with secondary data because it is to these sources that a market researcher turns first. In fact, many research questions can be answered at the least expense from secondary data before more costly original (primary) research is conducted.

Secondary Research First

Secondary research simply involves going to already published surveys, books, magazines, and the like and applying or rearranging the information in them to bear on your particular problem or potential opportunity. You do this before you undertake any primary research.

For example, say you sell tires. You might reasonably guess that sales of new cars three years ago would have a strong effect on present retail sales of tires. To test this idea you might compare new car sales of six years ago with the replacement tire sales from three years ago.

Suppose you found that new tire sales three years ago were 10 percent of the new car sales three years before that. Repeating this exercise with car sales five years ago and tire sales of two years ago and so on, you might find that in each case tire sales were about 10 percent of the new car sales made three years earlier. You could then logically conclude that the total market for replacement tire sales in your area this year ought to be about 10 percent of the new car sales in your locality three years ago.

The more localized the figures you can find, the better. For instance, while there may be a decline nationally in new housing starts, if you sell new appliances in an area where new housing is booming, you obviously would want to base your estimate of market potential on local conditions. Newspapers and local radio and TV stations may be able to help you find this information.

There are many sources of secondary research material. You can find it in libraries, universities and colleges, trade and general business publications, and newspapers. Trade associations and government agencies are rich sources of information.

Internally Generated Sources of Secondary Data

Departments within each company compile huge amounts of information for achieving their goals. These data can be particularly valuable to a variety of market research projects and should be made available to the marketing department. For example, financial information can be used to compare a firm's product costs with the competition's. Sales records reveal not only existing customers, but new buyers who had never previously composed a target market. Production records and customer complaint files may unearth a previously unnoticed problem with product quality. The following is a partial list of sources of secondary data:

- □ Financial statements
- □ Budget allocations for various departments
- □ Accounts receivable/accounts payable logs
- □ Sales call reports
- □ Sales compensation figures
- □ Sales records typically broken down by customer, product, and size of order
- □ Distributor/retailer reports
- □ Customer service files
- □ Production reports and schedules
- □ Inventory records
- □ Strategic plans and other top management documents

Externally Generated Sources of Secondary Data

Eventually, the market researcher will exhaust the internal supply of information and look to sources outside the company. The amount of external data is almost limitless, so it's important for the researcher to pinpoint information needs in advance and be familiar with the sources that best serve the requirements. Here is a list of general categories of external sources of secondary data. (See Appendix D for a more comprehensive list.)

- □ Government reports and statistical tabulations
- □ Business and trade press
- □ Trade associations

☐ Private company documents (press releases, product literature, annual reports)
☐ Commercial information services (Standard and Poor's, A.C. Nielsen)
☐ Special reports (Survey of Buying Power)
☐ Online data bases
☐ Standard reference works (Reader's Guide to Periodical Literature)
☐ Market research agencies

Utilizing Secondary Data

How a company makes use of secondary data will depend largely on its line of business, research needs, and market and corporate strategy. But there are some general guidelines and examples of how both internally and externally generated secondary data can be applied to highlight potential new marketing opportunities.

1. Internal records can show the size of a company's most profitable customers, their location, size of orders, and their industry. This data can be used to set new sales targets, realign sales territories, set minimum orders, and redirect promotion and advertising to companies in growth-oriented industries.

2. External data (such as census figures) provide all kinds of information about industries, population trends, community growth and level of income, ethnic and racial data, developments and changes in lifestyle patterns, and shifts in the importance of various geographic regions, for example. This information can be essential for targeting new customers, determining site location for new offices and factories, and providing new product strategies.

Advantages and Disadvantages of Secondary Data

The cost factor is the primary reason secondary data are attractive. Information generated from company records is free and many published reports can be had at relatively low cost. In addition, secondary data can be screened and studied at a fast pace, provided the researcher knows what he or she is looking for. Finally, much information can be obtained only in secondary data form—from census information, for example.

But secondary data cannot comprise all the market research. For one thing, information designed to serve a particular purpose may not be appropriate when used in a different context, or it may not be exact. For another, the information may be inaccurate or out-of-date.

Next, Primary Research

Primary research on the outside can be as simple as asking customers or suppliers how they feel about your product or service, or as complex as the surveys done by professional marketing research giants. It includes among its tools direct mail questionnaires, telephone or "on the street" surveys, experiments, panel studies, test marketing, behavior observation, and the like.

A company cannot truly know who its customers are or how they feel about its products, services, prices, advertising, etc., by relying solely on secondary data. For example, sales records may show that a product is slipping badly in the Southeast region, but may fail to provide an adequate explanation for the poor showing. Could it be that field reps covering that territory were poorly trained? Have customers started buying a new competitive product of superior quality? Is the distribution channel at fault? Has a cutback in advertising expenditures had a particularly damaging impact on the Southeast region? These are the types of key questions that can only be answered by primary data—information collected for a specific purpose and in a specific format. While some primary data can be gathered from within the organization (direct communication between managers), the major sources of primary data are:

- □ The market environment, namely customers, potential customers, competitors, and industry experts.
- □ The distribution chain, such as wholesalers, retailers, manufacturers, suppliers, and agents.

Primary research is often divided into "reactive" and "nonreactive" research. *Nonreactive* research is a way of seeing how real people behave in a real "market situation" (i.e., how they move through a store and which displays attract their attention) without influencing that behavior even accidentally.

Reactive research (surveys, interviews, questionnaires) is probably what most people think of when they hear the words "marketing research." It's the kind best left to the experts, since you may not know the right questions to ask. There is also the danger either that people won't want to hurt your feelings when you ask them their opinions about your business, or they'll answer questions the way they think they are "expected" to answer, rather than the way they really feel. If you feel you can't afford high-priced marketing research services, ask nearby college or university business schools for help.

There are two basic methods of collecting primary data: communication and observation. *Communication* seeks to obtain data by posing questions to a targeted group. This can take the form of personal or face-to-face interviews, telephone surveys, and mail questionnaires. *Observation* pertains to the viewing of customer habits and behavior in the field or laboratory, either directly by individuals or indirectly by cameras or video apparatus. While it is essential for market research personnel to be thoroughly versed in primary data collection techniques, nonmarketing managers will enhance their decision-making capabilities by knowing what these methods are designed to achieve. Here, in digest form, is a description of each technique.

Personal Interviews

This method is intended to sample a predetermined group of individuals' responses to a series of questions. Often, this method is used to test customer receptivity to a new or modified product or service. Personal interviews can take the form of door-to-door questioning, interviews in selective locations, such as shopping malls or at trade shows, and depth and focus group interviews.

Depth Interviews

These are structured and allow respondents to talk freely about a topic, with a minimum of questioning. Focus groups are composed of panels of 8–12 participants, including consumers and industry experts, who sit around a table and discuss a subject introduced by a specially trained moderator. Participants are free to exchange views, but the discussions are recorded or videotaped for subsequent viewing and analysis.

Telephone Interviews

Spurred by advancements in telecommunications, telephone interviewing has become perhaps the most popular form of collecting primary research data. This method is most often used when the researcher wishes his sample to be a random part of the population, when the series of questions is fairly short, and when face-to-face contact is either not necessary or not desirable. What's more, telephone interviews can be easily monitored and controlled. They are generally conducted from the interviewer's home or from a central location, such as a hotel or office.

Mail Surveys

In this technique, the researcher or company sends a targeted or random audience a questionnaire, cover letter, instructions, and a self-addressed return envelope. Mail surveys are generally used for relatively large samples and where the information requested can be clearly communicated in writing.

Recommendations for an Effective Survey

It is important not to lose sight of the fact that the goal of market research is the production of a comprehensive information bank to be used in the planning and decision-making process. Since the survey is the major vehicle for gathering primary data, managers must be confident that surveys yield accurate, timely, and clear information. Therefore, top executives should insist that researchers incorporate these suggestions:

1. Precisely define the survey's goals.
2. Identify the sample group and delineate the scope of the survey by yardsticks, such as industry, SIC codes, regions, and population segments.
3. Keep the survey as short as possible.
4. Make sure questions are clear, easy to answer, and unbiased.
5. Break down long or complicated questions into shorter, more concise questions.
6. Use the multiple choice format as much as possible.
7. Make sure the survey is clean and professional looking.
8. Provide a short but reasonable deadline for returns.
9. Write a cover letter that encourages people to respond, and provide clear instructions for filling out the survey.
10. Test the survey out first on a small sample to uncover any bugs.

11. Offer an incentive, such as participation in a contest.
12. Try to find if there are any problems with the survey topic and anticipate any flaws in the responses.

Data Collection by Observation Method

Some marketing purists believe that observing customer behavior is a more objective method of data collection than is communication through personal, telephone, or mail surveys. And while in certain instances watching a consumer actually buy a product or utilize a service can provide useful information, this technique is expensive, time consuming, and must be conducted by highly skilled observers. Furthermore, it is rigid in the sense that consumers do not provide information on their attitudes and motivations.

Marketing Research Limitations

Marketing research is limited only by your imagination. Much of it you can do with very little cost except your time and mental effort.

Strategic Decisions Through Information Banks

Just as marketing is taking the lead in management's attempt to grapple with an unstable business environment, so too is market research assuming an increasingly prominent position both inside the marketing domain and outside to all company functions responsible for planning strategy. Decisions so integral to shaping the future course of the company—those that center on the fulfillment of customer expectations, the response to domestic and foreign competition, and the absorption of new technology into existing systems and new products—cannot be made by gut feeling, intuition, or hypothesis. They require reliance on information and facts. But haphazard data gathering and analysis will not necessarily lead to effective decision making. The compilation and interpretation of data must be made an integral part of the organizational structure.

Marketing Research and Commercial Intelligence: What Is the Difference?

The terms marketing research and commercial intelligence have sometimes been used interchangeably. But there is an important, perhaps even fundamental, distinction. Market research is concerned with all external forces: customers, markets, economic, social, and political conditions, and the competition. Commercial intelligence is chiefly concerned with competition. It may be defined as the gathering and analyzing of publicly available information about competitor capabilities and proposed actions that are essential to planning short- and long-term strategies. In some quarters, commercial intelligence has acquired a bad name because it has been erroneously confused with "commercial espionage," which, of course, involves unethical or illegal attempts to gather information about the competition.

Setting Up a Commercial Intelligence Network

While commercial intelligence is but one facet of market research, the business climate in scores of industries—industrial, consumer, service—is dictating a new significance of intelligence-gathering operations. According to the top executive of a fast-food chain, "The main thrust today is taking business away from the competition, and that fact, more than any other, is modifying our business." What it all adds up to is that knowing the competition is basic, not only to marketing executives, but to top executives of every persuasion. Competitive considerations should be a component of most strategic decisions—whether to introduce a new product, build a new plant, raise prices, increase R&D expenditures, or step-up recruitment of top-notch managerial candidates.

The "competitive analysis" has become a standard section of the marketing plan. But the analysis is only as good as the information on which it is based. In the past, relatively small and midsized firms shied away from the compilation of competitive information mainly because of their preoccupation with day-to-day operations, but also out of fear that intelligence gathering is a timely and costly process. Of late, the mystique that only corporate giants can engage in intelligence has been largely debunked. More of the smaller firms have found that some forms of intelligence are free for the asking and others can be had at a relatively modest investment.

Below is a list of ten suggestions that can either serve as a starting point for a company that has never had an intelligence-gathering program or as a review and monitoring aid for firms seeking to extend their current system.

1. **Identify your competition.** Never assume that you know who the competition is, since companies, both foreign and domestic, are constantly trying to crack new markets. Similarly, the strength of individual competitors fluctuates in many industries. Don't assume that competing firms are those that market identical products. For example, candy manufacturers compete with ice cream firms for the snack food buyer.

2. **Periodically buy your competitor's products.** Read the labels and directions for information about changes in the product. Tear the product apart and analyze its components. A toy manufacturer found that its competitor was able to cut prices because it substituted cheaper plastic parts for metal.

3. **Instruct field reps to provide feedback information on the competition.** It should be part of the sales rep's job to find out as much as possible from purchasing agents. The sales manager or assistant sales manager should compile and analyze the reports from the field for distribution to marketing and other interested top departments.

4. **Have top company managers talk with key customers.** They may be willing to share information about competitor products and services.

5. **Find out what information is available under the Freedom of Information Act.** Ask department heads for a list and description of reports they must file with the federal government. Chances are, your competitors will be filing similar documents to fulfill their regulatory and legal obligations. This data can reveal much about the company's products and labor utilization.

6. **Protect your own information from security leaks.** For example, request that the government bar disclosure of your sensitive documents under agency trade secret exemptions. Beef up internal security to prevent unauthorized individuals from gaining access to proprietary information on company plans, products, and processes.

7. **Constantly be on the lookout for data about competitors in the general, business, and trade press.** Examine not only articles, but also advertisements and new product listings. Columns announcing staff changes and job changes can point up competitor weaknesses and strengths. Even help-wanted ads can tell you a great deal. To attract executive talent, some companies include information on plant assets, production schedules, relocation goals, hiring plans, and marketing strategy (including the development of new product lines).

8. **Consider subscribing to a clipping service or hiring a market research firm.** Clipping services can keep you abreast of competitor activities in various regions of the country. They scan newspapers, financial journals, and trade journals for articles on specified competitors. Market research firms are more expensive but provide an enormous amount of data on publicly held companies. They gather data on everything from patents filed, profit and loss statements, and new plants to labor contracts, lawsuits, and biographical information on top executives.

9. **Never miss the opportunity "to pick the brains of industry observers."** Trade association executives, reporters from the trade press and other experts can supply inside information on an informal basis during discussions at industry trade shows, meetings, and seminars. It also pays to cultivate relationships with security analysts and stockbrokers. Their job is to follow specific industries and particular companies so that they can advise their institutional clients. Generally, they represent a well-informed source of information.

10. **Store all your information in a "commercial intelligence" file or data base if you computerize the information.** This way data will always be easily accessible to you and other top managers.

Organizing and Interpreting Market Research Data

Most managers are not statisticians. True, they should be able to work with numbers and charts in performing their jobs, but detailed computations of raw market data are best left to the marketing department staff professionals. Nonetheless, the nonmarketing manager can gain special insight into the company's customer base, degree of competition, and market potential by understanding the basic data analysis methods, particularly the value they have in helping to interpret what's happening in the business environment.

Whatever role the manager plays in data analysis, he or she should watch out for the following traps that could undermine the entire market research effort and lead to conflicts and problems in planning company strategy:

- ☐ Inaccurate or incomplete raw data which can foul up the analysis process and lead to wrong conclusions.
- ☐ A biased researcher or analyst who may use data to support a preconceived idea or conclusion.
- ☐ "Seat-of-the-pants" analysis by managers who guess at the meaning of raw data instead of using an objective method of analysis.
- ☐ Insufficient funding and staffing of the market research project, leading to just a token study of data.
- ☐ An expectation that analysis will uncover major new markets or sales opportunities when, in effect, it yields less dramatic, but nonetheless useful, information.
- ☐ The inclination to emphasize favorable data and ignore problems posed by unfavorable information.
- ☐ The tendency to get bogged down in details without a careful evaluation of what the figures mean to corporate plans and decisions.

Information Technology and Market Research

Few would argue with the proposition that today's computer, with its immense data retrieval, storage, and analysis capabilities, is making major progress in satisfying business's almost insatiable appetite for information. But many managers are just beginning to understand that the key to the computer's value to a company is not so much the technological wonders it offers as it is the way the computer is applied to solve business problems, both operational and strategic.

Uses of the Computer in Market Research

What is the role of the computer in marketing applications? In answer, remember that marketing needs information of all kinds for planning market strategy. A review of the Market Research Checklist (later this chapter) offers just some of the major areas where computers are used to provide the requisite data. In addition, the list below reveals marketing applications of the most prevalent type of computer—the micro or personal computer.

1. Word processing of letters and reports
2. Market data files and statistics
3. Product data files and statistics
4. Customer listings and requirements
5. Sales performance data
6. Industry and economic statistics

7. Planning and budgeting worksheets
8. Sales forecasts
9. Financial analysis
10. Access to data bases

To the marketing manager, access to the growing number of online data bases is one of the most important capabilities of the personal computer. It puts at the executive's fingertips up-to-date demographic, competitive, technological, economic, and other data both as statistics and as the insights of industry and economic experts. A 1983 study by Link Resources Corp., a New York–based market research and consulting company, lists the following marketing-related uses of online data bases:

□ Market forecasting
□ Market share analysis
□ Industrial statistics/news
□ Price analysis
□ Product positioning
□ Product movement data

□ New product planning
□ Sales/advertising analysis
□ Demographic data
□ Search for business literature
□ Company financial information
□ Company news

How Computers Solve Marketing Problems

Many companies buy or lease computers without fully understanding how these technological marvels can be employed to solve business problems, and for good reason. While the computer manufacturers' reps or dealers are well versed in the units' capabilities—both in terms of hardware and software—at best, they will have only a general idea of the particular problems of a particular business. This leaves it up to company managers to harness the computer's power to the maximum benefit of their companies.

Information Overload

Though marketing managers have, and will continue to, reap many benefits from the data resources of the computer, they must guard against the danger of collecting information for information's sake, rather than using the data to serve company objectives. A firm can be so inundated with research data that it loses its ability to separate the meaningful from the useless and is rendered, in effect, immobile for purposes of making decisions. According to one marketing expert, "We've got a huge amount of data, and management can be overwhelmed by all the numbers." For this reason, marketing executives will be called upon to streamline their data-gathering activities. The job of non-marketing executives will be to make clear to marketing precisely the kinds of information necessary both for establishing and carrying out company objectives.

Sales Intelligence

If one thing is certain about the field of selling, it's that you can't know everything. People and products change, and so does the economic climate. Thus, ever more sophisticated selling skills are required.

To sell anywhere near your peak effectiveness, there are certain things you must know, some things you should know, and other things it would be good to know—about your competition, your product, and your customer. These are the basic elements in every sales situation.

The following checklist examines some of the elements of sales intelligence, asks you to rate this information in terms of your job, then suggests ways of analyzing this data to develop a sales strategy for each important customer.

In the checklist on pages 76–84, the first column asks you to rate the importance of the particular data required to answer each question. This in turn will show how much time you should spend on the other four columns (if it's must-know information, for example, you will want to spend a great deal of time evaluating it, the possible effects on the sales situation, and proposed courses of action.)

Sales Intelligence Checklists

When evaluating the information, you will want to separate fact from hearsay, and make your assumptions based on a realistic appraisal. Then consider, in column three, to what extent you are at an advantage or disadvantage, and, in column four, what effect the data is likely to have on the actual sales situation. Once you determine this, in column five you can plot a course of action.

Caution: In considering possible courses of action, try to choose those that are most promising in terms of long-range objectives and avoid attractive short-range methods that jeopardize objectives. In the actual sales situation, be prepared to exploit advantages and simultaneously anticipate and meet disadvantages.

Observation: Always be alert for new information that will add to your store of sales intelligence—intelligence that in long term will mean more sales.

Data Analysis Checklist:
Methods and Significance to Planning

I. Sales Analysis
   A. Purpose—to classify sales by product or category, figure unit, and dollar totals. Compare results to previous and anticipated figures to evaluate performance.
   B. How achieved—divide figures into various classifications, usually regions or type of product, and use automated equipment.
   C. Value to the company—clearly reveals weaknesses and strengths in the sales operation.

II. Market Share Analysis
   A. Purpose—reveals a company's competitive position and provides a check on sales performance (for example, sales analysis shows a 15 percent increase in sales, but market analysis reveals 25 percent growth in the targeted market).
   B. How achieved—figure out total market sales by dollars and units, then find company sales by dollars and units, then get the percentage of company sales in relation to the total market sales (market figures available from syndicated data firms).
   C. Value to the company—helps the company measure performance of the marketing department, analyze customer trends, and plan market strategy.

III. Distribution Analysis
   A. Purpose—to evaluate outlets selling a company's products.
   B. How achieved—review data, such as type, size, and location of outlet, outlet sales of company products, outlet's inventory, and shipments to outlet.
   C. Value to the company—reveals weaknesses or problem areas, such as inventory buildup. Highlights success of particular outlets. Similar strategy can be adopted by others.

IV. Profit Cost Analysis
   A. Purpose—to show a company why too much money is going out and not enough is coming in despite strong sales and market figures.
   B. How achieved—use gross margin system (final selling price less cost of goods sold), natural expense system (profit is percentage of income earned more than costs for materials, labor, and overhead), and/or function cost system (all costs of markets are compared with income produced to yield amount of profit).
   C. Value to the company—helps sort out profit producing items from nonprofitable items.

V. Sales Force Analysis
   A. Purpose—to appraise performance of the sales force.
   B. How achieved—analyze selling costs of sales force as a percentage of sales volume for a particular period (analysis should include unit sales by each rep, expenses of each rep, gross margin gained, number of calls, etc.)
   C. Value to the company—allows firm to identify sales reps contributing the most and least to profits, detect superior work patterns, plan training, compensation, etc.

VI. Break-even Analysis
   A. Purpose—to establish a relationship between product income, cost, and sales volume by showing the amount of income necessary to yield profits equal to costs.
   B. How achieved—use the following formula.

$$\text{Break-even Point} = \frac{\text{Fixed Costs}}{\text{Ratio of gross margins to sales}}$$

Sales Intelligence Checklists
Competition Intelligence

	Importance of Information MK |SK |WTK |NTK	Your Evaluation	Advantage or Disadvantage AA |PA |PDA |ADA	Possible Effect on Sales Situation	Proposed Course of Action
What is their financial standing? Is it so precarious that they will sell at prices that just pay for operating costs?					
What is their bargaining position? Are their products highly sought after? Is their inventory position good?					
Can they afford to give the service you can give? Can they afford to provide better service than you can provide?					
What are their selling practices, i.e., what strategies and tactics are they known to pursue habitually?					
Who specifically is your competition? Who actually calls on the customer? Are they capable?					
What are their personal strengths and weaknesses? What do they have in common with your customer?					

Does your customer sell to your competition?								
Is your customer located in the same city as your competition? Will this be used as a selling wedge?								
Do any personal relationships exist between members of your competitor's organization and your customer?								
Do your competitor and your customer have social, fraternal, ethnic, trade, or financial relationships?								
What are your competitor's promotional plans?								
Did your competitor get the last order from the customer? Why?								
How would you rate your competitor's distribution?								
Does your competitor have access to information on your customer that is not available to you?								
Does your competitor's organization permit them to operate more rapidly than you can?								
Do your competitor's representatives sell the "whole line" or do they have to tie in with other suppliers?								

(Continued)

77

Sales Intelligence Checklists
Competition Intelligence (continued)

	Importance of Information MK |SK |WTK |NTK	Your Evaluation	Advantage or Disadvantage AA |PA |PDA |ADA	Possible Effect on Sales Situation	Proposed Course of Action
Does your competitor have research facilities or do they imitate?					
Can your competitor see the customer more often than you can?					
What marketing strengths and weaknesses does your competitor have?					
Who are your competitor's key customers? Will they influence this customer? In what way?					
What poor experiences has your competitor had?					

Key: MK = must know, SK = should know, WTK = well to know, NTK = nice to know.

AA = assured advantage, PA = possible advantage, PDA = possible disadvantage, ADA = assured disadvantage.

Product Intelligence*

	Importance of Information MK |SK |WTK |NTK	Your Evaluation	Advantage or Disadvantage AA |PA |PDA |ADA	Possible Effect on Sales Situation	Proposed Course of Action
Is your competitor capitalizing on the performance of one outstanding product or service?					
What extra values do your competitors claim for their product?					
Is their product custom-built for this customer or are they offering standard equipment?					
Has their product ever been used in this application before? Will it perform? Will it stand up?					
Does their product surpass yours or is it inferior to yours in any respect?					
Is their product adaptable to other uses than the primary application the customer has in mind?					
If intended for resale, is it attractively packaged?					

(Continued)

Product Intelligence* (continued)

	Importance of Information MK |SK |WTK |NTK	Your Evaluation	Advantage or Disadvantage AA |PA |PDA |ADA	Possible Effect on Sales Situation	Proposed Course of Action
Does their product (or yours) have hidden values not readily apparent by inspection?					
If for resale, does it require excessive display or storage space?					
Are you or your competitor about to introduce new models or new products while you or your competitor are attempting to sell the present line?					
Will your competitor's product require the customer to train his or her people? Will sale of your product require the same?					
Are any patent or copyright problems involved?					
Is either your competitor's products or yours so revolutionary that they will encounter resistance, skepticism, or doubt?					

Is its design harmonious with other items used by the customer?						
Are price incentives or new pricing techniques involved?						
What is the identification of your competitor's product (and yours) in the mind of your customer?						
What features do you anticipate your competitor will "push"?						
What features does your competitor have that you cannot match?						
Which do you have that your competitor cannot match? Which are most important to this customer?						
Does your competitor's product have any bad features you can demonstrate easily?						

Key: MK = must know, SK = should know, WTK = well to know, NTK = nice to know.

AA = assured advantage, PA = possible advantage, PDA = possible disadvantage, ADA = assured disadvantage.
* If you sell a service instead of a product, you should be able to transpose many of these questions into your terms.

Customer Intelligence

	Importance of Information MK |SK |WTK |NTK	Your Evaluation	Advantage or Disadvantage AA |PA |PDA |ADA	Possible Effect on Sales Situation	Proposed Course of Action
What kind of business is the customer trying to run?					
What is the customer's key reason for buying (buying motive)?					
Is the customer short-term or long-term oriented?					
What is the customer's reputation in the market today?					
Is the customer currently making a profit? Is he or she satisfied with it?					
Does the customer put any profit aside for improvement of his or her product or place of business?					
What is the customer's current size? Rate of growth?					
What are the customer's prospects for future growth?					
Is the customer's cash position fluid?					
Does the customer have funds committed to other projects? How important are they to him or her?					

How is the customer's credit rating and past performance on meeting obligations?							
If the individual with whom you must do business must in turn sell to others in his or her organization, what information, help, or arguments does he or she require from you?							
Specifically, who makes the buying decisions in the customer's firm? Who are the key influences?							
Does the customer have a bad habit of spreading business among suppliers? If so, what is his or her reasoning?							
Does his or her annual report indicate that the customer is planning on expansion? Has he or she set up reserves for research?							
Is he or she in a rising or declining market?							
Is the customer's position in his or her market (or industry) improving?							
How long does the customer usually take to write off such purchases as your product represents?							

(Continued)

83

Customer Intelligence (continued)

	Importance of Information MK |SK |WTK |NTK	Your Evaluation	Advantage or Disadvantage AA |PA |PDA |ADA	Possible Effect on Sales Situation	Proposed Course of Action
How much is he or she affected by fluctuations in business?					
What is the customer's philosophy on inventory investment?					
Is it a heavily regulated business?					
What losses has the customer suffered? How recently?					
Do you have other customers by whom he or she is favorably impressed?					

Key: MK = must know, SK = should know, WTK = well to know, NTK = nice to know.

AA = assured advantage, PA = possible advantage, PDA = possible disadvantage, ADA = assured disadvantage.

C. Value to the company—helps in setting pricing policy, since different prices for a product will yield different results (in addition, a change in any one variable—prices, sales volume, or fixed costs—changes the break-even point).

VII. License Plate Analysis

In many states license plates give you information about where a car's owner lives. You can generally get information from state agencies on how to extract this information from license numbers. By taking down the numbers of cars parked in your location, you can estimate your trading area. Knowing where your customers live can help you aim your advertising for best effect. Or, how about tracing your competitors' customers using the same approach to win them for your business.

VIII. Telephone Number Analysis

Like license numbers, telephone numbers can tell you the areas in which people live. You can get customers' telephone numbers on sales slips, from checks and credit slips, and the like. As noted before, knowing where your customers live can give you an excellent idea of the way they live and what they like.

IX. Coded Coupons and "Tell Them Joe Sent You" Broadcast Ads

You can check the relative effectiveness of your advertising media by coding coupons and by including phrases customers must use to get a discount on some sale item in your broadcast ads. This technique may also reveal what areas your customers are drawn from. Where they read or heard about the discount offered in your ads will also give you information about their tastes.

X. People Watching

You can learn a great deal about your customers just by looking at them. How are they dressed? How old do they appear to be? Are they married? Do they have children with them? This technique is obvious and most owner-managers get their feel for their clientele just this way. But how about running a tally sheet for a week keeping track of what you're able to tell about your customers from simple outward clues? It might just confirm what you've thought obvious all the time, but it also might be instructive.

Market Research Checklist: Areas of Coverage

The key to effective marketing research is neither technique nor data—it's useful information. That information must be timely; your customers' likes and dislikes are shifting constantly. You'll never know everything about a particular problem anyway. It's much better to get there on time with a little than too late with a lot. If you spend too much time gathering too much data going for a sure thing, you may find your marketing research is nothing but garbage.

I. Customers: Opinions, Attitudes, and Behavior
   A. View of the company

B. Product acceptance, performance, and demand
C. Sales and order mechanisms
D. Delivery modes
E. Product servicing (warranties)
F. Price
G. Credit and collection procedures
H. Quality
I. Impact of promotion and advertising
J. Purchase motivation

II. Markets: Characteristics and Trends
A. Size, location, composition, industries, geography, and demography
B. Distribution (sales territories, agents, distributors, dealers, jobbers, etc.)
C. Opportunities for development or expansion of market share

III. Competitors
A. Identification (as groups and individually)
B. Products or services
C. Policies
D. Strategies
E. Sales and distribution mechanisms
F. Advertising and promotion
G. Pricing
H. Support services
I. Customer relations
J. Profits (current, past, and future projections)
K. Cost breakdowns

IV. Business Environment
A. Economic conditions and trends (international, national, regional, and local)
B. Social conditions and trends (population, urban/rural, lifestyle, education, health, welfare, and safety)
C. Political conditions and trends (legislative, regulatory)
D. Scientific and technological advances (materials, equipment, processes, and R&D expenditures)

8

Market Analysis

The purpose of market analysis and market planning is to acquaint yourself thoroughly with all aspects of your market so that you can formulate a plan to capture a share of it. It is the precursor to developing marketing strategy. Some processes overlap, but strategy uses the data generated during analysis to determine and generate the detailed information needed to develop specific strategy.

Marketing analysis will help you to estimate the size of your market today, next year, and for five years or more into the future. It will help you to identify your current and prospective customers as well as your competitors. It also will help you select target markets and estimate market share and sales. A market plan will help you to define your complete marketing strategy. Market planning will help you to put together sales projections as well as make you aware of what may be required to accomplish them. Market analysis and planning will help you to set prices for your product that the market will support.

One key to success for any business is to find a need—not partially or haphazardly, but completely. Does your product fulfill all requirements of a market need? If you were serving the American family sedan market, for example, it would be absurd to introduce a compact car that delivers only 10 miles to the gallon with a top speed of 200 miles per hour. The targeted customers would obtain their needed transportation, but many other market needs would be unsatisfied, particularly in a society that demands fuel consumption of 40 miles to the gallon and sets a speed limit of 65 miles per hour.

A full understanding of the various types of industries, the product life cycle, the competitive nature of the industry, and the various risks a business can encounter is essential to a sound marketing plan and is part of the analysis process.

Beginning with the business environment, you need to determine the specific industry you are competing in. Although this might not seem important, it can be a decision that affects your company for years to come. By defining your industry, you are also defining your competition. A classic example is the American railroads. During the early 1900s, the railroad owners ruled the country. They possessed all the wealth and power in the United

States. Still, they only saw their business as the railroad business, instead of the transportation business. Once the airplane was invented and grew in popularity and the interstate highway system was built, the railroad industry began to decline. In the early years, the railroad owners did not see these innovations as a threat. They limited their competition to other railroads and did not expand their operations to compete with the airlines or highway system. In the end, such a narrow definition of their industry caused a deterioration of both sales and profitability. Today, not only are the smart companies in the transportation industry competing on a transportation basis, they are also competing by providing lodging, food, and entertainment services as well. Avis has even gone one step further. If you rent a car from Avis and plan to fly United, you can leave your bags at the Avis counter and Avis will see that they get on the right flight. This is an example of a nonprice competitive strategy that companies are adopting. Hotels, airlines, and rental agencies are establishing promotional relationships with the various credit companies like VISA and American Express. Because many consumers use credit cards to pay for their travel, this relationship is a natural one. The two companies can share the cost of promotions. For every dollar spent on the credit card, both companies gain.

Various business types are structured to satisfy different market needs. These differences in purpose cause differences in internal financial and operational (asset) needs. In the following paragraphs we will examine these differences in internal needs.

Manufacturer: The major working assets of a manufacturer are plant and equipment. The manufacturer needs a tremendous amount of capital (long-term debt or equity) to finance investment in the plant and equipment. The manufacturer is affected by all the stages of the operating cycle from purchasing raw materials and producing inventory, to sales and accounts receivable. Besides needing long-term financing for fixed investment, the manufacturer also may need short-term debt for seasonal financing needs, such as an increase in inventory before Christmas, and the subsequent increase in accounts receivable as credit sales to customers rise seasonally. To be successful, the manufacturer needs to pay close attention to selling prices, production expenses, size of inventory, receivables, and payables.

Wholesaler: The major working assets of the wholesaler are inventory and accounts receivable. The wholesaler's need for long-term capital is based on the typical operating cycle: the purchase of inventory, the sale of that inventory, and the collection of accounts receivable. The longer the cycle, the more capital will be required. (The wholesaler will always have inventory and will always have receivables. These are called permanent current assets and need to be financed with long-term debt or equity.) The wholesaler's investment in fixed assets, such as plant and equipment, is modest and is usually limited to a warehouse and office. Like the manufacturer, the wholesaler also might need a short-term loan for seasonal increases in inventory and receivables. To be a successful wholesaler, it is critical to concentrate on price, inventory size and selection, administrative expenses, and receivables.

Retailers: The largest working asset of a retailer is inventory. Typically, the retailer rents space and sells the product directly to the consumer for cash or on credit cards. As such, the retailer's need for capital is limited and depends on the cost of fixtures installed and the size of his or her permanent inventory.

Just about the only financing a retailer should need is short term debt to support seasonal fluctuations in inventory. Aspects of a retailer's operation that are critical to the operation of a successful business are prices, selling expenses, general office expense, the size of inventory, and accounts payable.

Services: Because a service business lacks any inventory to speak of, the largest working asset or resource a service business has is its personnel. They are the business! Typically, the employees are paid on a current basis while the services the business offers may take several months to complete. It is important that personnel be managed efficiently and kept to a minimum. The need for capital is usually limited and is based on the cash needs of the business until it reaches the point where its sales support its expenses. Due to the nature of the business, there is usually only limited investment in fixed assets, other than possibly a computer system. Financing needs on a long-term or short-term basis are limited. To be successful, a service business needs to control administrative expenses and payroll.

Now that you have a firm understanding of the various basic business types and have established what industry you will be competing in, you need to gain a working knowledge of the various stages a business will go through in its lifetime: the product life cycle.

Product Life Cycle

The product life cycle can be broken into four stages: introduction, growth, maturity, and decline.

The *introduction stage* is when a product or service is first introduced to the customers. This can either be a whole new industry or a new business within an existing industry. Typically, you will be trying to gain recognition for an unsought good and your customer will most likely be an innovator. (You might want to review the characteristics of these categories!)

The *growth stage* is when sales are expanding and new competitors are entering the market. In this stage, you will be trying to establish some kind of brand loyalty and your customer profile probably will be that of the early adaptor or early majority.

These two phases are the most risky stages in the product life cycle. In the introduction stage, you face the possibility that no one will want the product or service and your business will fail. In the growth stage, you will experience widening acceptance by customers of your product, but you also will face new competition as more and more companies want a piece of the business. It is this growth stage where competition is fierce, prices are cutthroat, and only the best competitors survive.

The recent shake-out of telephone companies and computer companies is a prime example of the fierceness of the competition.

If your new business is in an existing industry, then you will be entering the market in the growth, maturity or declining stage of the product or service's life cycle. In the *mature stage*, there are usually only a few strong companies that dominate the market, and entry into that market is often difficult because of the amount of money required to begin a new company. This is because customers have already developed a strong brand loyalty for the existing businesses. On the positive side, in a mature industry, there is an established demand for the product or service. A business with a slight product differentiation or strong marketing strategy can gain a portion of the market. In this stage of the industry, and stage of your business, prices are somewhat constant and profits are adequate but not high enough to attract new competition.

The final stage of the product life cycle, the *declining stage*, is characterized by decreasing sales and companies leaving the market. Typically, a company in this stage is liquidating inventory or other assets in an attempt to raise additional cash. Eventually, either the company will go out of business or the specific product or service within the company that is in the declining stage will be withdrawn from the market.

There is hope, however, for companies in the declining stage of the product life cycle. Some examples of strategies to extend the life of an industry, business, product, or service include:

A "take-off" is designed to send the product into a new phase of customer acceptance. It is based on the strategy of encouraging more frequent usage by existing customers and more varied usage by current customers, attracting new customers, and finding new uses for the existing product. Some good examples of this strategy might include Listerine, which now promotes its product as more than a mouthwash, it's also a plaque fighter; and Arm & Hammer Baking Soda, which is now more than a leavening agent for cooking or a toothpaste, it is also a refrigerator and room deodorant. Other examples of take-off strategy include the recent commercials for Oldsmobile, touting "It's not my father's Oldsmobile," and the Frosted Flakes ads encouraging adults to "come out of the dark" and admit it's OK for adults to eat Frosted Flakes. In the case of the Oldsmobile commercials, they are trying to create a new image and thus a new market for their line of cars; Kellogg's is trying to attract a prior market that has quit using its product.

"Dynamic adaptation" is the maintenance of existing markets through package changes, imaginative advertising, trade deals, and the ability to anticipate competitors' actions. A recent example of dynamic adaptation is the resurgence of wine coolers, such as the ever popular Bartle & James brand. With nothing more than new names and packages, they are closely related to Boone's Farm strawberry wine of 15 years ago!

"Recycling" is the repeating of the entire product life cycle, but not to such a dramatic extent as the first time through the cycle. This is accomplished through advertising, product improvement, and/or price adjustments. The example that best illustrates recycling is the Apple II. The original Apple IIe peaked in sales during 1984, at which time Apple introduced the Apple IIc, a smaller and cheaper version of the widely accepted IIe. Now the most popular version of in-home personal computers has again been expanded with the introduction of the IIGS with its improved speed and graphics capabilities. Through these changes, Apple has extended and improved the product life cycle of its popular Apple II series personal computer. Another classic example is the Oreo cookie. After sales reached maturity, Oreo introduced the Double Stuff, followed by Oreo ice cream in vanilla and chocolate flavors, and the Big Stuff, which is nothing more that a huge Oreo. Most recently, Oreo has introduced its best product yet, the fudge covered Oreo!

The strategy of "stretch and harvest" is the extension of the product life cycle without major changes or expense. These are usually products that lead the industry and have a major market share. They need little advertising or price concessions. Here, the company normally limits research and development or advertising cost and reaps the greatest amount of cash from continued sales. A prime example of this strategy would be 3M and Scotch tape. Although the tape has been around for years, by limiting expenses, 3M maximizes profits from continued sales of this staple product.

Pricing Strategies of the Product Life Cycle

There are many pricing strategies for the four stages of the product life cycle. Some of these strategies are:

Introductory Phase: Due to the high cost of research and development that is usually associated with a new industry or product, initial prices are usually fairly high. This pricing is consistent with the consumer who typically will be the first to try the new product; the early innovator who is young, has excess spending cash, and has a need for excitement.

Growth Phase: Because of the intense competition of this phase, pricing is usually set by you and your competitors trying to under price each other. This type of price competition is why only the best run and most efficient companies succeed at this stage and so many other companies fail.

Mature Phase: Due to the mature and stable nature of the industry, pricing is fairly competitive and is set by the industry. Pricing will allow those who operate efficiently to earn a profit, but not be so high as to attract many new competitors.

Declining Phase: Pricing strategy usually followed in the declining stage sets prices below the market to get as much product sold as possible. Once you have reached this point, you have either stopped spending additional money on advertising or product development, or you have quit production altogether. Anything you sell is just cash flow.

Marketers must learn to identify and avoid the common mistakes that prevail in pricing decisions. Here is a list of the more common pricing mistakes:

1. **Basing pricing decisions only on the costs of doing business.** Other influencing factors are ignored, such as competition, the law, the changing culture, and consumers' own attitudes about prices.

2. **Increasing price because of a sudden supply shortage and excessive demand.** Buyers soon feel that they are being gouged and temporarily exploited with this weak position, and they don't forget this short-sighted seller.

3. **Keeping prices constant even when conditions have changed in the marketplace.** The result is too high or too low a price.

4. **Determining pricing policies and procedures in a vacuum, thus ignoring their impact on the marketplace.** Pricing strategies must coincide with the desired objectives that are sought from the planned marketing strategies. A low price, for example, may damage a company's image as the seller of quality merchandise.

5. **Ignoring communication channels between marketing, finance, and accounting personnel.** Pricing-related decisions dictate interdepartmental interaction and cooperation on a steady basis.

6. **Failing to define authority and responsibility for pricing decisions.** The accountability for pricing actions and associated rewards or reprimands must be pinpointed.

7. **Ignoring the premise that pricing is an art but still requires a systematic, objective approach.** To survive, marketers must try several pricing alternatives under different conditions and then carefully monitor their results within a dynamic environment.

A successful pricing strategy is highly dependent on tapping key and well-developed sources of pricing information. Pricing research should become a habit, a natural way of doing business. Components of the research process are study and analysis of financial/cost accounting data, use of public plus proprietary secondary data, and primary data collection techniques used for pricing research. Primary research could include experiments, test marketing, focus group interviews, and surveys on consumer pricing perceptions and expectations. Pricing research studies enable the marketer to be more on target with establishing and correlating prices with overall organizational objectives. Previously, pricing studies and scientific analysis for pricing decisions took a secondary role within the corporate community. Today, economic and competitive conditions have elevated pricing research to a higher status. Top managers now frequently demand it.

Symptoms of Problems with Pricing Structure

Here are a few of the problems confronted with price setting:

- □ Rigid target pricing that guarantees certain profits but is out of line with industry norms.
- □ Excessive number of complaints, from both customers and salespeople, about prices higher than those of the competition.
- □ Above-average inventory write-offs because merchandise is not moving.
- □ Constant brand switching by consumers of other companies' products.
- □ Failure of the company to win a fair share of bidding contracts.
- □ Constant feeling of having lost in the negotiating of final prices.
- □ Inability to pinpoint costs and profit contributions for individual products or business units.
- □ Constant price cuts and price wars.
- □ Repeated reaction to price moves of the competition.
- □ Competition on price alone.
- □ High number of markdowns.
- □ Consumer confusion over actual quoted prices.
- □ Too many pricing points that alienate or confuse buyers.
- □ Lack of customer loyalty; constant badgering by customers for the lowest prices.
- □ Failure to do a management audit within a reasonable period.

Determining Product Price

The following questions should be asked when determining the pricing structure of a product:

1. Who is the target market?
2. How sensitive is the target to prices?
3. Who is the competition? How financially strong are they?
4. What are the relevant costs of marketing and producing this product? What are the potential break-even points and return on investment or profit margins? What are competitors' financial variables and goals that could influence prices?
5. Are there any legal, political, or other government constraints in price setting?
6. What impact does the prevailing economic cycle (such as inflation or deflation) have on setting price?
7. What role does price play in consumer behavior?
8. How important is price in the marketing strategy of the product?
9. How often are review and modifications of pricing strategies needed?
10. Does the company follow through with pricing studies to see if it has developed effective pricing strategies?

Steps to be followed in setting prices:

1. Identify the organization's long- and short-term financial and qualitative objectives. The strategic objectives will help give guidance to the specific pricing objectives that must be formulated.
2. Explain realistic marketing objectives.
3. Figure out which groups of consumers are viable market targets.
4. Formulate and evaluate pricing objectives. These objectives may deal with costs, competition, consumer demand, and image categories.
5. Analyze, forecast, and monitor the many variables that influence pricing decisions. A team of managers can evaluate the strengths and weaknesses of the company's pricing practices.
6. Implement and sell the pricing decisions to internal and external groups. There must be conviction and commitment among personnel, such as salespeople and brand managers.

Marketers Must Be Sensitive to the Pricing Issues

Marketers must keep in mind the following items and answer these questions when determining product price:

1. Careful breakdown and examination of cost data is part of the pricing process.
2. Pricing strategy must consider the expectations and preferences of other channel members and probable cash flow problems.
3. Marketers must learn to determine how sensitive the marketplace is to a price increase or decrease.

4. Marketers must communicate the reasons and logic for a price change. There is often a valid and logical reason for raising prices. Marketers must first convince their sales force of this necessity, since salespeople are on the firing line with customers.
5. Is there a positive correlation between higher prices and consumer perceptions of better quality?
6. Selective pricing strategy is sometimes desirable to enhance accountability and controls.
7. Loss leaders should reinforce a company's desired image and lead to sales of other products.
8. Marketers must carefully analyze all pricing allowances, trade allowances, and special deals to channel members.
9. Marketers must know the conditions and factors that dictate either a skimming or penetration pricing strategy:

Skimming
Large number of buyers; inelastic demand
Unique product
Consumers unable to compare value
Economies of scale not possible
Product under patent protection
Advanced technology niche
High development costs for competition
Elite/prestige market target that equates high price with high quality

Penetration
Large market share desired when possible
Product very price sensitive
Economies of scale feasible
Immediate and wide exposure desired
Desire to discourage competition (low-margin markets)
Product easily copied
10. With many high-priced items or industrial capital goods, the marketer may have to price according to the economic orientation of consumers.
11. Leasing may be a feasible pricing option.

Pricing is described in greater detail in the Chapter 9 Marketing Strategy section that covers the strategic analysis of marketing functions.

The strengths and weaknesses of the customer service function must be objectively monitored and measured. Marketers must develop the degree and type of services that are desirable in the marketplace. Quick delivery of a product may seem essential, but consumers may place more value on reliability, durability, accuracy, or higher quality.

Creating and monitoring service policies, objectives, and performance standards will enhance the service department. Admittedly, certain intangibles and service variables are difficult to quantify. But those areas that can be measured (such as cost/benefit ratio of adding more service technicians) should be.

The following are key criteria to be considered in an objective service function audit:

- ☐ Durability of product
- ☐ Reliability of product
- ☐ Length of downtime of product sold
- ☐ Service support level while product is in use
- ☐ Training of seller's service personnel and buyer's employees who are using the product
- ☐ Current and future service capabilities (is the company keeping up with advanced service technology?)
- ☐ Response time to customer calls
- ☐ Service support for technicians and dealers
- ☐ Number of service outlets, their geographic distribution, and the quality of service representatives
- ☐ Level of inventory and number of spare parts for products
- ☐ Warranty terms
- ☐ Cost versus profit trade-offs between level of services offered and degree of customer satisfaction

Management must further decide if it should treat the service area as a cost or profit center.

Marketing executives must learn to unbundle the service components and evaluate each. How does each service component contribute to profits, costs, sales, cash flow, goodwill, loyalty, dealer cooperation, and future growth?

Service personnel, like other marketing/sales personnel, should be rewarded with schemes. In many firms good service representatives, like good salespeople, are now being recognized with prizes, free trips, bonuses, points, and other rewards. Some are also getting commissions for helping to sell lucrative service contracts. Customer service can be used to create new business while still keeping current accounts satisfied, and thus can become a profit contributor instead of a necessary but costly evil. Staffing and training programs may be implemented to teach service personnel effective selling techniques while also updating them on technical aspects related to servicing different product lines. Service technicians should be troubleshooters, knowing how to repair equipment as well as how to handle angry customers.

Consumer Behavior

Marketing might be fundamentally defined as "satisfying consumer demand while maintaining social responsibility." The two basic parts of this definition are consumer demand and social responsibility. Only by understanding why people act the way they do and buy the things they buy, can you fulfill the first part of the definition and successfully sell your product or service. Compromising social responsibility is one of the pitfalls you must avoid while being successful in satisfying consumer demand.

The best example of the possible conflict between these two goals is the current public debate over cigarettes. Smoking is extremely harmful to a consumer's health. The result is legislation requiring designated smoking areas, strict product warning labels, hundreds of pending liability suits against manufacturers, and even the recent advertising of Northwest Airlines touting no smoking on some of their flights.

Social responsibility can even include the way you promote your product. While no one is crying out for Anheuser-Busch to stop selling Bud Light, recently there has been public outcry against their choice of Bud Light's popular representative Spuds McKenzie. Consumer groups are complaining that because Spuds clothing and stuffed animals are being produced and sold to children, this advertising appears to be saying to children it is OK to drink beer. Although Anheuser-Busch is not producing the products and has not officially licensed any other business to produce them, the products can still be found in almost all children's stores and at fairs around the country. Unfortunately, Anheuser-Busch is still faced with the social pressures associated with these promotions.

The need to discuss consumer behavior or individual habits is not always evident. Yet, when you remember that no matter what type of business you are in, the final decision to buy or not to buy is made by an individual, you realize that the better you understand the decision-making process, the better you can sway that process.

When trying to understand your customer, you need to ask yourself the following questions:

1. Who is your customer?
2. What does he/she want?
3. How does he/she make the purchase decision?
4. How does he/she like to be sold?
5. What does he/she think of your competition?

Questions are the foundation of understanding consumer behavior. It is helpful to break consumer behavior into two distinct states: physical and psychological. The physical state includes sex, age, weight, location, and size. The psychological state deals with the consumer emotions.

The two primary emotions you need to consider are a person's motives and perception. According to Maslow (a much-quoted psychologist), motives are what cause people to act. They occur in five distinct phases in decreasing order of importance. The first and most important motive is the need for survival, food, clothing, and shelter. Since a person is concerned about survival, he/she won't be interested in any other activities such as going to the movies or buying a new TV.

The next phase is an individual's safety, security, and stability. A person likes to know where his or her next meal is coming from and that his or her family will always be taken care of. This is the emotional force that drives people to purchase insurance and to save money.

The third phase is a little less concrete. It is the need to be loved, wanted, and accepted. This emotional concept helps to explain why people buy clothes and sports cars such as Porsches. People like to be admired and envied.

The fourth phase that governs a customer's motives is esteem and social acceptance. Most people want to belong and be associated with a group. This need to be associated with a group is illustrated by the number of baseball caps people own and wear, ranging from college and professional teams to Budweiser beer. This is also the same emotional force that drives customers to purchase name brand products such as Coke or Apple computers.

The fifth and final phase is the hardest to define. It is the need to achieve "self-actualization;" the ability to "reach one's own fulfillment." This is perhaps the best way to understand why people climb Mt. Everest or fly around the world nonstop.

Several of Maslow's phases may apply at the same time. While clothing and transportation are essentials for survival, the type of clothes people wear and the cars they drive are also a function of the need to belong or the image a person wants to portray. Currently, the major theme for Chevrolet is that their products are the "Heartbeat of America." This follows Chevrolet's classic theme of a few years ago that portrayed Chevrolet products as American as baseball, hot dogs, and apple pie. Chevrolet is portraying their product as being associated with rural, traditional America. On the other hand, Pontiac is currently promoting its line of cars with the line "We Build Excitement." This approach is an attempt to satisfy the need for self-fulfillment. Notice that none of these promotions say a thing about any of the cars' features or price. They are strictly targeted at the consumer's emotions.

In Maslow's conceptual framework, all human emotions (fear, nostalgia, insecurity) fit into one of these five categories, and a person will fulfill personal demands based on the descending phase of emotions. For example, an unemployed construction worker will probably be concerned with survival and security and will not respond to messages based on self-actualization. It is important to understand that each phase has its own marketing strategy to arouse customer awareness and usage.

The psychological state that you will encounter is how a person perceives, senses, or recognizes stimuli (your packaging, advertisements, signs, or sales approach). Once your advertisement has been seen by a potential customer, he or she will unconsciously screen the message and either accept, reject, or distort it. An individual's perception is affected by personal experiences, capacity to remember, and social attitudes. This state of perception is important because it affects what a potential customer will accept as true, what he or she will associate with, and ultimately, what he or she will remember. By targeting the correct group of customers and using marketing techniques that will be accepted and remembered, you can increase your chances of effectively selling to potential customers.

The physical and psychological state of an individual creates wants and needs. A want is a condition that arises out of the messages that a person remembers (perceives) and is based on psychological emotions. These wants can be affected by individual taste, attitudes, culture, environment, and social pressure. A need is a condition that requires satisfaction and is usually based on the physical state (you *need* food, but *want* steak, for example).

Demand is a want or need that is also accompanied by the ability to satisfy that want or need. The customer must not only want or need your product, but must also be able to pay for it, either with cash or available credit. Which product a person will choose to satisfy that demand will be influenced by income, then personal taste and availability of substitute products, and finally by price. Based on these ideas, a person may need a car, want a Mercedes, but only afford a Yugo. This person does not have demand in the eyes of Mercedes and they would be wasting their time trying to sell him or her a Mercedes 350SL. The final ingredient to demand is the willingness to buy. Although some people are extremely well off, no one can have everything they want or do everything they would like. A consumer might be able to afford that Mercedes, but only if he or she does not take the usual ski trip this year. For everyone, there are trade-offs. The key is to convince the consumer that your product will offer sufficient satisfaction to make your choice worthwhile.

As consumers build demand, they go through what is called the consumer adoption process. The five stages of consumer adoption are: 1) awareness, 2) interest, 3) evaluation, 4) trial, 5) adoption. A customer cannot feel a need for a product or service until he or she is aware it exists. In this phase, you need to develop a strategy to inform the customer of your product's existence. Once the customer is aware the product exists, you must develop an interest in that customer for your product. You must make the customer want to try your product for the first time if it is a new product, or try your product instead of a competitor's. In trying to persuade the customer to try your product, you must offer a basis on which to make that decision. The customer must be able to see some type of satisfaction or reward for buying your product. Once the customer has tried and likes your product, he or she should adopt it as a satisfaction for a specific need that he or she feels. When the customer feels that need in the future, it is hoped, he or she will again buy and use your product.

Consumer Adoption Process

The consumer adoption process is the idea that certain people will accept and use your product in different stages of behavior based on varying personalities. These classes of adoption in the order of the greatest willingness to try your product are innovators (2.5 percent of the total market), early adopters (13.5 percent), early majority (34% percent), late majority (34% percent), and laggards (16 percent). (These percentages are based on the natural "bell curve" distribution.) It is important to remember that each of these groups generally has different traits that separate them. These traits might include social and ethnic background, age, race, family stage, and geographic location. Innovators tend to be young and well educated and are able to understand and apply technical information to their decision process. They also tend to be mobile and have significant contacts outside their local social group. They typically rely on impersonal and scientific information rather than emotional promotions.

In contrast to innovators, early adopters are usually well respected by their peers and are in positions of leadership. They tend to be younger, mobile, and more creative than the later adopters. Typically, they respond better to direct salespeople and are an extremely important class of consumers because of the respect they have for the following groups.

The early majority likes to avoid risk and will wait to consider a new product until the product has gained some sort of positive following from early adopters. When the early majority is trying a product, the product is probably well into the growth stage. Typically, the early majority consists of company employees with young families. Their ability to accept risk is limited due to their limited time in the work force and the need to raise a family and build net worth.

Members of the late majority are older than the early majority and are skeptical and cautious. They have experienced various disappointments in life and are cautious about trying anything new. Often, it is only social peer pressure that forces them to adopt a new product. This category tends to ignore promotional messages and relies more on other late adopters for guidance.

For a marketer, the laggards are almost a lost cause. They tend to be much older, less educated, and are lower income earners. They will stick with the same old product even though consumers around them have changed products long ago. They do not respond to marketing messages and only look to other laggards for guidance.

It is essential for you to identify the group that you intend to try to sell to, and organize your marketing plan according to the traits of that group. You can create the right marketing message to reach successfully the group you have identified.

Consumer Spending Factors

It is important to understand the economic factors that affect how people spend their money. The more money an individual has in savings, the less the individual will need to set aside for savings from his or her current income. The less money saved, the more income available for leisure items such as travel, entertainment, and sporting goods, and the greater potential to purchase those higher-priced durable items like cars, appliances, and housing.

Closely related to personal savings is personal debt that includes personal loans, car loans, house loans, and credit card balances. The further in debt an individual is, the less money he or she has available from current income to spend today. Heavy debt limits the consumer's ability to borrow additional money for such items as cars and appliances.

Another factor that relates to savings and debt is the expectation people have about their income, prices or inflation, and product availability. If consumers expect prices to rise, they will purchase and put into inventory goods they feel are a necessity. Similarly, if they expect their income to rise in the future, they are likely to borrow and spend money based on that future expected income.

No discussion of debt or savings is complete without an understanding of interest rates. Historically, traditional savings accounts earned a fixed 5.25 percent or 5.5 percent rate of interest, and consumer debt for cars and homes were also at fixed rates. However, in the early 1980s, as banks were deregulated and interest rates were in essence higher than normal, consumers were able to take advantage of new investment accounts such as interest checking and money market accounts. Consumers were able to take advantage of the higher rates on savings while still paying lower fixed rates for preexisting car and home loans. According to Stephen S. Roach, a senior economist at Morgan Stanley & Co., floating rate investments at the end of 1983 outnumbered floating rate loans by a margin of 7–1. Yet, by the end of 1987, the margin had dwindled to 4–1. Included in these new variable rate loans were home mortgages (approximately 60 percent of all new mortgages) and variable rate home equity loans ($20 billion at the end of 1985, and $75 billion at the end of 1987).

Also in the decision to spend money today or in the future, is the number of products with longer lives (durable goods) that people own. Because of the nature of the product, durable goods are generally expensive. During hard economic times like a recession, people tend to put off the purchase of durables, such as cars and appliances. Still, as the economy improves and people have more money to spend, they begin to replace older durables that are beginning to wear out. Once older durable goods have been replaced (everyone has new washers & dryers, cars, refrigerators, television sets, and stereos), consumers will begin to spend money on leisure activities such as travel and entertainment. They know they won't have to replace those major appliances for years to come.

Finally, the decision of how much and when to spend money is affected by personal taxes and people's attitudes toward the need to save for the future. The higher the taxes (whether they are personal, business, or add on taxes) the fewer dollars people will have to spend on goods and services.

Savings and debt affects the demographics of consumers. Young couples and those with families tend to have higher debt levels due to purchasing cars, housing, and education. This group is affected more severely by an upswing in interest rates than the older family which had established itself, has less debt, and has the opportunity to build assets over a longer period of time.

Summarized below are the factors that influence consumer spending:

- ☐ Liquid asset balances
- ☐ Durable goods balances
- ☐ Expectations of income, prices, and product availability
- ☐ Debt levels
- ☐ Attitudes toward savings
- ☐ Taxes

Defining the Target Market

Now that you understand a customer's physical and emotional demands, you can begin to define the group of people you consider to be your target market. A target market is that group of people you believe have demand for your product and that you want to sell to. In defining that market, you need to consider who will be making the actual purchase decision, who will have an influence on that decision, and who will decide when and where to buy the product or service initially and on a repeat basis. Traditionally, men have made the buying decision on such items as cars and stereo equipment, though these purchases may be used by the wife. Women have typically decided on the household appliances and furnishings. However, in today's society of two-income families, women are also playing a major role in the purchase decision of traditionally male-dominated purchase items such as stereos, televisions, and automobiles.

To define a target market, the target market must be:

- ☐ Identifiable
- ☐ Measurable

□ Economically accessible
□ Stable over time
□ Have adequate buying potential
□ React uniquely to a marketing effort

Demographics

Demographics are studies based on research by the national census, local governmental agencies, and private firms. These studies list such items as average income, average age, average family size, and a variety of other information about consumers who live in a given geographic area. Excellent sources for demographic studies include your local Chamber of Commerce, the local newspaper, your state's Department of Commerce, and the local library, as well as your local radio stations.

As a business owner/manager, you must develop a "profile" of your primary customer or customers. These will be the people you believe have demand for your product or service and will be making the purchase decision. Excellent sources to help you determine your appropriate profile are the various industry associations and trade publications. For example, one of the major publications for the scuba diving industry is *Skin Diver Magazine*. The media kit for the magazine states that the "average" subscriber fits the following profile:

Male	86.0%
Female	14.0%
Average Age	34.7 years
Attended College	82.7%
Average Household Income	$48,000
Professional/Managerial	68.4%
Traveled Over Seas in Last Three Years	60.6%
Average Amount Spent on Dive in Past 12 Months	$1,598
Average Investment in Equipment	$1,710

Although this "average" subscriber is not characteristic of all scuba divers, you now have a customer profile with which to base your product line selection (depth and breadth), pricing objectives, promotional message, media channels, and location selection.

In quantifying this group, you want to determine the number of people in the group, what they have in common, how much money they have to spend, and how you can effectively solicit them for sales. The answers to these questions will be based on those psychological and physical states previously discussed. To determine the size and location of the target market you have identified, you will need to use what are called demographics.

Demographic Shifts Potential

An analysis of current population and business trends paints a picture of a substantially different mix of buyers in year 2000. These developments will force marketers to emphasize different types of products and services, alter their advertising appeals, and adjust every aspect of their marketing.

Shifting World Population

Today the industrial democratic world comprises about 15 percent of the planet's population. If the current birth rates continue, the percent will be down to about 12 by the year 2000; by mid twenty-first century, only 7–8 percent of us will live in the industrialized democratic world. Thus proportionally there will be a lot more consumers in the less developed countries (LDCs) and Eastern European (previously Soviet-bloc) countries than there are today. More items will be aimed at those buyers, and a different mix of products will be offered.

Key Changes in U.S. Demographics

In America, the youth market will fade and the proportion of traditional two-parent households will continue to decrease. Higher levels of education will mean fewer unsophisticated, easily influenced consumers. The work force will include more women and fewer young people, and changing job patterns will lead to different buying patterns. U.S. consumers will command substantially greater resources than they do today. Booming entrepreneurship and a greater proportion of service providers will affect the mix of products and services created and sold in the business-to-business arena.

Here are some specifics:

Aging Population
By the year 2000, the dominant consumers will be in the 40–60 age group. Fifty percent of them, versus 25 percent today, will have had some college education. Because of the "birth dearth" of the 1970s, there will be about 20 percent fewer employees in their early 20s than there were in 1975.

Increasing Affluence
Based on a conservative 1.5 percent annual income growth, American households will have about 30 percent more disposable income in real dollars—if the U.S. continues to be able to provide jobs for most adults.

Fewer, but More Affluent, Traditional Households
The proportion of husband-wife households will drop from about two-thirds today to less than half by the year 2000. Single-parent and single households will be a very large market. Although fewer proportionally, husband-wife households—many enjoying second incomes—will increase in affluence. By year 2000, more than one-third of married couples aged 45–55 will be earning $50,000 or more.

Influx of Working Women
Experts see no letup in the movement of women away from the home and into the work force. With "reentering" women added to recent female graduates, most entry-level employees will be women.

Proportion of Minority Employees
About half of America's population growth is now due to immigration. In the near future, work force entry rates for minorities—both immigrants and native-born—are expected to exceed those of white native-borns by 100 percent.

Growth in Service Employment
Goods-producing jobs are expected to remain static at about 25 million, while goods production increases. Most employment growth will be in the service sector. Economist Audrey Freedman of the Conference Board in New York, predicts that the service share of U.S. employment will increase from about 70 percent today to 80–85 percent by year 2000. Note that during the 1990s, fully 75 percent of all jobs will require some form of technical training.

Actions to Take
There are hundreds of adjustments you might make to get ready for the coming demographic shifts. Some of the more important actions are:

☐ Target LDCs and, politics permitting, Eastern European markets. That's where more and more consumers and businesses are going to be.

☐ If you supply products or services for the baby or youth markets, develop new offerings for the third world. Your domestic and free-industrial-world markets are static or shrinking; those in South America, Africa, and Asia are rapidly expanding.

☐ Develop more offerings for 35–65-year-olds. No matter what your product or service, ask yourself if and how it should be modified to appeal to tomorrow's more mature population. If you run a restaurant, for example, think about possible changes in the menu, decor, and background music.

☐ Bear in mind that tomorrow's prime American consumers won't be a good market for playpens, baseball gloves, first homes, cheap beer, or high-interest auto loans. They will be interested in home improvements, golf equipment, travel services, fine wine, and investment advice. They will also be a big market for health foods, pharmaceuticals, cosmetics, hairstyling products, exercise and recreation facilities, cultural products and events, and educational materials and courses.

☐ Develop more offerings for the well-to-do. Higher incomes, especially in the dominant older segment of the American population, will create a demand for all kinds of luxury items. Quality and "status" products and services will sell well. Astute marketers will provide well-appointed motel rooms, artistically sculpted appliances, fruits ripened to perfection, and flawlessly served restaurant meals.

☐ Or, go for the low end of the market. The poor and low-income consumers will continue to need food, clothing, shelter, and entertainment. With increasing numbers of marketers aiming for the affluent, the lower-income segment could prove a profitable, less-competitive target for companies that can produce goods and provide services cheaply and efficiently. These products and services also might find ready markets in LDCs.

□ Target single households. Package your rice, bread, carrots, or beefsteak in smaller units suitable for one person. If you run a hotel or restaurant, plan your facilities to make an unaccompanied person feel welcome. If you deliver a product or service to the home, don't assume that someone will be there to accept it during the work week. Set up hours or methods that accommodate the workers who live alone.

□ If you're in construction, take advantage of the market for less-expensive small living units. If you're in banking, consider creating new instruments catering to the unmarried. Remember, single people will account for half the U.S. households. You can't afford to ignore the market created by their needs.

□ In business-to-business sales, get ready to face more women buyers. Eliminate all traces of male chauvinism from your promotional materials and sales presentations. By year 2000, a greater proportion of decision-makers—purchasing agents, office managers, plant supervisors, and executives—will be female. Already, 50 percent of business-to-business direct mail purchases are made by women.

□ Pay more attention to ethnic minorities. Thanks to their increasing presence in the work force, many of them will have plenty of money to spend.

□ Develop products and services that will help fill the gap caused by the dearth of young workers. Certain labor-intensive industries now rely on youths to fill their low-wage service jobs. Industries such as fast-food, health care, hotel, travel, and banking are hard-pressed to operate as usual. They will welcome labor-saving innovations ranging from self-service methods to robotic devices.

□ Elevate your promotion and product development a notch or two in sophistication. Your prime U.S. audience will be older, wiser, and better educated. Place more emphasis on the product itself; don't count on good packaging alone to make the sale. Also, cultivate a more mature image for your firm and your offerings.

□ Refocus your sales training. Coach your representatives to place much more emphasis on needs analysis, problem solving, and technical explanation. While closing skills will still be essential in the year 2000, the consultative approach to selling is the wave of the present as well as the future.

□ Develop more convenience products and services. Higher incomes and more working women will create an increased demand for easy-to-prepare foods, labor-saving gadgets, and disposable (though recyclable) items of all kinds. There will be a ready market for appliances that can be fixed or replaced without the need for expensive, inconvenient repair services. More and more busy people will want things done for them—shoes shined, dogs walked, children tutored, trips arranged, finances managed, and backs massaged.

□ Aim products at small new organizations and home-based businesses. A good portion of tomorrow's wealth may be spent not on luxury items but on entrepreneurial investment in an independent future. The continuation of today's corporate instability, combined with a rise in affluence, will spark a boom in part-time entrepreneurship.

□ Increasing numbers of executives and professional people, feeling insecure in their corporate positions, will venture out on their own. Most will start by moonlighting. As a result, there will be a great demand for home-office business machines, equipment, and furniture. All kinds of industrial products and services—storage trays, assembly lines, banking instruments—will be downsized for this market.

□ Aim future sales at service organizations. If your product line is geared to manufacturing customers in the U.S., get ready for harder times. Or, adapt your offerings for the service sector. For example, if you launder uniforms for production workers—many of whom will be replaced by automation—ask yourself what you could do now for the people in offices.

□ Cater to the growing "active retired" market. Because of golden parachutes and layoffs, more and more people in their 50s and early 60s are leaving traditional employment. Those who can afford it and are so inclined will enjoy an extended period of active leisure. Others will venture into new mini-careers as consultants, twilight entrepreneurs, volunteers, or part-time workers. By the year 2000, they will constitute a market segment that's well worth targeting.

In concluding the discussion of consumer behavior, it is important to remember that people make the final buying decision based on how they perceive your product or service. Those perceptions are grounded in their personal emotional state. Unfortunately, it is not enough that your product or service is the cheapest, best, or most available. It must also be perceived as the socially correct one. The same is true for the business customer. Although he or she will place more objective importance on quality, service, and price, everyone wants his or her business to be perceived well socially. They all want to be able to say, "I bank at Barkley's" or "Yes, I have IBM computers."

Now that you understand how people behave, you need to understand the various categories of goods people have to choose from. Because of various prices, availability, and size, different emotions come into play for each category. Traditional marketing defines these various groups of consumer goods in varying product categories.

Market Segmentation

Once you decide who to include in your target market and have located it geographically, you can choose among three primary segmentation strategies to reach that group: demographic, geographic, or psychographic.

"Market segmentation" is one of the buzzwords that has, of late, worked its way into popular business jargon, taking its place alongside such classics as "management-by-objectives," "zero-based budgeting" and "reindustrialization." But unlike its noble predecessors, segmentation is not being touted as the cure-all for what ails the private sector. It is, however, gaining widespread recognition as a prerequisite for strategic and market planning. The notion that all a company has to do to reap profits is to mass market a "better-built mousetrap" has finally been put to rest. Today's marketplace has cracked into literally hundreds of different pieces—a fact made only too clear by the 1980 Census. For example, any one shampoo that would audaciously be targeted at the general population would inevitably wind up a wash out. To be successful today, the product must be formulated, packaged, advertised, and distributed with one goal in mind—to win the acceptance of a clearly defined market segment. Thus, the shampoo would have to appeal to a particular group, such as quality-conscious consumers or working women.

To forward-thinking executives charged with plotting their companies' growth, the task of market segmentation falls naturally between the research and the planning functions in the strategic process. Research, as we have seen, provides the raw data about the marketplace—the customers and competitors. Segmentation, the prelude to planning, enables companies to zero in on who their customers might be by dividing the marketplace into clearly defined groups based on demographic, geographic, psychographic, and other factors. Simply defined, a "market segment" is a group of customers with similar or related characteristics, with common needs, wants, and motivations who can be expected to buy a product or service that satisfies these needs and wants. Once market segments have been crystallized, executives can begin to plan strategies on how best to tap the potential of each targeted group.

Ongoing evaluation of market segments is essential to strategic and market planning. Market segmentation is, by no means, a one-time procedure. That is because markets are constantly segmenting and resegmenting themselves as customers change their lifestyles and needs, and as competitive pressures work to influence customer expectations. These dynamic conditions pose a challenge to managers entrusted with planning strategy. The challenge is to anticipate change, and understand how these changes will affect the market segments they will use for planning. Consider, for example, how the American household, long the favorite target of marketers, has changed in the recent past. Previously, the American family consisted of a working father, house-wife-homemaker, and two children. The 1980 Census, however, revealed that only 7 percent of 82 million households fit this mold. In families with children under 17 years of age, 54 percent of the mothers worked, either full-time or part-time, outside the home. Households have generally shrunk in size with over 50 percent consisting of only one or two persons. The vastly altered makeup of the household and other population segments has forced marketers to redirect efforts to previously unattractive groupings. For example:

☐ Single men now head about 10 percent of all U.S. "households." This is almost twice as many as in 1971 and means that marketers cannot ignore the fact that single men must cook, clean, shop, do laundry, and furnish their homes.

☐ Men and women over 50 years of age account for nearly 20 percent of the U.S. population. To a large extent, this group was previously ignored by companies because of the stereotype that the group lacked sufficient income to be a significant marketing factor. But now consumers 55–64 years old have a per capita income 30 percent above average, work more than was previously thought, and are better educated.

Thus management's function is to uncover the "patterns" at work in the marketplace and define the market segment or segments for its business. The goal here is to find out which groups of customers will react positively to a given product or service and how many customers comprise each group. When the objective is achieved, the entire executive team will be in a much better position to plan strategy than would be the case without a precise delineation of market segments.

Segmentation and the Competition

A total picture of the marketplace cannot be attained simply by keying into the company's particular market segment. Also required is an analysis of the competition's market segments. Management must be prepared to make assumptions about how its rivals view their markets in order to:

1. Understand the competitive arena
2. Recognize their competitors' objectives and anticipate their strategies
3. Plan counterstrategic moves

Segmentation and R&D

One of the least noticed, but far from insignificant, contributions of segmentation is in the area of research and development. As R&D costs escalate and the number of technical options to explore increase, market segmentation is called into play to direct R&D efforts in the fulfillment of market requirements. As noted before, the interchange between marketing- and R&D-oriented managers is critical to the development of innovative programs that are both practical and profit-making. Companies inevitably emerge as winners if they take scientific and technical discoveries and convert them into new or modified products judged by the customer to be superior to the competition. With both the risks and rewards being so high, the role of market segmentation in guiding R&D can hardly be ignored.

Segmentation and Potential Markets

The markets for products and services are characterized not by uniformity, but by diversity. In fact, one might easily argue that no two buyers or potential buyers are alike in all respects. However, groups of buyers share needs and wants and, in this way, are important to executives for both setting marketing objectives and formulating strategy. By grouping customers with common characteristics into market segments, management can gain at least some degree of homogeneity. Thus, whatever basis the company uses to segment its market, the final segment should include groups of prospective customers who are as similar to each other as possible within each group. Here are the most prevalent ways of segmenting the market:

☐ **Demographic.** This is the oldest and most common form of segmentation. It is the study of population, and groups consumer markets into such variables as geographic location, income, age, sex, education, stages in the family life cycle, religion, race, and social class. Industrial markets are segmented demographically by geographic location, kind of business, and size of potential customer's company.

☐ **Geographic.** Although geographic location is a subset of demography, it merits special attention because it is the most widely used approach to segmentation. Companies will often want to tap markets in proximity to production facilities, metropolitan or rural markets, and regions with different climates or cultural/sociological factors. Geographic segmentation is especially attractive to marketers because areas can be easily identified.

☐ **Psychographic.** In this method, potential customers are segmented according to their lifestyle so that buying behavior can be predicted. One aspect of psychographics focuses on individual consumption patterns. The thinking is that an individual expresses his/her personality and projects a chosen lifestyle through the products consumed. Another psychographic approach calls for clustering consumers according to common AIOs—Activities (work, hobbies, sports, social events, entertainment, reading, social and professional clubs, community groups), Interests (family, home, community, books, clothes, recreation) and Opinions (politics, religion, social issues, business, education, world affairs).

☐ **Buyer benefits.** This approach concentrates more on the consumer as an individual rather than as a statistic and seeks to identify the motivation behind purchasing decisions. For example, a buyer benefit segmentation of the automobile market would include size, looks, ease of handling, gasoline mileage, and reputation for quality and price.

☐ **Rate of usage.** In this method, a company segments its market according to the amount of products consumed by various customers. The classifications include present heavy users, present light users but potential heavy users, present light users who will remain light users, nonusers who are potential heavy users, and nonusers who are potential light users. Usage rate segmentation can be of great value only if the reasons for usage variation are spelled out and analyzed. Differences in usage can usually be traced to demographic factors such as age, income, and size of household.

Business Market Segmentation

Although it is sometimes difficult to relate business customers and consumer behavior, you need to remember that all decisions are made by individuals and all individuals are motivated by emotions. In the business environment, those emotions might be self-improvement, greed, or the desire to impress others. We would all brag about buying an IBM but might not discuss our purchase of a Samsung computer. Many of the same branding techniques used to convince consumers hold true for business customers as well.

Businesses can be grouped demographically just as individuals are. The groupings might include geographic location, annual sales, number of employees, years in business, ownership of property, and business sector (service, retail, wholesale, or manufacturing). For instance, a new business might not be in need of a computerized accounting system but would need a monthly bookkeeper. A well-established business might need a sophisticated, computerized accounting system and would only require the services of an accountant on an infrequent basis.

Basic to the market segmentation process is the division of potential buyers into either consumer or industrial users. The consumer's aim is to buy for either personal or household consumption, while the industrial user purchases to further the production of the company's goods.

Consumers generally buy in small quantities, over short periods of time, and in a relatively unsystematic manner. Industrial users buy in large quantities according to a systematic buying procedure. In addition, consumers devote only a relatively small part of their time to buying, while industrial customers usually employ full-time purchasing agents.

Segmentation of consumer markets emphasizes the demographic, geographic, and psychographic approaches. For example, breakdowns by sex and age may be critical in segmenting markets for cosmetic and grooming aids. Lifestyle is a critical segmentation technique in marketing certain food products while geographics, level of income, and occupation are key categories for furniture and automobile manufacturers.

The segmentation of industrial markets emphasizes geographic location, kind of business or activity, size of customer, and purchasing procedures. Thus, industrial marketers will segment their customers by geographic clusters or sales territories. The SIC (Standard Industrial Classification) is a valuable means of categorizing all industrial users into major groups and subgroups, and permits segmentation by kind of business or activity.

Segmentation by size of customer is highly desirable since the amount of material or equipment purchased by a company of 50 employees will be significantly less than the amount purchased by a firm of several thousand employees.

Finally, purchasing procedure can be a vital segmentation method to some industrial marketers. For example, an original equipment buyer will normally follow a more complex purchasing procedure than if he or she were buying the same product as a replacement.

Product Positioning

When viewed strategically, market segmentation often entails pinpointing those parts of the market with exploitable differences in customer requirements and expectations, selecting those areas for a major marketing initiative, and designing a product or service to gain a competitive advantage in those segments. The essence of product differentiation is the development of readily apparent distinctions between a company's product or service and those of the competition in a particular market segment. The difference may be in performance, quality, price, availability, or service, for example.

Once those differences are in place, the company can position its product for maximum competitive advantage. Positioning is the process of developing and maintaining a distinctive "niche" in the market segment. Positioning helps the company to establish a clear, and hopefully positive, image of the company itself, its product, performance, or specific attribute as distinct from the competition. Thus, for example, 7-Up was able to capitalize on its position as the alternative to Cola beverages by using the term "unCola." Avis promoted the point it was the number two car company but "We try harder." In the highly competitive fast-food business, Burger King differentiated itself from McDonald's with its "Have it your way" message and Kentucky Fried Chicken boasted of being "Finger-lickin' good."

Streamlining the Market Segmentation Procedure

As a forerunner to the planning of market and corporate strategy, the market segmentation process is prone to two undesirable and extreme tendencies:

1. It may attract only fleeting interest by the corporate planning staff and thus get shortchanged in terms of market department resources
2. It gets the necessary recognition, but becomes mired in extraneous detail and implausible readings of who customers are or should be.

To find the middle ground for your company and make the most profitable use of the segmentation procedure, consider these suggestions:

1. Focus on classifying customers by their needs and wants. Make sure to select product, price, and quality factors most appropriate to your firm's line of business and available resources.
2. Identify the major advantages and benefits sought for each customer grouping. Use input from market research and your firm's commercial intelligence network.
3. Select the most significant approaches to segmentation. For consumer marketers, these include age groups, income level, family size, and lifestyles. For industrial marketers, these include industry served, technologies, and purchasing practices. For both consumer and industrial marketers, include size, location, buying patterns, competition, and distribution channels.
4. Isolate and evaluate the potential and real impact of outside or environmental factors, among them, economic, social, political, and religious.
5. Draw up a tentative list of market segments. This should be the natural consequence of the previous steps, if clear patterns of customer behavior have emerged.
6. Test chosen market segments against predetermined criteria for evaluation and make a final selection.

7. Describe each final market segment. The document should not be too long but should be detailed enough to paint a complete picture for use in the strategic planning process.

Market Segmentation Facilitates the Planning of Strategy

As we shall see, business planners must work with all kinds of variables—economic factors, competitive considerations, pricing, new product development, emerging technologies, and legislation—in setting and carrying out company objectives for survival and growth. The entire process can be greatly facilitated if the proper homework is done in dividing the potential market into meaningful and measurable components. Here is a rundown of some tips on segmentation that the corporate manager will want to consider before beginning to participate in strategy planning sessions.

1. Focus on a segment that will give your company the opportunity to be a major player. The segment should not be too large —that would raise the eyebrows of the competition, yet not too small either—that could lead to early market saturation.
2. Make sure the segment is characterized by uniform customer needs. This will enable your company to design a quality product—one that measures up to customer expectations. It also reduces the risks and costs of new product development.
3. Do as much field testing as possible of new and existing products. This exercise, though potentially costly, will keep you in touch with the ever-changing attitudes, behavior, and demands of the particular customer grouping. It also serves to direct the R&D effort and results in products that have longer life cycles.
4. Don't allow sales and advertising to stray to other segments. These departments and personnel should keep their efforts directed solely to the selected market segment. By building strength within a narrow segment, your company will eventually gain a reputation for expertise and quality. Sales reps should call only on qualified customers within certain geographic areas and not be tempted to spend time on marginal accounts. Keep in mind that sales and service people have been trained to respond to the needs of a particular type of customer. Major deviations will only lead to a decline in sales.

The first market segmentation strategy is the most broad: not defining a specific market. You attempt to sell to everyone. Although this sounds good and should result in the greatest sales, it is usually unrealistic. Because each group of consumers perceives their wants and needs differently, each group needs to be solicited with a specific message that will cause them to remember and purchase your product. If a message is too general and vague, although a broad range of consumers sees it, no one group will remember and act on it.

The second approach to market segmentation is called differentiated marketing. It is the attempt to modify your product and marketing efforts so that you solicit two or more segments simultaneously. The Levi's "501" promotions are an excellent example. By using various ethnic groups and both sexes in its commercials, Levi's solicits several specific markets individually, but all in the same advertisement. The solicitation is only aimed at people in the age group of late teens through early 20s. Another good example of classic market segmentation is the Chevrolet Cavalier car commercial. Aimed at the young (35–40-year-old) housewife, the ad shows a young mother with a Cavalier full of children. The children get out and she drives away while the voice-over asks, "How do you change a Cavalier from a family car into a sports car? You just drop off the kids."

These are two examples of successful target marketing. Examples of unsuccessful attempts can be just as useful. Volkswagen built its reputation in America with the Beetle or "Bug." With this car, Volkswagen created the image of an inexpensive car to buy and maintain that was also fun to drive. Over the last decade as foreign car sales in America have exploded, sales of Volkswagen cars have lagged. The reason for this poor performance is best illustrated by the current models of Volkswagen and their commercials. The two predominant models of Volkswagens are the Jetta, a family car, and the Golf (ex-Rabbit). Both are offered in basic models and in sports models that come with expensive, high-performance enhancements. Although they are excellent cars, they are comparatively expensive and are advertised as sport coupes. This positioning is not exactly in line with Volkswagen's classic image of cheap, inexpensive transportation!

The third most limited segmentation strategy is called concentrated marketing. This is the selection of one, or only a few, closely related target segments. For example, BMW targets young, upwardly mobile professionals in its TV commercials that stress looks, performance, and prestige.

Checklist for Evaluating Market Segments

1. **Customer groupings.** Is each market segment comprised of a group of customers with similar or related characteristics, common needs, wants, motivations, and expectations? Are their patterns of acceptance, preference, and demand reasonably homogeneous?
2. **Size and composition.** Is the size of the segment—in terms of number of customers, price level, and purchase frequency—large enough to justify special strategic attention?
3. **Natural distinction.** Is the segment recognizable as a natural division of the marketplace or is it contrived only to encompass different customers who can't be grouped as a class?
4. **Relation to other segments.** Does this grouping hold up by itself, or are there confusing overlaps, crossovers and conflicts with other segments that would impede the formulation of market strategy?
5. **Competitive influence.** Can competitors in this market segment be easily identified? Can their activities and planned strategies be continuously tracked?
6. **Time and growth flexibility.** Will the market segment change dramatically in a relatively short time? Does it present sufficient room for growth? How will changing patterns in the marketplace alter the future composition of this segment?

7. **Other options.** Was adequate attention paid to other market segment possibilities? Were they discarded for the proper reasons?
8. **Viable opportunities.** Does this segment facilitate selection of business opportunities, buttress the new product planning effort, help guide R&D, reveal ways of modifying the current offerings, and point out possible obsolescence?
9. **Decision making.** Does the market segment provide useful input on which decisions can be made regarding financing, facility expenditures, developmental programs, and human resources planning? How does the segment facilitate decisions on the selection of sales and distribution channels, promotion and advertising targets, and service support facilities?
10. **Market positioning.** Does the segment pinpoint and encourage exploitable differences in customer requirements, clarify possible niches, and allow the company to differentiate itself from the competition?
11. **Marketing orientation.** Will the choice of market segments enhance the understanding of marketing's role among the company's top decision makers? Does it serve to foster an appreciation of marketing's actual and potential contribution to corporate strategic planning? Does the segment aid all managers in separating the practical marketing objectives from the impractical?

Competition

The largest business risk every company faces is competition. Although you have no control over your competitors' businesses, you can minimize risk from competition by offering the best product or service at the best price (quality), holding costs to a minimum, and staying abreast of current changes in customer demand and your industry. By sticking to basics and never losing sight of your true target customer, you can fend off attacks by larger competitors into your market, and probably even beat them on their turf.

A recent example of the small competitor beating the large competitor occurred in the computer war between IBM and Apple. Traditionally, Apple targeted the home and educational market for their Apple II series of computers. With the PC Junior, IBM attempted to enter this market. Although the Charlie Chaplin commercials were effective, Apple's countering commercial was superior. Apple's commercial began showing the stack of computer manuals needed to operate the IBM computer. Next, a single manual needed to operate the Apple floated down onto the table. Apple had realized that the home market wanted an inexpensive and easy-to-use computer. In contrast, IBM offered a scaled-down version of the business model IBM PC. It was too expensive and too difficult to use for the home market. Within a few years, IBM withdrew the PC Junior from the market. Today, Apple is attacking IBM on its home turf, the business market. With the Macintosh computer and its unique capabilities, ease of use, graphics, and compatibility with major software packages, Apple is making significant inroads in the business market and rapidly expanding its share of that market.

Knowing and Analyzing the Competition

Marketing executives must become fully aware of the competition. Many new and challenging forces, such as government deregulation, industry crossovers, foreign competition, acquisitions/mergers, and high technology advancements, have blurred competitive demarcations. It is no longer a simple task to find where competition lies. A prime example is the consumer financial services market—competition exists among banks, stockbrokers, savings and loan companies, insurance firms, retail chains, and so on. A formal approach to analyzing the competition is a major obligation for marketers.

Management must answer certain key questions periodically to stay competitive. No organization is an island unto itself. It must have a keen awareness of current and future competitive changes. A handy checklist of questions can serve as a basic reference scheme for managers.

Competitive Analysis Questionnaire

1. Who are our stiffest competitors? Are they becoming stronger? Weaker?
2. Do we recognize the limits of our own competitive position?
3. In what markets or product categories are we gaining market share? Losing market share?
4. How can we exploit out competitors' vulnerabilities? Which specific firms provide us with additional selling opportunities? What will be the costs and resulting profits if we take share away from them?
5. How can we overcome our own competitive weaknesses? Are any firms exploiting our weaknesses?
6. What competitive defensive and offensive strategies provide the greatest opportunities? Do the targeted consumers know about our competitive strengths?
7. Are new competitive entrants, including foreign ones, on the horizon?
8. Are many competitors leaving the industry?
9. How attractive is the industry outlook?
10. Does our remaining in a certain industry or product category coincide with our strategic plan?

When analyzing the strengths and weaknesses of your competition, you should compile a brief business assessment of each competitor. Some factors to review include:

Product or Service
1. How is the product or service defined?
2. How is it similar to yours and others?
3. How is it different from yours and others?
4. Does the competition specialize or offer variety?
5. Does the competition cater to the mass market?
6. What features of your product are superior in satisfying your targeted market?
7. What strengths or weaknesses of your competition can you exploit? (You might make the slow pouring of Heinz ketchup a weakness.)

8. How does the competition use changing technology to improve their product?
9. What quality image does the customer associate with the competitor?

Price
1. What is the competitor's pricing strategy?
2. Is the competitor higher or lower priced?
3. What is the competitor's gross margin and net margin for similar products?
4. Does the competitor offer terms or discounts?

Place
1. Where is your competition located?
2. How does their location compare to yours?
3. What are the strengths and weaknesses of the location?
4. Do they have room to grow?
5. Do they have more than one location?

Promotion
1. How does the competitor advertise?
2. How much do they spend on advertising?
3. What is the message they are trying to convey and does it relate to their target market and the demand of that market?
4. Is the competitor's advertising effective?

Management
1. How strong is the competitor's management team?
2. What is their background or experience?
3. How do they get new key employees?
4. Do they have in-house training?
5. How do they compensate their employees?

Financial
1. Is the competitor profitable?
2. What volume are their sales and how much market share do they have?
3. Do they spend money for research and development?
4. Are they properly capitalized and how strong is their cash flow?

Analyzing Risks

It is essential that any discussion of the business environment include the various kinds of risks a business will face. In researching risk, it is important to remember that it is impossible to anticipate all possible risks and to alleviate those risks. As a business manager, the best you can do is to identify as many of the potential risks as possible and anticipate solutions to handle them before they occur. The best strategy to alleviate risk is to diversify. Use multiple suppliers, sell multiple products, attempt to keep up with new technologies, and purchase insurance for those risks you can insure against, such as fire, theft, and illness.

Risk can be broken down into two major categories: business and environmental.

The category of business risk can be further broken down into subcategories. The first and perhaps the riskiest subcategory is the cost structure of the industry that is directly related to the amount of fixed assets or capital required to operate your business. As discussed earlier, the amount of capital required is determined by the type of business you own and the structure of the market. In general, the more capital your industry or business requires, the larger your fixed expenses will be. If you wanted to compete with MicroSoft, you would need tens of millions of dollars to open your business. You would need to purchase or build a large development organization and buy an expensive amount of equipment to produce competing software products. You would have debt and rent payments that would be fixed whether you produced ten software products or a thousand. The dollars you would lose each month that you didn't produce and sell your break-even volume of software products could rapidly force you out of business.

The completely opposite example is the accountant that begins his or her practice. He or she locates in a small office with minimum rent, leases a computer for $300 a month, and the only other expense is time. The overhead or fixed expenses are minimal. Because they are so low, the accountant is able to pay these expenses out of savings until reaching the break-even point. The larger your fixed cost is, the more you stand to lose before reaching break-even. Although there is nothing you can do to minimize this risk, it is important that you recognize it exists and plan for it by having sufficient capital (equity or your personal savings) to allow you to pay those fixed costs for a sufficient time until your business can reach break-even.

The next subcategory of business risk is the cyclicality of the industry. Is your business a seasonal business or are your sales steady throughout the year? If your business is highly seasonal, you face the risk of having to estimate your inventory and cash needs as the season begins, matures, and finally comes to a close. Typically, in the retail clothing business, you need to order your fall inventory in June, your winter inventory in September, and so on. The risk you face is two fold. You face the possibility of buying too little inventory and selling out early. The second part of the risk is that customer attitudes change and the styles you ordered won't be popular. The best way to minimize these risks is to plan ahead, gain as much expertise in your business as possible, and be conservative. Planning ahead means to deal with as many suppliers as possible and to negotiate the ability to get additional inventory quickly or to return to the supplier inventory you can't sell. In being conservative, it is better to be short or run out of inventory and make a profit than to sell your surplus inventory below cost and wipe out profits.

Another subcategory of business risk is profit margin (the percentage of net profits to sales) versus the volume of sales. A good example of this risk would be to compare a grocery store and a jewelry store. The grocery store sells its entire inventory every other day; however, net profit margin is only 1 percent. The business makes its money through high sales volume. The grocery store owner is able to determine changes in customer demand quickly and adjust for those changes within a few days. The jeweler, on the other hand, holds a piece of jewelry on average 90 days before selling it. Because of the amount of profit made on each individual item, the jeweler only has to sell a few large items to equal the profit of the grocery store. However, risk occurs in the jeweler's inability to detect changes in demand quickly and to adjust marketing strategies for these changes quickly. The grocery store owner can see a slowing in business within two days and adjust immediately. The jeweler will need 90 days to make those same adjustments. The only way to minimize the profit-volume risk for the jeweler is to have surplus cash to support operations until buying habits can be adjusted.

Continuing with business risk, you need to understand how your business depends on complementary industries. If you were a plumbing contractor or a hardware store owner, your business would prosper or starve depending on how the housing industry performs. As new homes are in demand, the housing industry grows and your business has the opportunity to succeed. However, as interest rates go up, tax laws change, and new home demand declines, you face declining sales over which you have no control. The best way to lessen your dependence on any one industry is to expand (diversify) your business. If you are the contractor, you can expand into home repairs. As new homes start to decline, people need to repair their existing homes. You are now working with two industries—new home construction and home repair. This is called horizontal diversification. Diversification can be further expanded by adding additional products or services and by entering new industries, such as yard sprinkler systems and swimming pools. Now, not only has the contractor added a new market segment for the same product, new products and additional target market segments have also been added.

A further subcategory of business risk is the vulnerability to substitutes that your business might face. This goes right back to the beginning when you defined your product or service. Unlike the railroad example, you need to see your industry in the broadest possible way. By doing so, you should be able to foresee changes. Instead of being hurt by them, you can take advantage of them to further expand your business.

Three more life-threatening risks you might face will come from your suppliers and customers. If you depend on any one of just a few suppliers, your business survival is at their discretion. If they raise their prices, you can be trapped into paying those increased prices. In today's low inflationary economy, you might not be able to pass those price increases on to your customers. If your supplier decreases trade terms from 60 days to 30 days, your cash flow will be hurt without you having any control. Finally, if your supplier only has a limited inventory, the ability to ship the amount you ordered might be restricted. The best way to minimize supplier risk is to spread your purchases over a number of suppliers.

The more you depend on others, the more risk your business faces. An excellent example of how small businesses can be at the mercy of third parties appeared in a recent *Wall Street Journal* article. The article reported that 30,000 longshoremen were on strike from Maine to Virginia. If you were a distributor who purchased your product from Germany and had it shipped through New York, you would find your business temporarily paralyzed.

Some of these ideas about a limited number of suppliers can apply to your customers as well. A good example is the lawn mower manufacturer whose only customer is a major retail chain. As the manufacturer faces rising costs of production, he or she attempts to pass those costs along to his customer. However, because the retail chain knows it is responsible for 100 percent of the manufacturer's sales, the chain can refuse to pay the increased prices. The manufacturer is faced with no sales or sales at the old price and greatly reduced profits. The best strategy is to have as many credit-worthy customers as possible. Although it is advantageous to have guaranteed sales and know you will be paid for those sales, it is not a favorable trade-off to lose control of your pricing to your customer.

Another major category of risk is the environment in which your business operates. Unfortunately, these risks cannot be controlled by you the business owner. These risks begin with the legal environment. Almost without warning, a local ordinance can invalidate your business license, restrict your business operations due to zoning considerations, or condemn your property in the public interest. As previously mentioned, a primary component of the definition of marketing is social responsibility. It is possible that manufacturers of cigarettes might be forced to cease production and be faced with bankrupting jury awards. On a local basis, in Florida, there was an entrepreneur who owned the rights to rent catamarans on the local beach. His business was located on a resort hotel's property. It was discovered that the hotel was in violation of several local ordinances and the rental concession was one of them. Unless the ordinances were amended, the owner of the concession would be forced out of business overnight!

Perhaps the most onerous legal environment risk that you, the business owner, face is legal liability. This potential disaster is the liability your business, and sometimes you, face for personal injuries or damage your business or employees might cause, even indirectly. Although you should purchase liability insurance, the cost of that insurance is increasing dramatically and might seriously impact on your business' ability to earn a profit.

Beyond the legal environment, you face such economic risks as inflation, recession, and rising interest rates. You cannot alter these risks, but you can decrease the effects they have on your company. By understanding how each will affect demand for your product or service, you can plan a strategy to minimize the impact of these risks on sales and profit. Perhaps the best strategy is diversification, offering many products or services to multiple market segments.

Finally, the last environmental risk you face is the environment itself. You need to assess how changes in climate, such as temperature and rain fall, will affect your business. Included in this category is the potential for catastrophes such as fire, floods, or drought. The best way to avert these risks is good planning, good management, and proper business insurance coverage.

The following worksheet is designed for you to assess the various potential risks your business faces and to assess the severity of those risks. In each category, check the appropriate level of risk your business faces. Those categories scored as moderately high or high must be given special consideration as you proceed with your business.

The next section describes the process of developing marketing strategy. These processes use the data captured through the market analysis as guides in developing strategies that reduce the competitive risk and give greater assurance of success in accomplishing corporate goals through marketing and sales. The process of developing marketing strategies expands on the marketing analysis processes as they relate to your specific product/service needs in the accomplishment of corporate goals.

Risk Worksheet—Industry Risk

	Lowest Risk	Moderate Risk	Moderately High Risk	Highest Risk
Cost Structure				
Industry Maturity				
Industry Cyclicality				
Profitability				
Dependence on Other Companies				
Vulnerability to Substitutes				
Regulatory Environment				
Suppliers (Price) (Availability)				
Production (Catastrophes) (Employee Relations)				
Competition				
Technology				
Distribution				
Management (Depth, Breadth)				

9

Marketing Strategy

The development of marketing strategy requires a broad knowledge of all the marketing processes. This section has been written to help in the understanding of these processes and their applications in the development of your product/service marketing strategies. These marketing processes are:

1. Meeting Market Needs
2. Specific Market Identification
3. Pricing
4. Marketing Channels
5. Promotion
6. Advertising Media
7. Principles of Selling

It is the purpose of the information presented here to help pinpoint possible weak items in a product line using available sales data. Decide what, if any, changes should be made in the product line(s) or prices, using available information from the subject industry and projected changes in the market. Evaluate a competitor's strengths and weaknesses. Use demographic data from various local publications and broadcasting stations to establish a rational marketing plan. Use information about the target audience to develop an appropriate advertising message. In short, use your market research and analysis to develop a strong specific marketing strategy for your venture.

Meeting Market Needs

In only two years, twenty million people visited the National Air and Space Museum in Washington, D.C. Sidewalk vendors do very well around the museum. With the enormous traffic, glittery trailers, and hawkers' shouts of "Hot Dogs Here!" "Fresh Pizza!" "Cold Ice Cream!" and "Hey, Souvenir!" the vendors have combined locations, products, and customers for steady profits. This shows the simplest and the ultimate in marketing and sales. All the elements of marketing are here—a plan, survey, product selection, pricing, location, advertising, and it is still the basic transaction, person to person, often with hectic bargaining. Marketing is such an all-inclusive concept.

As the operator of a small business, you can control some elements of marketing and sales more closely than others. Obviously, if you are already in business, you have made basic decisions about what your product will be; you have established basic prices for your goods or services; and you probably have some ideas about how to promote your business and your product, including the sales methods to use in presenting your goods and services to the ultimate users—your customers.

Marketing involves not only making the initial decisions about each of the above elements, but also reviewing those decisions periodically to be sure that your business is operating as profitably as you had planned.

If you are now operating a business, you already have a basic idea of what your product/service is. Your selection of a business was based upon some prior experience with that product—either an idea you had or a skill that you possessed. You wanted to go into business for yourself so that you could put your ideas into practice and take advantage of the potential income that results from operating your business.

Product Definition

When defining precisely what your product will be, whether goods or services, you must first evaluate the potential market where you intend to do business (market research and analysis), whether it be a neighborhood, city area, or the international marketplace, and then tailor your line of products to the needs of that area. For example, if you were planning to open a record shop in a predominantly student-populated neighborhood, you would want to find out whether those particular students listened to classical, jazz, hard rock, or other types of music. You also would want to know if most students preferred discs, cassettes, or albums. Would they need accessories such as compact disc cartridges or blank tapes?

Reevaluation and Change

Once the decision about your product or service line has been made, it must be constantly reevaluated (ongoing market analysis). Use your sales and inventory records to determine which items sold quickly and returned a good profit. These same records can help you spot slow-moving or unpopular items so that you can remove them from your inventory and replace them with more profitable items.

You also must be able to anticipate changes in either your market or your product so that you can react to them to ensure your continued success. Changes can come in many forms. Your basic market can shift in character; for example, the neighborhood constituting the market area for the record shop can become older (or younger), causing the demand for certain types of music to change.

Your product can change due to technological advances, changes in fashion or taste, or changes in general economic conditions.

Know Your Customer

"Beauty is in the eye of the beholder." This old adage can be applied to any characteristic of the product or service that you sell. The dress you sell is only beautiful if your customers think it is. The shoes you sell are comfortable only if your customers think they are. The storm windows you sell are economical only if your customers think they are. Your opinions, the opinions of experts, or sometimes even the facts are of secondary importance in selling your product or service. What the customer thinks is of primary importance. Certainly, facts or expert opinions can and should be used to influence your customers' thinking. But, in the final analysis, only their own thinking will determine what they buy.

Customer-Oriented Product Decisions

The easiest and most profitable products or services to sell are the ones your customers want to buy. Although their buying habits can be influenced through a manufacturer's advertising effort or your persuasiveness, the surest path to marketing success is to identify your customers' needs and desires and shape your line of products or services accordingly.

Competition

No aspect of marketing can ignore competition; not research, analysis, strategy, or planning. Just as competition affects the price you charge for your product or service and the methods you choose to market it, competition also influences the line you will offer.

Competition can frequently alter your marketing decisions. To market any product or service effectively, you must know your competition and the advantages that they offer, as well as the advantages that you offer or the steps you must take to gain a competitive edge. Too often, people tend to look upon competition solely as a question of price. Yet a competitive edge often can be gained in other ways, such as offering better customer service, a superior location, or more effective advertising. Marketing support activities such as credit availability, product service, warranty, customer advice, or a more attractive buying atmosphere also can help you gain a competitive edge. (These marketing support activities will play a greater role in the competition of the future—when service will be the only real competitive advantage.)

To protect yourself from competitors, you must stay a step ahead in every aspect of your marketing operation, including the selection of your product or service line. Frequently, this requires a further definition or review of what you are selling.

The record shop mentioned earlier must realize that it is in the recorded music business, not just the record business. The recorded music business includes cassettes, compact discs, and albums. The "record" shop that didn't offer these items would soon lose business to competition.

Furthermore, the record shop must assess its competition in other areas. Perhaps some are offering stereo equipment or car stereo equipment that the shop also might consider offering its customers (product mix). Or perhaps competitors offer customers the opportunity to preview records before buying them. Some competitors may offer more personal service. And, of course, some competitors may simply offer lower prices.

Granted, competition cannot always be met in every way in which it is possible to compete, but the small businessperson must continually be aware of the competition and what it is doing so that lines can usually be tailored to provide a uniqueness that will appeal to the market you are trying to reach, whether that uniqueness is in product selection, service, price, location, or another quality.

New Products or Services

There are times when, based upon your analysis of previous performance, industry trends, or market conditions, you will want to consider adding to or modifying the products or services you offer.

Market Tests

Since the ultimate test of the value of any new product or service is your market's reaction to it, you are usually well advised to make some sort of market test before committing yourself to any major change in your line. For example, a women's dress shop may be interested in adding a higher priced designer group, a sporting goods store might be considering the addition of camping equipment, or a restaurant might be considering supplementing its basic "meat-and-potatoes" menu with quiche or crepes. In each case, a tryout for a predetermined period can give you an idea of the likely success of a major commitment.

One factor must be borne in mind when conducting a market test of a new product or service. This is whether or not you expect the added line to create additional sales with your present customers or to attract new customers. The purpose of the change must be known so results can be properly evaluated.

For example, if a fast food shop added salads to its basic hamburger menu, there may be little gain if this simply makes salad customers out of hamburger customers. In fact, it might even reduce the average sale, resulting in a loss. However, if it causes hamburger customers to buy a salad also, or if it attracts new customers to the shop, it probably will prove to be a profitable addition.

Promotional Support

If the change in your product line is expected to increase sales among present customers, they must be aware that you are offering the additional product. In other words, your sales force must make the effort to suggest the new items to present customers as they purchase your current offerings. Also, announcements must be made, perhaps in the form of in-store signs, window displays, or advertisements.

If a product innovation is expected to attract new customers, some form of promotional effort must accompany the introduction. Otherwise, the "new customers" will have no way of knowing that you are offering them the product and your effort will be wasted. While the cost of the promotional effort may exceed the profit potential of the market test, the knowledge gained can be rewarding in the long term. It will alert you to potentially profitable products while deterring you from investing in those that offer little hope of marketing success.

As discussed previously, a market test is generally conducted for a predetermined length of time. For instance, a sandwich shop may offer homemade soups for two months to see how well they are received. After the two-month period, the sales checks can be analyzed to see if soup is being purchased in addition to a sandwich or instead of a sandwich. After this analysis, a decision can be made about whether the addition of soup to the menu has increased profits sufficiently to warrant becoming a permanent offering. Similar examinations of test results can be made for almost any product or service being considered.

In marketing, trial and error is often the most practical decision making technique. The men's clothing store that stocks only blue shirts will never know the profit potential from other colors. In fact, the owner may think that blue is the only color men buy because blue is the only color the store ever sells. The easiest product to sell is the one that the public wants to buy. You will never know what they want to buy unless you give them a chance to buy it.

Pricing

Price is one of the most effective marketing tools you have to promote your business. Price conveys an image of your business, affects demand, and can be a competitive and target market segmentation tool.

When considering what price to charge for your product or service, realize that price should not be based on the cost to produce or obtain plus some profit. Rather, price should be solely based on the value of your product or service to your customer. If that price does not generate the necessary profits, then changes must be made or the product line discontinued.

Establishing prices involves three primary considerations:

1. Your Cost
2. Your Competition
3. Your Customer

In normal circumstances, cost can be considered a minimum price. Certainly, when closing out a product line or reducing a surplus in inventory, you may temporarily sell below cost. But pricing below cost can never be a continuing formula for prosperity. Nor can selling at your cost be expected to make you prosperous.

Pricing should follow directly from the company's overall goals and objectives. Every marketing strategy will have its own related pricing strategy. One strategy is to "skim the cream" in the introduction phase by charging high prices when competition and substitutes are minimal. Another strategy is to "match competition" by pricing slightly under competition to expand market share, keeping in mind that profit is the primary goal of any "for-profit" business. A final strategy is to underprice the market substantially to keep out competitors. These strategies can be categorized into three areas: profit margin, sales, and status quo goals.

Profit-oriented goals include a specific net profit percentage or profit maximization. The first is a percentage goal and the second is a dollar value goal.

The first goal might be to obtain a 10 percent net profit on sales that would bring in $10,000 on sales of $100,000. The second would attempt to earn $15,000, a higher profit, on sales of $200,000 that would be a 7.5 percent (lower) return.

Sales-oriented goals attempt to reach a specific dollar or unit sales-growth objective, despite profit percentage or value. A sales-oriented goal also might be to obtain a specific market share. Typically, these goals are used to introduce a new product to a new market. Profit goals can be established later when the company has a consistent sales volume and customer base.

Status quo pricing is an effort to match the competition and not "rock the boat." This is usually the goal in a mature market where competition can be based on other competitive marketing features such as promotion, place, and packaging.

If you cannot sell below cost, then how far above cost can you sell? This will be influenced by your competition. Perhaps your product has certain advantages that justify a higher price. Perhaps you plan to sell below competition to capture the largest possible share of the market. But there is a delicate balance involved in selling below competition. Will the increased number of units sold result in enough additional profit to warrant cutting prices? And, will a lower price give your products an unfavorable image?

How will your customers react to prices higher than competition? Will they recognize the advantages of your product and pay the premium? Can they be persuaded by salespeople that your product is worth a little more?

On the other hand, your product may be no better than that offered by competition. Nor can you point to any significant advantages in the product support that you offer such as service, delivery, or credit terms. How large a discount will be necessary to attract customers away from your competition? How much will it cost to tell the market that you sell for less?

Pricing decisions affect your company's cash flow, profitability, and growth rate. They influence the size of your advertising and promotion budget. Finally, they create an image for your company. Because of this pervasive influence, chief executives should make their firms' basic pricing decisions. Pricing is a complex process; it is not a responsibility to delegate to even the most competent subordinate executive. To get a better idea of the use of pricing in business strategy, the following is a description of various pricing strategies and their applications.

Establishing a Pricing Policy

How much will you charge your customers? How much will your customers pay? You must deal with these critical questions when you introduce a new product or bid on a new job, add a product to an existing line, sell in a new market, learn of a price change by a competitor, adapt to inflation or recession, or adjust your price as a product matures.

Naturally, the type of business you are in affects these decisions. A company with a standardized product line, such as office furniture, need not make a pricing decision with each order. A job shop, on the other hand, produces everything on special order and makes pricing decisions with each sale. Despite such differences, each business requires some guidelines that will control pricing decisions. Without sound guidelines, two things are likely to happen:

□ Short-term business pressures may depress prices. Such factors as meeting your competition, pleasing established or key accounts, needing to recover cash, attracting new customers, and using spare capacity all tend to force the business executive to accept lower prices to maintain or increase volume. Once prices are lowered, it is hard to raise them again.

□ You may rush into bad pricing decisions. Say that demand is weak for a key product and your inventory and carrying charges are high. Here, a snap decision to lower prices would not spark demand if your customers already have high inventories.

There are many pricing guidelines that apply to all companies and they should be used as a basis for your decisions.

Set prices according to your market, not your costs! Your market will pay a reasonable price for your product or service when it satisfies what the market needs. Your costs, in other words, do not determine what your customers will pay. Instead, costs are simply the floor below which you cannot make a profit.

Establishing a Price Floor

The first step in pricing is to determine your product cost, the floor below which prices cannot fall.

All costs can be classified as variable or fixed (overhead). Variable costs are the out-of-pocket costs or costs of doing business that you incur with each product unit you sell. They include the purchase price of goods acquired for resale, sales commissions, and any product preparation charges such as alterations or delivery costs.

Fixed costs are the costs of being in business. These costs include such items as rent, administrative salaries, equipment depreciation, and office expenses. They go on from month to month with little variation due to sales.

Consider a product that sells for $1.00. You buy it for $0.50, pay a $0.06 commission on every sale, and incur delivery costs of $0.04 on every sale. Each time you sell one unit you realize $1.00 in revenue and incur $0.60 ($0.50 + $0.06 + $0.04) in out-of-pocket costs.

Each $1.00 sale provides $0.60 to pay your variable costs. The balance of $0.40 ($1.00 − $0.60) contributes to covering your overhead and, once your overhead is covered, produces a profit.

Unit Contribution

The difference between the selling price and the variable cost can be called the unit contribution.

Unit Selling Price	$1.00
−Unit Variable Cost	−.60
=Unit Contribution	.40

Break-Even Point

A product with a variable cost of $0.60 per unit and a selling price of $1.00 has a unit contribution of $0.40 ($1.00 − $0.60). If fixed expenses are $1000 per month, you can determine the number of units that must be sold to cover the fixed expenses. This sales volume is called the break-even point, and is calculated as follows:

Break-Even = Fixed Expenses/Unit Contribution
Break-Even = $1,000 / $0.40
Break-Even = 2,500 units

If sales are less than 2,500 units, you will show a loss for the month. For every sale above 2,500 units, you will show a profit of $0.40.

A company needs a system that tracks product costs. It is the only way to know which products make money and where to look if a product needs to shed costs. It is also a tool to estimate losses, and if they are severe, to know when to jettison the product.

Some executives use cost as their base when determining prices. Such cost-plus-a-profit pricing has serious problems. For example, insufficient fixed costs may be allocated to a core product that has a cost-plus price. In this way, you could be lulled to inaction by a product's strong margins only to discover that operations have slipped into the red. In addition, cost-based pricing:

- ☐ **Ignores the upside of your market.** Your cost for an item will tell you the minimum price you can accept. If this cost is too high, weak demand will require you to produce the product less expensively or drop it. On the other hand, cost-plus pricing will not tell you if you have priced too low and if your customers would pay more.

- ☐ **Underplays demand.** Customers of fashion, gift, and novelty items pay high prices for products they consider desirable. Remember the lesson of the pet rocks. Demand, not supplier cost, determines what customers will pay.

- ☐ **Is undercut by variable costs.** Companies with cost-plus pricing systems price up from a product's standard costs. But, if there is inflation or decreases in volume, actual per-item production costs rise. These companies risk profit squeezes.

Marginal Pricing

When you use marginal pricing, you add to your price only your cost of producing and selling extra volume. For example, a company that manufactures humidifiers may price the sale of 2,000 humidifiers at $40,000. But, for an additional 500 humidifiers, the company prices at cost—$7,500. At this price, there are no profits on the extra volume.

A marginal pricing deal makes sense for companies that periodically have spare capacity. Then management may decide on a marginal deal to keep its work force intact. So that these cost-based deals do no undermine your regular prices, permit them only when:

- ☐ You make the decision. A salesperson should not be allowed to authorize any marginally priced sales.
- ☐ You do not sell your spare capacity to an existing customer.

☐ You receive cash up front.

☐ You do all future business with the company at your regular prices.

☐ You will recover out of your price any capital expenditures you incur while performing the work.

Caution: A deal with a marginal price poses a serious threat to your company. Regular customers may hear of it and demand the same at-cost price. As a result, back away from any marginal price deal that you cannot keep confidential.

Unless you manage your salespeople properly, some of them may develop bad habits. For example, they are likely to perceive their jobs as simply getting business, not getting business with the smallest possible price concession. They also may make price concessions without getting reciprocal concessions from customers. Or, it may become a habit to treat certain discounts as automatic: "Oh, paying cash? That's another 2.5 percent off."

To prevent these pricing habits from emerging in your sales force, consider four simple management measures:

☐ **Make it difficult to lower prices.** Have your salespeople discuss every discount with their managers. This will encourage them to sell the benefits of your products, not the price. When salespeople have to struggle to give discounts, customers have to struggle to get them.

☐ **Circulate a periodic list of discounted sales.** Use policy announcements, promotions, and salary reviews to express your displeasure with discounted sales. Salespeople will work to keep their names from the top of this periodic list.

☐ **Favor rebates over discounts.** Rebates are a useful method for lowering prices. With them, the buyer gets the lower price only after its purchases reach a negotiated level. Until this level has been reached, there is no price concession to lessen your company's cash flow.

☐ **Make your salesperson the negotiator.** Regardless who has made the decision, your salesperson should be given the responsibility of offering the discount to the customer. When the sales manager offers the discount to the customer, it undercuts the salesperson's ability to take a tough bargaining stance on price in the future.

Pricing for a Competitive Advantage

Setting a competitive price for a product is a two-stage process. First, you design and market a product for a particular group of customers—a market segment. Here, you set price by what these customers will pay, not by your costs. Second, you create a pricing system that strengthens your product's appeal to your buyers. To do so, you may offer periodic volume discounts or special services with your product without pricing higher than your competitors. In every case, you choose a price that makes your product the most appealing to your buyers.

Always keep this fact in mind: a competitive price boosts product sales without necessarily being the lowest price in the market.

A market leader often builds a market from scratch. As that market grows, the leader maintains customer loyalty with good quality, value, and service. A key to this success is the company's ability to sell and service its products on a broad basis.

You can use your industry's market leader as a pricing yardstick. In general, companies price below the market leader. The obvious reason is that their reputation, products, or support services are not as strong, and they must offer a lower price to attract customers. In consumer product industries, for example, the number two brand in volume usually is priced about 5 percent below the market leader. Other companies generally price about 7 percent below the market leader. On the other hand, you can price over the market leader if your product is discernibly different and your sales force can sell this difference to your customers.

Three pricing strategies exist that help companies minimize or avoid pricing competition with the market leader in their industry:

- □ Price and market your products relative to competitors who are not market leaders. Then, compete by promoting the superiority of your product's quality, design, service, and so on.

- □ Use a loss-leader strategy to build a reputation for low prices in your market. To do so, offer selected high-volume items at very low prices. Then push these products hard. This strategy gives your lower-priced items high visibility. As a result, you develop a reputation for low prices with your customers.

- □ Undercut your market leader's price by no more than 10 percent to 12 percent. In general, a market leader responds with its own price cuts when a competitor beats its prices by 15 percent. Then a market leader tries to win key customers from you.

Buyers, not sellers, start most price wars. They know when the market is soft and when their suppliers need business. Purchasing agents then work the phones until they find suppliers who will lower prices. After securing this price concession, they maintain that prices are weakening while they negotiate with you.

Purchasing agents exert downward pressure on prices even when demand is stable or strong. They will often say to your salespeople: "Sorry, we have a better offer elsewhere." As a result, you need a competent pricing coordinator who can verify purported movements in prices. Only then can you make informed pricing decisions.

If there is indeed downward price movement, make concessions to buyers only after reviewing your company's financial situation. If your company needs to maintain sales volume, you may decide to offer a large, but temporary, discount. Or, you may negotiate lower prices on selected items with big volume buyers. One point is crucial: don't ignore rumors of declining prices. If you do, your sales force may be unable to respond competitively and you may lose customers. Still, thoroughly check out the rumors before responding.

Managing in a Price War

In a price war, suppliers lose control of the competition in their market and must quote the lowest price to get business, which in turn drives prices downward even further.

To make sound decisions when prices are volatile, you need reliable up-to-date information. Otherwise, you may postpone critical actions that the company must undertake to survive (for example, laying off employees). Again, the best way to get useful information for pricing decisions is through your pricing specialist.

Executives have several options in a price war. At small companies, they can try to influence the market through their trade association. They can leave the market—the sooner the better if this is the decision. Or they can adjust to lower prices. Consider these choices:

- ☐ **Impose a hiring freeze.** When necessary, order layoffs. Make sure your remaining employees are your most productive ones.

- ☐ **Strip your core product to its basic form.** Sell it at a rock-bottom price. Then charge your customers for extra features and for services like delivery, installation, and maintenance.

- ☐ **Raise price on low-volume or slow-moving products.** This will compensate somewhat for the rock-bottom price of your core product.

- ☐ **Create a deluxe version of your core product that your sales force can show.** Encourage customers to upgrade their purchasing to this deluxe and more expensive version.

- ☐ **Add to your invoices the cost of services which you do not now itemize** (for instance, long-distance calls you have made for customers).

- ☐ **Avoid giving credit.**

Make Short-Term Pricing Decisions with a Long-Term Pricing Perspective

Each pricing decision you make should be based on your company's need for stable margins, controlled competition in key markets, the loyalty of key and established customers, and your desired return on investment.

Make Your Prices Only One Consideration for Your Key Customers

In most businesses, 80 percent of sales come from 20 percent of the customers. So that these key accounts do not exert uncontrolled downward pressure on your margins, you must find special ways to hold their business. If you are a supplier of industrial resins, this may mean offering better backup services than those provided by the competition. If you are a realtor, it may mean developing an expertise in managing commercial projects.

Start High

Established and familiar products are more sensitive to price than new products aimed at new markets. In general, your customers will be willing to buy new products based on their technology, performance, capabilities, and reliability. In new markets, price is secondary. Be ready to respond to heavy price competition, however. When Texas Instruments introduced its TI99/4A home computer in 1980, the retail price was about $1,000. It dropped to $199 in two years because of intense price competition from other computer manufacturers.

Delegate Limited Pricing Authority

To respond quickly to new product developments and opportunities, a top executive needs to build clear pricing authority into the chain of command.

Such authority, still, should be limited to short-term price decisions. Short-term price changes are usually slight and temporary, in exchange for larger volume. Long-term decisions generally involve significantly more volume, in exchange for price concessions that permanently lower gross margins. These long-term decisions should be made at the highest possible management level.

Although salespeople in certain industries commonly have some discretion in pricing matters, it is usually best not to give them pricing authority. Many companies also give salespeople only general information on account profitability. The reasoning behind this is that if a salesperson knows a bottom-line price, buyers may sense this and push toward it when negotiating a price concession. Or a salesperson may willingly go to the bottom price to close a sale.

Raising Prices

Ultimately, demand, not your costs, sets your prices. As a result, not every supplier with rising costs can raise its prices. But, if rising costs are the reason you are contemplating a price increase, your competitors are probably feeling the same cost pressures. Under such circumstances, a company that increases its prices usually sees its competitors match its move.

Let your salespeople know the timing of impending increases. When informed, they can pass news of the coming price increase to customers. This helps customers prepare their businesses for the higher price. It also gives them the option of stocking up at today's lower price. When should you raise prices? In general, increases will meet the least resistance when they:

- [ ] Coincide with the beginning of an industry's new season or a company's new product introduction.

- [ ] Take effect during an industry's strongest selling season.

- [ ] Occur during an industry boom or an upturn in demand.

- [ ] Match increases by competitors. In this situation, don't wait to follow the competition upward. Delay will simply spotlight your increase. Besides, if you delay, some customers may think you have raised prices twice.

Preparing Your Sales Force

A meeting or series of meetings with your sales force is an effective way to announce a price change. Present the increase positively, the same way you would expect your salespeople to present the increase to customers. If the increase is substantial, you may unveil new sales tools, perhaps a revised presentation, that will help your sales force counter price resistance.

Even when a price increase is small, salespeople appreciate some corporate support. One valuable type of support you can give is a standard memo for customers that discusses the increase. Effective memos are often in a question-and-answer format and contain variations on these points:

☐ Since your last price increase, you have lowered some costs for your customers. For example, your company may have negotiated lower prices successfully with its shippers and passed the savings on to your customers.

☐ Your price increase matches or is less than your cost increases. Here, you must remember to disclose costs selectively. Don't disclose productivity improvements or reductions in your overhead that allow you to absorb some costs without reducing your profit margin.

It is also a good idea to consider how much notice to give your sales force. If you have any choice in the matter, you should consider the following factors.

A "confidential" advance announcement can provide certain benefits. It gives the salespeople a chance to use the information to their advantage: to close sales or encourage larger orders and to score points with some or all of their customers. There's no doubt that for many members of the sales force, this opportunity will take some of the "curse" off the increase. There are also drawbacks, however, of which you should be aware:

☐ As with a formal announcement to customers, there is bound to be a temporary spurt of business at the old lower price, which borrows from volume at the new, more profitable price.

☐ To the extent that certain salespeople build their entire presentation around "price," they may abuse the confidential information. Good sales managers know who these salespeople are, and must give them special attention.

☐ You must assume that any "confidential" announcement to your people will quickly become an announcement to the competition. Thus forewarned, competitors may gain an edge with some segments of the market.

☐ Finally, there is the possibility of a last-minute change in your plans before your announcement to customers, but after advance word to your salespeople. If some sales have been made based on an imminent price increase that fails to materialize fully, the reputation of the individual salespersons and the company can be damaged.

A simultaneous or nearly simultaneous announcement, on the other hand, is bound to cause some resistance among your sales force. If they are given the information at the same time as customers, they can still take some advantage of the period before the effective date of the increase. But, an announcement that is truly "effective immediately" for both the sales force and the market leaves no room whatsoever for maneuvering.

Gaining Customer Acceptance

Certain rules of thumb help companies avoid buyer resistance to their price increases. Buyers, for example, are more accepting of an increase that is less than the rate of inflation. They are usually more receptive to small, semiannual increases than to one high-profile, annual increase. They are generally put off by price lists that show the prices of all products moving upward.

Sometimes companies cannot take these simple pricing precautions. The sales force then must be ready for tough buyers' resistance. For example, a purchasing agent for a major customer may refer to a memo from his or her chairperson. "This memo says we can't accept any price increases for six months," the purchasing agent claims. In such situations, instruct your salespeople to be adamant on the price increase but flexible on nonprice variables like service. With a major customer, you may agree to a limited moratorium on the price rise, provided the customer places his or her usual order.

When a company anticipates major resistance to a price increase, a public relations effort can pay off. You may want to try the strategy of floating rumors in the trade press of substantial impending price increases and then announcing actual increases that, though high, are less than rumored. Proponents of this strategy say customers frequently feel relieved and are usually willing to pay the new price.

Announcing the Price Change

If yours isn't a field where prices frequently change, or if you are not in a regulated industry where price changes must be published, a brief review of some problems that come up in the mechanics of announcing a price change may prove useful. What's the best way to make the announcement? When should the change be made effective?

A higher price isn't an ideal candidate for general publicity or advertising. Certainly, customers and prospects need the information; but there's usually no need to call general attention to this type of management action. There are several ways to inform various categories of buyers, some better suited to your purpose than others.

Frequently, circumstances will dictate your actual choice. If you sell directly to many customers, who typically order from a catalog or stock sheet, you have no practical choice except to send every customer a price change notice. Or, if the timing is appropriate, the new price can simply be listed in a new catalog.

On the other hand, if all your sales are made through personal calls by your sales force, there may be no need to announce the change except through the material your salespeople carry. Each customer will then learn of the change when it's time for his or her next sales or account servicing call. If there's room for choice in this area—and you are not illegally discriminating against selected customers—here are a few of the basic rules to follow:

- □ **Customers should be notified before announcements are made to the press, industry associations, and others**. Whatever other announcement means you use, a prompt notice to customers should precede it whenever practical.

- □ **Consider the trade press.** Although you will want to notify your sales force, customers, and distributors first, don't assume that this rules out the need to inform the specialized media that covers your industry. Unless you are in direct, continuous contact with all your present and potential customers, they may learn of your price changes from secondhand information that may be inaccurate, distorted, and generally unfavorable.

☐ **Aim for thoroughness and accuracy.** In preparing your announcement and selecting the trade publications that are to be used, be thorough and accurate. Any announcement that is vague, ambiguous, or incomplete will cause misinterpretation, with results that can be very harmful. Any publication that you have reason to believe won't report your changes accurately or in sufficient detail should be avoided; an advertisement (where you control all copy) may be a more prudent method.

☐ **Be cautious about notifying competitors.** Notifying competitors—even informally—is dangerous. Be sure that you let your competitors know only through your trade association, the trade press, or another indirect medium, not directly. Company-to-company exchange of price information of any sort can get you into serious trouble under the federal antitrust law.

Picking the "Effective Date"

Theoretically, you have only two choices: the price change will be effective immediately, or on a future date specified in your announcement. In practice, still, there are several variations on these simple alternatives.

Generally, announcing a price increase "effective immediately" can be a good way to handle it. In many fields, however, such a simple change isn't practical because it takes time to notify all concerned. There also may be complications in ordering, production, labeling, and other practices that dictate a delay between notification and effective dates. For many companies, therefore, the question isn't one of whether the increase should be immediate or effective in the future, but how far in the future, and at what stage of the selling/distribution process it can be applied.

Even if you aren't forced to choose a delayed "effective date," you may choose the time lag because:

☐ **Your customers like it.** It gives them a chance to place more orders at the old price, or liquidate their present stock. If you sell parts and components in the original equipment market, a delay gives your customers some extra time to plan through the effects of your price exchange on their pricing structure.

☐ **Your competitors won't like it.** If they've already made their upward move, it means they lose some additional price-conscious business to you during the "under-the-wire" period. And, if they are planning to follow this time, your delay prevents them from using price differential as a selling point.

☐ **Your sales force will like it.** Although it is only a temporary factor, the delay is still a selling point. And, the experience of most firms has been that salespeople can often merchandise a "grace period" to everyone's advantage. Much of the sales volume developed in this manner is likely to be "borrowed" from the near future. But, there are likely to be lasting gains as well, in sales to existing customers of items they may not have otherwise bought, and in sales to new customers who are attracted to the price opportunity.

One detail to be considered is whether your price change takes effect as of date of shipment or date of acceptance of the order. Usually, traditional industry practice will dictate the way you handle the changeover. If your special circumstances leave the choice open, you will want to be sure you weigh the pros and cons of both options. In any event, be certain that you consistently insert the appropriate wording in your sales contracts, order forms, etc.

Disguise Price Increases

There are good reasons for disguising or understating price increases for particular products. These include a company's need to foster a certain sales mix or to maintain the volume of a core product. In such situations, there are many tactics you can use to raise prices discreetly:

- □ **Change the product package.** In 1985, Chrysler included certain optional equipment such as factory windshield wipers as standard equipment on some models. As a result, customers who would not ordinarily have purchased this equipment paid more.

- □ **Discontinue your cheapest models.** This is not a direct increase, but it raises a company's price floor and makes products in the middle of your company's price list look less expensive.

- □ **Keep popular optional equipment out of the list price.** For certain products, 90 percent of buyers may order certain optional equipment. If you keep this optional equipment out of the list price, the product looks less expensive to most buyers. If you raise the price of this popular optional equipment, it does not affect your list price.

- □ **Unbundle the cost of special services from the product.** Pass on all hidden costs to your customers. A good place to start: overtime costs on rush orders.

Additional Information

Miscellaneous fragments of information occasionally improve a company's pricing decisions. Among the most valuable sources of miscellaneous information are:

- □ **Your employees who have contact with customers.** Shipping clerks, repair personnel, customer service specialists, and others have contact with your customers. Sometimes their contacts provide information on how your services or products compare to those offered by your competition. You and your pricing specialist should periodically have informal conversations with these employees. Among the key things to look for are whether the product features you market to customers are ones that your customers value the most and whether your competitors over- or under-price their products.

- □ **Government contracts.** Federal, state, county, and municipal governments usually buy products through bidding. The winning bid then becomes public record. Information your pricing specialist can acquire on a winning bid includes: price, volume, credit terms, extra charges, guarantees, and warranties.

☐ **Market studies.** Industry surveys sometimes have broad information on pricing trends that may improve your pricing of individual products. Organizations that publish surveys of industrial and consumer markets include Predicasts, Inc. (Cleveland, Ohio) and Business Communications, Inc. (Stamford, Connecticut). Research organizations concentrating on particular fields include Knowledge Industry Publications (White Plains, New York—Communications) and Business International Corp. (New York City—Exporting). Finally, Find/SVP (New York City) publishes and annually updates a reference guide to commercially available market and business research reports.

Don't Leave the Decision for a Price Hike Up to the Competition

For most small manufacturers, the overriding consideration in establishing prices—in addition to margin over costs—is the competition. Still, there are other considerations that may lead to a different but effective pricing strategy:

☐ **Quality.** Chances are you've instructed salespeople to promote product quality to buyers. But, have you hesitated, because of competition, to build quality into your prices? You may find that your accounts often keep records on product life, downtime, operating costs, on-time delivery, and service response time and capability. If this is the case, simply write a form letter that can be personalized and send it to all accounts, asking that they share with you their experiences in these areas. This effort will produce enough documentation to support a higher price for one or more product lines.

☐ **Market differences.** As competition becomes increasingly onerous for many U.S. original equipment manufacturers (OEMs), they are bringing price pressure to bear on their suppliers. Detroit, of course, is the outstanding example, but it is happening throughout the industrial sector. If you are caught in that squeeze, the business you do in replacement parts can help you recoup. Distributors who market replacement parts to jobbers or to small end users may be more amenable to higher prices than are OEM accounts. Although this should be checked out thoroughly with your counsel, generally, since the product is customized enough to make it clearly different from the OEM version, violation of the Robinson-Patman Act should not be a problem.

☐ **Long-range planning.** If your company has come up with a product innovation that has found market acceptance, you may have set its price at the low end of the possible range to discourage competition from following quickly. Sometimes, of course, that is the appropriate strategy. But, if the product is one with a relatively long projected life cycle, then the total dollar advantage of a higher price over the years may suggest that this is the most profitable course to take.

☐ **Competitive history.** In some industries, particularly declining ones, price competition can be fierce, even in the face of rising costs. In other industries, however, that is not the case. Therefore, if your costs are climbing, and your standing in your industry is solid, you might find that raising prices gives you breathing room, rather than trouble. The competition, who is probably caught in the same cost squeeze, is likely to follow the leader.

The applicability of the foregoing factors will differ from industry to industry, and even from company to company in the same industry. However, such factors are so fundamental to any firm's profit picture that they bear consideration.

If you choose to raise prices, document your reasons to salespeople. They usually resist having to ask a higher price.

Short-Term Profits: Not Always the Primary Consideration in Pricing

After the lean profit years of the recent past, immediate improvement in profitability is high on the priority list of most executives. Thus, when it comes to setting prices, maximum return is likely to be the major consideration. There are situations, yet, in which a company's overall strategy at a given time may demand a different mission for price setting:

☐ **To increase market share.** Price cutting, which need not be drastic, can be used in two ways to attain a larger piece of the market. First, a company can make significant inroads to underselling the competition constantly in areas where the company has the lion's share of the business. You can add to your advantage, in places where you do best, by providing distributors with price promotions. Says one manufacturer of metal partitions, "Giving our top distributors something to run with not only rewards them and reinforces our relationship with them, it also creates results for us we might not otherwise achieve."

☐ **To head off competition.** A major computer service bureau used price reductions to deter a well-financed newcomer. "There was no way we were going to keep them out," recounts the company president, "but we were going to slow them down, and add to the big nut they already had accumulated to get into the market." The result: the newcomer withdrew quickly from two large geographic regions and is making slow progress where it continues on the offensive.

☐ **To avoid the price chaos.** A so-called orderly market, where margins are reasonable, can be thrown into disarray if one or two firms adopt a program of drastic price cutting. In such a situation, a New England maker of printed circuit boards found himself spending much time adjusting his price schedule up and down as two competitors attacked his position with "ridiculous promotions about every three months." Finally, he let it be known in the trade press, and by direct mail, that his salespeople were authorized to meet any price challenge without even checking with the home office. "I'm sure some accounts took advantage of our posture," he says, "but in the end, the throat-cutting ended," and again reasonable price practices—and margins—prevailed.

☐ **To enhance the company image.** When a company's costs drop, it can simply enjoy the increased margins that follow, or can reduce prices accordingly. One Midwest manufacturer of flow control equipment reports that he always responds instantly to a cost reduction with a matching price cut. "The competition always follows eventually," he says "but apparently they figure that waiting 30 or 60 days gives them more cash in the till. And, maybe it does. But, what we have is even better—a reputation for strict corporate integrity. I can't measure the dollars that gives us, but I know the number is not small."

A company must calculate the results carefully, of course, before it adopts any pricing strategy. It is especially important to look at both short- and long-term consequences.

When choosing a pricing strategy, there are many pricing dimensions you can tailor besides the basic price of the product. Included in pricing are discounts, which can be based on single order quantities, cumulative quantity orders, or on specific products. The owner might choose to use seasonal discounts to move more of the product during slow times of the year. Discounts can be used for either consumer goods or industrial products. Perhaps the best known discounts are the "frequent flier" discounts being offered by the airlines.

Trade-in allowances are an effective way of lowering the final price to the customer without actually lowering the list price. Trade-in allowances are given for used goods when similar new products are purchased. They are standard in the automobile industry and in other industries that deal in industrial and durable goods. For instance, IBM has offered trade-in allowances for old IBM PCs when you purchased an IBM Personal System/2 (PS/2). By reducing the effective price through trade-ins, IBM hoped to induce its current customers to switch from PCs to the new and less established model. IBM hoped that once these customers tried and liked the PS/2, they would spread the word, inducing others to purchase the system at full price.

Coupons are another effective way of tailoring your pricing strategy for the consumer market. Coupons can be mailed directly to consumers' homes, delivered in local papers, or offered at the point of purchase. Many cost-conscious consumers shop only for those goods where they can use discount coupons. Coupons are an effective tool to reach various markets with the same product through pricing.

Similar to coupons are **trading stamps**, such as S&H Green Stamps. After a certain number of books of stamps have been collected, the consumer takes them to a local retailer and exchanges them for merchandise. Retailers either buy the trading stamps from a stamp company or offer their own stamps. An example is Winn Dixie with its yellow "Frequent Buyer Stamps" that were redeemable in lower prices at Winn Dixie stores or at other local outlets like RAX Roast Beef chains.

There are many pricing terms available to firms selling to industrial customers. One term is **freight charges**. The question is who pays for them, the customer or the seller. **"Free on Board"** (F.O.B.) indicates the seller is responsible for the cost of loading the goods onto the vehicle. The customer then immediately takes title to the goods, is responsible for all freight charges, the cost of unloading, and any damages that might occur in transit. This can be easily changed so that the seller pays all transportation cost and is responsible for all losses until the buyer takes physical possession by changing the terms to **"F.O.B. Delivered"** or **"F.O.B. Buyers Factory."** Another way of pricing freight charges is to charge all customers within a specific zone a standard freight charge for that zone. The seller actually pays the freight charges but bills the customer a standard charge. These strategies work well when a business is selling to firms near its production facilities, but is sometimes too expensive to allow sellers to compete with other producers in distant markets. This situation can be alleviated by what is known as **freight absorption pricing**, which means the seller's delivery charges will meet that of the local competition.

Included in pricing strategy are sales terms and credit. Sales terms allow customers to take a discount if the invoice is paid within a specified period of time. A typical discount might read like 2/10, net 30. This means the customer can take a 2 percent discount if the invoice is paid within ten days; but the entire invoice is due within 30 days. Customers buying on credit create accounts receivable. The terms of these accounts can range from cash on delivery (C.O.D.) to due in 30, 45, 60, or 90 days from the date of delivery.

When deciding a pricing strategy, you need to remember the emotional impact of prices. For psychological reasons, all prices should end in an odd number. Also, it is difficult to persuade people to pay more than what is considered the customary price for something (the newspaper is always 25 cents during the week and 50 cents Sunday). Finally, for most people, price equals quality.

Competing Through Price

Price cutting is always risky. But, if you take this risk, be bold. Except for trade discounts, announce your action in the trade press. Do a special mailing to your market. At the same time, use your lower prices to pry volume business and key accounts from your competitors. When doing so, you can offer four kinds of price discounts: promotional, trade, quantity, and cash.

Promotional Discounts. When demand for a product matures, the market usually divides into segments. For personal computer manufacturers, for example, these segments include office workers in big companies, independent business owners and employees, home users, students, and schools. When companies do not skillfully match product features to the needs of a market segment, or there are too many suppliers with similar products aiming for the same segment, both buyers and sellers place a heavy emphasis on price. In these markets, promotional pricing is common. When used effectively, the supplier sells the discounts, not the price. Or, a supplier boosts a perception that something is free—a free printer with your personal computer, for example—not the total price of the product package.

Promotional pricing helps a company hold its market position, move excess inventory, or create interest in slow-selling lines. In addition, it can help a company's distributors increase sales. In general, promotional pricing is most effective for companies that sell necessities, not fashion items or novelties.

Further, it improves sales for goods that have quality reputations more than for goods that the market considers substandard or flawed. At the same time, most companies do better selling excess inventory outside their regular markets than giving a promotional price to regular customers. Why? Promotional pricing for regular customers pressures competitors to lower prices and may start a price war; it conditions buyers to shop for the best price, not the right product; and it makes selling without special deals a difficult task for your salespeople.

Before you offer a promotional discount, make sure it will achieve your goals. For example, assume you want your distributors to sell more to the end user. Here, you will need some system for monitoring distributor sales. Also, the timing of your promotional discounts must coincide with seasons when your distributors buy less from you. Otherwise, they may simply order more this month at your discounted price and then cut back on purchases of your products in succeeding months.

How much money will you allocate to a promotional pricing program? How will you apportion that money among your products? How will you time this expenditure over the year? Begin with this year's advertising and promotion budget. Decide what media (sales literature, space advertising, direct mail, etc.) you will need to support your sales effort. Then allocate your money between advertising and promotion. If you are a brand leader in your market, you may try to underscore your strong reputation by apportioning most of your money to advertising. If you are battling for distribution in a fragmented market, as much as 80 percent of your budget may fund your promotional sales efforts.

Next, divide the year into congruent sales and promotional periods. These are the same length as your sales cycle—say, a visit to a customer every two months. Then create a different promotional scheme for each sales period. Have one promotion that features a heavy discount on a major product. Offer minor discounts on one or two additional products. In the next two-month period, shift your promotions to other products. This way your sales force always has something special and new to interest customers. If appropriate, time your promotions so that the products your sales force pushes align with seasonal needs in your markets.

Caution: Underscore the fact that each discount you offer has a strict time limit. If you are soft on this point, your customers will pressure you to continue a discount through the next sales call. In this way, buyers fix promotional discounts in a company's price structure and hamper the flexibility of the company's sales force.

You can also preserve your company's margins while you sell products at promotional prices. How? Buy from suppliers who will give you special prices or allowances on their products. Then pass your savings on these products to your customers. Here, contact key suppliers in the early stages of your price promotion planning. You can then settle on products from one or more suppliers that you will buy in volume and at deep discount. Note that in a recession, companies use this strategy to keep both cash flow and sales volume strong.

Trade Discounts. Companies primarily discount their prices for two reasons. First, they discount to achieve business goals, such as moving extra inventory or raising visibility in their markets. If you take this approach, be sure that a discounted price will achieve its goal. A discounted price for plywood won't stimulate demand from homebuilders if home mortgage rates are high. Second, companies discount because it is their industry's convention. If your company is in this situation, follow these pricing rules:

- □ **Vary your discount order sizes from those of your competitors.** This will make simple comparisons between discounts difficult and discourage your customers from approaching your products solely based on price.

- □ **Avoid publishing your discounts.** Published discounts restrict your negotiating flexibility. Further, your biggest customers will demand a discount on your published discount.

- □ **Create a two-tier discount system when industry convention forces you to publish your discounts.** In this situation, set your price list high and publish small discounts. This gives you the opportunity to offer special discounts to all customers and discretionary discounts for key customers.

- □ **Periodically revise your discounts.** Otherwise, standard discounts take root in your price list. These become an additional negotiating point when you try to raise prices.

Pricing a product at a discount can sometimes be a useful tactical tool. A telephone interconnect company may sell, at full price, a leading brand of telephone switches used by large companies. At the same time, it may heavily discount prices for its telephone switches aimed at small firms. Why? The tactic could lower the profitability of other suppliers selling primarily in the small-company market and forestall their entrance into the big-switch market.

As usual, management must be certain before it decides to compete or forestall competition through pricing. In the case of the interconnect, the tactical discount could spread from the small-switch to the big-switch market and weaken margins on its strongest products.

Quantity Discounts. You give your customers incentive to place larger orders when you offer quantity discounts. You can offer these discounts on a cumulative or noncumulative basis, but cumulative discounts tend to concentrate a buyer's purchases on your company.

Companies that offer quantity discounts face three problems. First, these discounts are hard to eliminate once they take effect. Second, customers who make purchases just below the quantity discount level—say, the bakery that orders 950, not 1,000 pounds of flour—frequently demand the discounted price. Third, these discounts lower profit margins. As a result, they fit best at closely held companies that are managed for maximum cash flow or companies with idle production capacity.

Companies frequently offer volume discounts when they attempt to shift important business from a competitor. A garment manufacturer, for example, may spread its shipping equally among three trucking companies. To knock out a competitor, one shipper may offer a 30 percent discount on business that will raise its current volume with the manufacturer by more than 50 percent. For top effectiveness, such a volume discount must have a limited duration, say, a year. Further, the manufacturer must agree to accept or reject the offer. If it goes to competitors for counteroffers, the three suppliers will be caught in a price war.

Quantity discounts can create problems for distributors. Microcomputer manufacturers, for example, offer quantity discounts to their retailers. To get micros at a lower per-unit price, retailers buy machines in more volume than they can sell. What they sell is very profitable; what they cannot sell, they transfer to the gray market, that is, nonauthorized dealers and mail-order suppliers. The resulting glut of micros depresses prices and causes cash flow problems for the retailers that are already in shaky financial shape.

Cash Discounts. A cash discount—a price reduction for a repayment a buyer makes within a certain period—is an expensive service to offer customers. For example, a common trade discount is 2 percent off the invoice if the buyer pays in ten days; the full payment is due in 30 days. If a buyer pays a $100 invoice in ten days and takes the $2 discount, the effective interest rate to the supplier for giving up $2 for 20 days is about 36 percent.

Industry practice requires many businesses to give cash discounts. However, when it is not bound by standard practice, a company can offer selective cash discounts with good results. Automobile manufacturers, for example, offer cash discounts when customers balk at a price increase. These cash discounts—frequently rebates, or a month or two moratorium on car payments—are, in fact, temporary price rollbacks. At the same time, they keep the list price up while bolstering sales of slow-moving models.

In theory, a cash discount accelerates customer payments and cash flow. But, if this discount is not part of an industry standard or the promotion of a weak product, it is wiser to borrow cash at the bank. Further, bank borrowing is confidential, while a cash discount signals buyers that a supplier needs sales. This can make it harder for suppliers to bargain successfully with buyers.

Effect of Discounting

If your company is forced into discounting, give your first-line sales executives very limited authority to move prices (no more than 5 percent from list). Give your area managers the authority to move prices by a slightly larger percentage. You and your top managers should examine any deals with price reductions more than these limits, particularly those for your key accounts. In all deals where you lower prices, follow these rules: Never publish the discount; always negotiate from the list price; and be sure your company gets something in return when you do give a discount.

Suppose you find that your product is not selling at $1.00. Therefore, you want to consider the possibility of discounting it to see if the lower price will encourage sales and produce an operating profit.

Consider the effect of various discounts. First, assume that you decide to discount your price by 20 percent, to $0.80 per unit. At this price, your average unit contribution would be $0.20 per unit ($0.80–$0.60). To break even, you would then need to achieve units sales as follows:

Break-Even = Fixed Expenses/Unit Contribution
Break-Even = $1,000 / $0.20
Break-Even = 5,000 units

Therefore, you must double your sales to 5,000 units to offset the effect of a 20 percent discount.

Now try a 30 percent discount of $0.70 selling price. At this price, your unit contribution is $0.10. Your new break-even point would be calculated as follows:

Break-Even = $1,000 / $0.10
Break-Even = 10,000 units

As you can see, successive discounts of 10 percent have greatly increased the number of units that must be sold to break even. Whenever you discount to promote sales volume, you should be aware of the added volume required to break even and be reasonably confident that the additional sales volume can be generated by the lower price.

Pricing Strategy for New Products

The nature of a new product, its mode of manufacture, or the maturity of its market dictates a new product's pricing strategy.

For a time, a new product that is unique may have the most advanced technology in its field. Provided there is genuine demand for the technology, a company can price such a product very high; the company then generates large revenue on low volume. In doing so, it accumulates substantial resources it can use to compete with when other companies enter the market and the price drops. A company that enjoyed recent success with this strategy is Intecom, Inc., the developer of a telephone switch that carries both voice and data transmissions.

Certain familiar products have mass market potential but are currently sold as luxury items to a small market. A company that spots this opportunity can retool its manufacturing for the mass market, substantially undercut the price of luxury suppliers, and succeed on volume. An example of a mass market product that began as a luxury item is the ball point pen.

Variations of established products that appeal to niche markets have special features that are geared to niche markets. For example, a company may equip an existing executive workstation with specialized transaction software. The company then markets the product to stockbrokers. The market niche will pay a fair price, provided the supplier's marketing convinces potential customers that the product has special value and the product delivers what its marketing claims.

Hard and Soft Pricing Information

The intuition of influential executives plays a major role when a company sets a price for a new product. But, executives do not rely solely on their market experience to set a price. They also must consider both hard and soft information on prices.

First, survey customers to determine what price they would pay for a proposed product. Watch out, however, because survey information is frequently misleading, since customers are offering an opinion, not actually buying the product.

Second, compare the proposed product to the product it will compete with or replace. If your new product has an important feature that distinguishes it from the competition, factor its value into your price. You can do this if you can provide a credible estimate of its value and are sure your customers will pay for the feature.

Finally, test the product at different prices in various geographic markets. Although such testing is expensive, it accurately shows the volume a company can expect at a number of prices.

Break-Even Analysis

When setting a price for a new product, you also must identify the point at which product revenues match product costs. To do a break-even analysis:

☐ Choose a price for the new product, say, $10.

☐ Identify the variable costs of the product, say, $8. Note that variable costs—labor and energy consumption, for example—are those that rise and fall with volume.

☐ Subtract per item, variable costs from price. The resulting number—$2 here—is the money generated by the new product that the company can use to pay fixed costs or to increase retained earnings. This is the product's contribution margin.

☐ Divide the contribution margin into the company's total fixed costs, say, $200,000. The resulting figure—100,000 units—is the number of units the company must sell to pay the product's costs.

Break-even analysis places potential products within actual markets. In the example above, company executives would compare their 100,000 break-even point to total market size—say, 5 million in annual industry volume. If they feel their product can capture 2 percent of the market, they can proceed, reasonably certain that the product will not lose money. Break-even analysis also helps executives review and adjust a new product's cost structure.

To illustrate, assume that your company is designing a vaporizer that you price at $20. In a meeting on the product's specifications, your engineer says that certain moderately expensive material improvement would make the vaporizer run more quietly, thereby differentiating it from other $20 models. To decide if you will make this improvement, review your break-even volume calculation. With higher variable costs, your break-even rises. Can you attain this higher volume? If you pass this added cost on to your distributors, does your break-even volume look reasonable for a $23 product?

Break-even analysis is a crude tool for pricing new products if it assumes that fixed costs remain fixed for any volume and that variable costs per unit are always stable. In practice, this is not so. As volume increases, repair costs rise; large purchases of materials lower variable costs. To reduce these inaccuracies, break-even analysis is best done on a microcomputer. Using a spreadsheet program, you can key in changes for fixed and variable costs at different volumes. This way, you can generate more break-even variations and develop more accurate information on new-product break-even volume.

Adjusting the Price of a New Product

If initial sales of a new product are disappointing, you probably should maintain the price while you review the product's marketing. Is it explaining how the product is different from the competition? Is it describing a service or benefit customers need or value? If you are confident that the marketing approach is sound, then consider these options:

□ **Lower the price.** A lower price raises a product's break-even volume. At the same time, lower prices can make significant increases in volume possible. The key consideration when looking at lower prices is whether you can do sufficient volume—that is, take enough business from current suppliers—so that the product will make money. If your analysis shows a breakeven volume you can reach only after carrying the product a year or more, you have an important decision to make. Can your company afford or risk this cash drain? If not, act quickly and drop the product now.

   To avoid this tough decision, test prices before you introduce a product to the entire marketplace. Testing does not need to be extensive or expensive. You can do it with a few valued customers through personal interviews, surveys, or even business-to-business focus groups in which people who are prime targets for your product are interviewed for their reaction to a new product or service.

   This will help you avoid dropping prices, or the product, within weeks or even months of the introduction. That can reflect badly on your company and other products or services you offer.

□ **Raise the price and reposition the product for customers who are less price-sensitive.** A company has to reformulate its distribution strategy when raising price and repositioning a product. A direct marketing company, for example, may have disappointing volume when offering high-quality lawn care tools through the mail. The next year, it may raise prices and move the products to upscale suburban retailers. Now, customers can handle the tools and retailers can sell value. The result can be greater volume and higher profits if your variable costs don't rise dramatically.

Appoint a Pricing Coordinator

Overall, your pricing patterns should see an occasional price moving down, but most should be moving up with enough frequency and regularity that your customers accept change. This is very difficult to achieve if you have no pricing specialist on staff.

   A pricing specialist should report directly to the CEO, and his or her work should not be reviewed by other managers, even if the job is not full time. A common mistake is to put the pricing specialist under the company controller or financial manager. Pricing strategy then tends to be too concerned with costs. Another mistake is to put the pricing specialist under the sales manager. Then, the pricing strategy is not sufficiently profit-oriented.

   The pricing specialist's job is twofold. First, he or she should establish information pipelines for costs, market news, and all other major influences on your company's prices. Second, the specialist should organize this information for you and your managers so that there is still a flexible and intuitive dimension to your pricing decisions. A job description may require the pricing specialist to:

☐ Collect important public information on, and from, major competitors. Review trade publications; collect price lists of major competitors; spot-check sales information from the sales staff; interview personnel newly hired from competitors; gather product and strategic information on competitors at trade shows; acquire public financial information, such as Dun and Bradstreet reports and annual reports on competitors; analyze competitors' products or services.

☐ Collect cost and payback information. Work with the financial manager or controller to develop sales projections and key financial ratios that show the effect of proposed price changes on cash flow, return on investment, return on assets, and product and company profitability; distribute to top managers the controller's break-even analysis and return on investment calculations for each proposed product; monitor standard costs and variances for each product or service.

☐ Collect pricing information from production, engineering, and purchasing departments. Monitor potential difficulties and opportunities in these departments that affect pricing. Example: production—potential economies of scale; engineering—alternative materials or designs that would lower product costs; purchasing—possible shortages or key materials.

☐ Maintain pricing input from other specialists. Secure views of advertising advisers, attorneys, and other specialists on pricing issues.

Pricing Strategically

An enviable role for any company is to skim a market. To do so, a company gears its product to that sector of the market that is least price-sensitive. Companies that are successful with this strategy price high and do well on a very small volume (for example, Ferrari in the sports car market). There are two keys to their success: they have a product that customers, not necessarily technicians, consider the best; and they keep down overhead and manufacturing cost.

Since there are few customers for whom money is not an issue, most companies do not price for the top of their markets. But, many successful small companies follow a related strategy: offer a product with special value to a particular market niche. If the product is something that segment truly values, the company gets its price. Producing for a market niche has two advantages for the small company:

☐ **Balanced competition.** If the niche is small, a large company cannot afford to enter the market. The reason is that without high sales volume, most large companies will not cover their overhead costs. As a result, there are seldom giant suppliers in these markets, whose economies of scale will drive down prices. A small company can, therefore, keep its prices up without the fear that a giant competitor will enter the market with lower prices.

□ **Niche market growth.** A small company can dominate a niche market. In doing so, it develops the customer contacts, experience, and reputation it needs to succeed. If the market later grows sufficiently to attract big companies, the small company probably will have grown as well, but it will have acquired these intangible assets to help it compete.

Set Pricing Targets

In niche markets, buyers still look for the best possible price. To counter this downward pressure on price, many executives set target prices for their products. These target prices are common in job shops and other businesses that negotiate a price for every sale.

A pricing system based on price targets tends to keep prices and profits up, helps executives evaluate sales performance, and links pricing decisions with long-range planning. The best way to use this approach is to:

□ **Determine your company's cost to do a particular job, offer a service, or produce a product.** Be sure to include all overhead. The result should be the lowest price you can accept, but not the base from which you price your work to the customer.

□ **Review your pricing of recent and similar jobs.**

□ **Consider the future.** Estimate how much volume your company can build with this customer.

□ **Set your target price.** Your review of costs, pricing history, and future business prospects will help you select a target price. It is sometimes best to set this price a bit high to allow room to maneuver. If you agree to drop your price slightly, the customer usually feels he or she has negotiated a good deal with your firm. Don't set your target price unnaturally high at the outset or your strategy will be obvious. Your customer will then feel that any price reduction is not genuine.

□ **Make sure the target price agrees with your corporate goals.** If you must choose between contracts, select the contract that meshes with other company strategies. For example, an executive who is managing for growth and cash flow would choose the job that brings the most revenue to the company, which might not be the job with the highest profit margin.

□ **Convey your target price to your salespeople.** If a job is important to your company, establish special pricing controls when you set a target price. For example, you may normally give your regional sales manager discretion to drop 7 percent below your target price. On an important job you may decide to approve all price concessions yourself.

□ **Insist that your salespeople average your target price.** If your salespeople have some pricing discretion, this policy works to keep prices up. Commonly, it forces salespeople to stop automatic price concessions they give to long-standing customers.

PRICING QUESTIONNAIRE

When formulating a pricing strategy, you must look at prices from several different points of view. You must consider costs, sales, volume, profits, and the practices of your customers and competitors. The following questions will provide information that is useful when devising your pricing policies:

1. Which of your operating costs remain the same despite sales volume? Which of your operating costs decrease percentage-wise as your sales volume increases?
2. What is the break-even point for your items or services at varying high prices?
3. When you select items for price reductions, what are the effects on profits?
4. What is your sales volume goal and can your prices help you reach it?
5. Do you have all the facts on costs, sales, and competitive behavior?
6. Do you keep records that will give the needed facts on profits, losses, and prices?
7. Do you review your pricing practices periodically to make sure that they are helping to achieve your profit goals?
8. Do your customers shop around, and for what items? How do they make their comparisons—by reading newspaper ads, store shopping, or hearsay?
9. Which items do your customers call for even though you raise prices? Which items do they leave on the shelves when you raise prices?
10. Have you decided a pricing strategy to create a favorable price image with your customers?
11. If you are trying to build a high-quality price image, do your individual price records show that you are selling a larger number of higher-priced items than you were 12 months ago?
12. Are you a "leader" or a "follower" in announcing your price reductions?
13. Do you try to time price reductions so they can be promoted in your advertising?
14. Do you use all the available channels of information to keep up to date on your competitors' pricing policies?
15. Is there a pattern to the way your competitors respond to your price cuts?
16. Do the items or services that you sell have advantages for which customers are willing to pay a little more?
17. Does your advertising and sales pitch emphasize customer benefits rather than price?
18. Are you using the most common competitive tools, such as service and credit terms?

Marketing Channels

The next consideration in preparing your marketing strategy is to decide how you are going to sell your product or service, where you are going to locate your business, and how you are going to get your product or service to the customer. The whole purpose of the distribution process is to deliver what the customer wants to a place he or she will buy it. For instance, Wilson Sports, Inc. produces millions of golf balls each year while an individual consumer will only need a relative few (depending on his or her golf game). It is the responsibility of the distribution system to allocate all the golf balls Wilson produces to all the avid golfers around the world. The process begins with the production of raw materials and progresses through manufacturing, wholesaling, and retailing. The process of production, distribution, and final sale is considered a **vertical channel**. A company's operations may include one or more of these activities: raw goods production, manufacturing, wholesaling, and retailing. For example, a tire company can be a rubber tree grower to tire retailer like Firestone or it can do less than all the functions in the channel like Michelin.

Besides being the physical distribution of goods, the distribution channel also can be a marketing tool. Indirect distribution marketing strategies relating to brand image include **extensive, selective,** and **exclusive** distribution. **Indirect distribution** is the process where a manufacturer sells to a wholesaler who sells to a retailer who ultimately sells to the customer. Most firms operate at one level in the distribution chain. The major reason companies do not control the entire distribution chain is lack of expertise and capital.

Often described at the "shot gun" approach, **extensive distribution** sells your product or service through as many retailers as possible without regard to image or competition. This type of channel works best for convenience goods such as soap, pencils, film, and other household goods. The intent is to sell through all responsible outlets where the customer would expect to find your product. For example, you might sell sandpaper through all the various hardware store outlets such as Home Depot, ACE, and the local hardware store. Consumers generally expect to find soap at convenience stores, drug stores, and grocery stores, but not in hardware stores. Batteries, on the other hand, might be found at these locations and provide a good example of extensive distribution.

Selective distribution is the broad category between extensive and exclusive. You want to reach as many potential customers through as many responsible outlets as possible, but you want to maintain some type of image. This approach attempts to reach more than one customer profile or target market. It does so by selecting specific outlets with specific images and then matching product selection and promotion to that image. Good policy here includes avoiding outlets with bad credit, poor service, a bad customer image, and a poor location. Selective distribution differs from extensive in that selective distribution subscribes to the concept that 80 percent of a company's sales come from 20 percent of its customers. There is no need to sell your product through every retail outlet under this distribution strategy.

Exclusive distribution (the rifle approach) is selling your product or service at a very limited number of retail outlets, either a single store or chain of stores. An example of this approach would be Ralph Lauren apparel being sold in such department stores as Burdines and Lord & Taylor, but not Sears or JC Penney. The objective of exclusive distribution is to reach a single target market. It usually requires strong dealer loyalty and active sales support from the dealer. Exclusive distribution is brand image conscious and is usually used in conjunction with a concentrated marketing strategy.

In choosing the appropriate distribution strategy, it is important to avoid distributing to competing channels. For instance, Jimmy Buffet has a line of casual wear that he sells in retail shops around the country as well as in his retail store in Key West. However, in Key West, his store is the only store where his Margaritaville line is sold. By limiting distribution in Key West, Jimmy Buffet avoids having his product offered in competing channels.

Direct distribution is the alternative to indirect distribution. Examples of **direct distribution** companies are Avon, Firestone, and Thom McAn. Each produces its own product line, ships to regional warehouses (replacing the wholesaler), and then sells directly to consumers through its own retail outlets. Firestone is perhaps the best among these examples. The company owns rubber plantations in Liberia, tire manufacturing plants in Ohio, and has wholesale and retail outlets throughout the United States. The benefits of direct distribution are control over supply of raw materials, control of distribution and quality, increased buying power, lower administrative costs, and ability to capture profits that would have been earned by other companies at the various stages of the distribution channel.

Both direct and indirect channels are considered **horizontal distribution** and are set up to sell your product or service directly to the customer. Which distribution channel you choose is dictated by your product definition, target market, and other marketing strategies. A good example of the importance of the right distribution channel is Izod Manufacturing. At one time, Izod was a leading manufacturer of highly image-conscious fashion wear. Sales of the Izod Lacoste brand peaked in 1982 at $150 million. Izod then began manufacturing lines of clothing other than their highly popular Lacoste sport shirts. Motivated by a desire to maximize sales, Izod expanded its distribution channel from just highly fashionable stores to major department stores and even K Mart. Not only was the golfer now wearing an Izod alligator, so was his caddy! As Paul Harvey would say, "Now you know the rest of the story." Izod violated its own exclusive distribution strategy.

How many of us have heard that for any retailer the three most important ingredients for success are location, location, and location! In choosing the right location, the three important characteristics are the demographics of the general area (within a three to five mile radius), visibility, and mix of other stores or outlets in the area.

When you consider renting from a strip or large shopping center, the first question to ask is "what are the demographics of that center?" The demographics should include, for example, the age, income, and race of the average shopper (consumer profile). The shopping center owner should include a customer count for the center as well as traffic counts for the bordering roads and intersections. You will want to know whether most of the people traveling these roads live in the area or commute to and from work. If they live in the area, they are more likely to stop and shop. If they are traveling between work and home, they are less likely to stop. These are questions you need to have answered before you start discussing rent. The cheapest rent won't do you any good if you don't have customers.

The next characteristic, visibility, is extremely important. Consumers hate to search for a business. They usually shop at a store they have seen and recall, one with a big unique sign outside or exciting window display. You may have the best mouse trap ever invented, but if your business is not visible from the street, you've lost 50 percent of your potential customers. Access and visibility are essential in attracting new customers.

Finally, you will want to make sure the image of your business and target customer profile are compatible with the other stores in the center. A local sporting goods store in Florida who catered to middle income families and team sports athletes went out of business. The center it was located in contained mainly specialty boutiques that catered to affluent older couples with grown children. Not far away, another sporting goods store in a shopping center that included K Mart and a movie theater was highly successful. This demonstrates the importance of image and customer profile compatibility between your business and your location.

DIRECT MARKETING CONSIDERATIONS AND CHECKLIST

Key review considerations:

- □ Know who your target is. Decide who your buyer is. It is not everybody, and you must have a clear picture of that buyer.

- □ Choose a strategy. Decide exactly what is most likely to persuade that buyer—fear or greed—and how you will invoke that motivation.

- □ Decide what your offer is. Your offer is not what you propose to sell, but what you propose to do for the prospect. Choose your main promise, and make that promise unmistakable.

- □ Focus on the main promise. Start with impact—the chief benefit promised, whether it involves fear or gain—by focusing sharply on it in your opening message. Don't dilute your opener by promising everything at once.

- □ Tell your story in the headline. Always use a high-impact headline and be sure that the headline clearly summarizes the offer and the chief reason for buying—the strategy. The copy following it must reinforce, not explain, the message in the headline.

- □ Add a reasonable number of benefits. Add other benefits in the copy, but make it a reasonable number. They help persuade the prospect, but overdoing it by promising too much leads to confusion and skepticism instead of motivation.

- □ Quantify. Find the means to state promises—benefits—in terms of quantities, for greater impact and credibility. Turn your facts into pounds, feet, numbers of people, miles, or other units of measure.

- □ Prove your case. Provide the evidence to make your promises credible. Use logic, testimonials, photographs, official reports, charts and graphs, or other backup evidence.

- □ Use more than one piece. Include at least a sales letter and brochure or broadside to tell the story. "The more you tell, the more you sell" is a general truth. Tell your story in as many ways as possible, with as many promotional pieces as possible.

□ Tell the whole story. In each promotional piece, retell the story completely, with different language and different perspectives for each.

□ Overwrite, then boil it down. Keep your copy lean—as tight as possible, without leaving information out—by writing as much as necessary to tell everything, and then going back to boil out all unnecessary language.

□ Make it all good news. Avoid anything unpleasant. Break price into palatable units such as "only $29.50 per month" and "less than 2 cents a page." If the item requires skill to use—a personal computer, for example—offer "simple instructions," "school children learn the basics in minutes," and other reassurances. If it's something with potential hazard—a kitchen appliance, for example—stress safety features such as automatic shutoffs.

□ Make copy easy to read and dramatic. Keep sentences and paragraphs short, and use white space generously. Use high contrast colors—black or dark colors on white or yellow paper. Use underlines, boldface type, two colors, circled items, marginal notes, and other devices that dramatize important points and make copy appear easy to read. Don't use these for motivating copy. What you promise and how you prove your case are the prime factors; nothing substitutes for them.

□ Use charts and graphs. Claims and reports are more easily understood, and more believable, when they are presented as (or with the aid of) graphic devices such as plots, charts, exploded views, and matrices.

□ Offer free gifts. Useful free gifts—cameras, radios, pens, and others—are highly motivating. Choose gifts that are appropriate for your anticipated buyers, and feature them prominently. But don't base your strategy or main appeal on the gifts. Your strategy is based on your offer—the main promise and the proof. The gifts should be a bonus extra.

□ Offer discounts. Probably nothing, not even gifts or the word "free," is as alluring as is the lure of a bargain—discounts, special prices, and special offers. Test after test verifies this.

□ Close frequently. Just as in face-to-face selling, you must ask for the order repeatedly. Remind your reader frequently of your offer and make it clear that he or she must take action—respond to your urging—to gain the advantages of your offer. Ask frequently for the order by advising and reminding the prospect of the action to be taken—"fill out the enclosed order form," "call the toll-free number," "come in for a free, personal demonstration," and similar closes.

□ Make sales letters informal and friendly. Use typed (not typeset) copy in sales letters, with ragged right margins (even if you use a word processor to compose the letter). Mark up the copy with a bold, felt tip marking pen to create underlines, circled items, and marginal notes.

□ Make it easy for the prospect to order. Arrange to accept credit card orders, in writing or by telephone. Enclose easy-to-use order forms—forms that require only name, address, credit card number, and checkoffs. Supply postage-paid response envelopes and toll-free telephone numbers.

□ Eliminate risk. Offer guarantees, trial periods, delayed billings or payments, or other measures to eliminate risk and display total confidence in what you offer. But don't overdo this or you begin to sound defensive.

□ Use a postscript in the letter. A prominent "P.S." gets attention and makes the letter more informal and personalized. Many direct-mail professionals make it a standing rule to use a P.S. in their sales letters.

□ Don't be a comic. Humor has its place, but is dangerous in direct-mail copy. It distracts the prospect, when you want to focus the prospect's attention. Often, attempted humor offends some people—a distinct hazard. If it is not truly humorous in the reader's opinion, it totally destroys the copy. It's safer, much safer, to shun humor completely.

□ Don't be clever. Bad copy is created every day by clever copywriters, people who believe that irrelevant puns, acronyms, and other clever gimmicks sell. They don't. Worse, they are often used for the right copy, the copy that would sell, and so are destructive. Forget cleverness and keep your eye on the ball—what you offer and why the prospect ought to buy.

□ Tell the prospect the price. You can't close an order, in most cases, without revealing the price. Make it as palatable as possible, but do tell it.

□ Test, test, test. Nothing is as reliable as actual results. Every mailing, large or small, should be a test mailing, and can be made so by establishing and keeping records that are designed to help you interpret results and put the information to good use in future campaigns.

The Checklist

The checklist following is a suggested form for planning and specifying major characteristics and elements of your direct-mail package. But it is general, and you will have to get down to more detail using other forms and lists supplied here for many of the items. Still, this checklist will serve you well as a preliminary planning tool and reminder of some key considerations. Refer to it repeatedly as you build your direct-mail package, to ensure that you have not allowed anything to slip between the cracks.

Each item has two boxes, one on the left and another on the right. Use the box on the left to decide what items you plan to incorporate or use in your offer. Use the one on the right to verify that you have done so.

You also can use this form as a guide for others. Check off the left-hand boxes as your specifications, and have them check the right-hand boxes as they complete each task.

General

□ Know who your target is □   □ Make copy easy to read and dramatic □

□ Choose a strategy □   □ Use charts and graphs □

□ Decide what your offer is □   □ Offer free gifts □

□ Focus on the main promise □   □ Offer discounts □

☐ Tell your story in the headline ☐   ☐ Close frequently ☐

☐ Add several benefits ☐   ☐ Make sales letters informal and friendly ☐

☐ Quantify ☐   ☐ Make it easy for the prospect to order ☐

☐ Prove your case ☐   ☐ Eliminate the risk ☐

☐ Use more than one piece ☐   ☐ Use a postscript in letter ☐

☐ Tell the whole story ☐   ☐ Don't be a comic ☐

☐ Overwrite, then boil it down ☐   ☐ Don't be clever ☐

☐ Make it all good news ☐   ☐ Tell the prospect the price ☐

☐ Test, test, test ☐

Package plan

☐ Sales letter ☐   ☐ Order forms ☐

☐ Brochure   ☐ Separate item ☐

  ☐ 3 x 9 ☐   ☐ Clip or tear off ☐

  ☐ 8½ × 11 ☐   ☐ Special items

  ☐ _____ ☐   ☐ Plastic "credit" card ☐

☐ Broadside ☐   ☐ Novelty item ☐

☐ Return envelope ☐   ☐ Discount coupon ☐

  ☐ Plain ☐   ☐ _____ ☐

  ☐ Postage paid ☐   ☐ Envelope copy ☐

NOTES:

_____

_____

Target population

GENDER:

☐ Male ☐   ☐ Female ☐

AGE GROUPS:

☐ Children ☐   ☐ Teenagers ☐

☐ Young adults ☐   ☐ Mature/middle-aged adults ☐

☐ Senior citizens ☐   ☐ _____ ☐

OCCUPATION(S):

☐ Students ☐   ☐ Housewives ☐

☐ Blue collar ☐   ☐ White collar ☐

☐ Craft workers ☐   ☐ Professionals ☐

□ _____ □   □ _____ □

MISCELLANEOUS:

□ Home owners □   □ Apartment dwellers □

□ City residents □   □ Suburbanites □

□ Rural residents □   □ _____ □

NOTES:

_____

_____

Strategy

MAIN MOTIVATOR:

FEAR   GAIN

□ Embarrassment □   □ Making money □

□ Health □   □ Getting an education □

□ Accident □   □ Learning a secure trade □

□ Failure □   □ Being popular □

□ Disaster □   □ Being more attractive □

□ _____ □   □ _____ □

NOTES:

_____

_____

Proofs of offer

□ Logic—rational argument □   □ Charts, graphs □

□ Testimonials □   □ Photographs □

□ Official documents □   □ Citations from documents □

□ _____ □   □ _____ □

NOTES:

_____

_____

Gifts and discounts

GIFT ITEMS:

□ Luggage □   □ Digital clocks □

□ Calculators □   □ Subscriptions □

□ Books □   □ Purses □

□ _____ □   □ _____ □

Discounts:

□ Package prices □   □ For prompt ordering □

□ Coupon enclosed □   □ _____ □

Notes:

_____

_____

Other considerations

Making it easy for the customer to order:

□ Separate order form □   □ Credit card ordering □

□ Toll-free telephone □   □ Postage-paid postcard □

□ Prepared order customer need only sign and mail □

□ Self-stick customer return-address labels □

□ _____ □

Revealing the price:

□ Break it into weekly or daily rate □

□ Unitize it on some other basis □

□ Accept payment schedule □   □ List several payment plans □

□ _____ □

Eliminating risk:

□ Money-back guarantee □   □ Guarantee of results □

□ Free trial period □   □ Delayed/deferred payment □

□ _____ □   □ _____ □

Promotions

A promotion is marketing stimuli (messages) used to generate demand for your product or service. The purpose of a promotion is to communicate to potential customers that you have a product or service that can satisfy their demands, to convince those potential customers to buy from you, and to compete successfully with other similar businesses. Your message will depend on the target market you identify and how that market will perceive the message you are trying to send.

The goals of promotion are simple: to inform, to persuade, and to remind. Because a customer must know a product exists before he or she can buy it, informing is probably the most important form of promotion. A firm with a distinctly new product might target its message to inform potential customers of the existence of a product. A business in an industry with established products needs to inform consumers of the existence of its products and also to persuade them to choose that firm over a competitor. However, if a firm is well known by consumers and has a positive image, all it may need to do is to remind the consumers of its existence.

Whatever the objectives of a company's promotional effort are, some specific, measurable results of promotion include:

☐ Increased sales
☐ Improvement of market share
☐ Creation or improvement of brand image
☐ Creation of a favorable climate for future sales
☐ Increased knowledge in the market about your business
☐ Creation or improvement of a competitive advantage of your business

The different types of promotion include advertising, publicity or public relations, personal selling, and sales promotions. The point of promotion is where your product definition, selected target market, and marketing strategies all come together. Which promotional strategy you choose will be determined by marketing decisions you have already made.

Personal selling is targeted directly at the final consumer, whereas advertising, publicity, and public relations are aimed at a mass or large target audience. The third broad category, promotions, is usually a back-up for personal selling and mass promotions. Which type of promotion you use is determined by the size of the target market, the emotional content of the message, and the need for direct feedback. Other factors that play a role in choosing which type of promotion to use are the availability of money to pay for promotions, stage of the product within its life cycle, type of competition, and nature of the product.

The following chart outlines the various sales promotions.

Final Consumers	Wholesalers	Internal Salespeople
Banners	Price Promotions	Contests
Aisle Displays	Promotional Allowances	Bonuses
Samples	Sales Contests	Meetings
Calendars	Calendars	Displays
Point of Purchase Displays	Gifts	Sales Aids
Coupons	Trade Shows	Training
Contests	Meetings	Materials
Trade Shows	Catalogs	
Trading Stamps		

Advertising

Advertising is communication by nonpersonal messages to selected large audiences for the purpose of soliciting or informing consumers. This includes such traditional forms as television, radio, print, direct mail, outdoor billboards, signs on mass transit vehicles, point of purchase displays in stores, and ads in the yellow pages. Which media you choose is based on the target market and cost per person receiving the advertisement. In advertising, no individual representing your business is communicating directly with your potential customer. As a consequence, advertising messages are limited to one-way communications. Advertising works well when your target market strategy is to solicit business from a broad market. However, it can become quite specific when you choose local media such as newspapers, radio, and television air time. Advertising can also be effective when your target market is specifically defined, but sufficiently large to make the advertisement cost effective. A good example is Pepsi advertising to the "Pepsi Generation," a target market of people in the U.S. defined by a specific age group and income potential.

How much to spend on advertising can be decided in several ways. The first method is the **marginal approach** and can be difficult to implement. The marginal approach entails spending to the point where the last expenditure on advertising equals the net profit on sales generated by that advertisement (usually, large corporations use this approach). A second method for determining how much to spend on advertising is the **available funds approach**— spending whatever you can afford to spend. Although probably the most commonly used method, the available funds method is also the most conservative. It is safe to assume that the more you spend on effective advertising, the more sales you will generate. In other words, if you make the investment in quality advertising, you will generate the sales to pay for the advertising. The next method to determine the amount to be spent on advertising is the **budgetary approach**, that is, spending a percentage of projected sales on advertising. If you want sales to reach a certain level next year, you need to spend a certain percentage on advertising during the year. The final approach is the **matching approach**—to match dollar for dollar what your competition is spending. This method is based on the assumption that equal spending will at least keep you and the competition at equal sales levels and market shares.

Advertising Strategy

Advertising is usually a significant aspect of a marketing strategy. Yet this promotional tool is often the one most misunderstood by management, especially nonmarketers. There are a multitude of misconceptions about managing the advertising function. Confusion may abound over the actual planning or developing stages and formulating the most effective advertising strategies.

Advertising is a tool that can help the organization achieve strategic objectives and goals. It can help to increase profits, sales, market share, or frequency of buyer purchases. It can help to generate positive feelings and thoughts about the organization and its products, services, or social contributions.

If used properly, mass selling can be a beneficial medium for demonstrating products or services. It also can educate consumers and other groups about various concepts or issues. Advertising can create awareness and influence attitudes. In essence, it is a communication medium that helps an organization relate to the market.

Advertising strategy has been emphasized for unused production or marketing capacity. A company may want to cover some costly overhead. Or it may need to deal with the nagging problem of a cyclical or seasonal business. Constant advertising may help to even out the peaks and valleys of a business.

A product with a short life requires more ad dollars. Repeat purchases become critical to the bottom line. New variables or objectives also might dictate more advertising dollars. For example, new competition, products, markets, channels, services, or operational problems will require advertising that is informative. In these cases an educational process is needed to create awareness while eventually obtaining the desired action from the advertising audiences.

Not only may advertising motivate marketing personnel—including the sales force—but it also may help to produce an excellent list of prospects, such as in a direct mail campaign. Mass selling also may help to supplement the scattered and dissimilar efforts of manufacturers' representatives, sales agents, and other groups who may not be actual employees of the organization but are selling arms of the firm.

Promotion of your products or services involves two elements, both of which relate your selling effort to your market:

□ What is your product message? Describe your product or service so that your customers will recognize the benefits they can expect from purchasing it.

□ How will you deliver the message? Select marketing channels that will reach your audience. Advertise to a large audience through radio, television, or newspapers. Use merchandising activities such as displays and product support activities. Use direct face-to-face selling. Or do you consider your location alone sufficient to attract all the customers that you need?

Frequently, a combination of efforts is necessary for success. Through advertising, you attract a certain number of potential customers to your business. Once there, displays and merchandising aids heighten the customer's interest in buying. Finally, a salesperson takes the time to present and demonstrate your product to close the sale.

All marketing, from large-scale advertising to direct person-to- person contact, must be aimed at satisfying the purchaser's buying motives. Therefore, the buying motives of the audience you are trying to reach must be understood before you can select the product message and media channel that will best serve your needs.

Buying Motives

Why do people buy? Not so much for the sake of owning specific things, but to satisfy certain basic needs or wants. Some of these basic needs include clothing to keep warm, food to avoid hunger, or medicine to relieve pain.

People's buying motives are also determined by wants. A desire for comfort or an interest in styling will often dictate people's preference in furniture, cars, and clothing.

As a marketer, you must convince potential customers that your product or service meets their needs and wants and that it satisfies one or more of their buying motives. You can do this only by relating your product to their needs and wants, and by proving how it will satisfy their buying motives.

Product Features and Benefits

The product or service that you sell may have any number of features that appeal to your market. A feature is usually a specific product characteristic. A temperature control could be a feature of a clothes washer. A remote channel selector could be a feature of a television set. A 1,000 watt capacity could be a feature of a hair drier.

But what do these features mean to the buyer? How do they satisfy buying motives? With somewhat simple products, the buyer is often familiar with the advantages that the features offer. In many other cases, you may have to explain how the features of your product satisfy the customer's buying motives.

Features Related to Buying Motives

Any description of features must be related to the prospect's buying motives. The temperature control of the washer provides protection for the owner's fabrics. The remote TV channel selector offers the convenience of channel changing without leaving your seat. The key words are protection and convenience—basic buying motives or benefits that people look for when they buy a wide variety of products or services, not just washers or television sets.

Suppose you sell insulated windows with flexible vinyl glazing. Mr. and Mrs. Wilson enter your store to look at insulated windows. They already know that insulated windows reduce heating costs because they have talked with other suppliers. Why should they buy yours instead of theirs? If you said, "Mr. and Mrs. Wilson, these windows have flexible vinyl glazing," their answer probably would be, "So what?" and a shrug of the shoulder, or "What is the price?" Flexible vinyl glazing means nothing to the average customer.

As a seller, you must explain the advantages of the flexible vinyl glazing in terms that show Mr. and Mrs. Wilson the benefits that they would realize. If you explain, "Flexible vinyl glazing won't chip and will not require painting," the Wilsons will recognize how this will preserve the appearance of their windows and eliminate the cost and inconvenience of maintenance.

Complicated Products

In today's world, products are becoming increasingly complicated; to prompt a customer to buy, technical features must be explained in terms of the increased satisfaction that they will bring to the owner. If customers do not understand how advanced, sophisticated features provide them with specific benefits, the technology and cost of these features are wasted.

Selling at Premium Prices

If you are selling a product at a premium price, it is particularly important to explain your product in terms of the benefits that it offers the customer. This must hold true in advertising, promotional materials, or selling directly to a customer.

Direct Selling and Your Product Message

Although not all products or services are sold person-to-person, an understanding of the direct selling process is often useful in explaining the key elements of any marketing message.

Customizing Your Marketing Message. Direct selling is the ideal marketing situation. When you are face-to-face with a customer, you have an opportunity to find out which specific benefits are most important to the particular customer. Then you can explain how your product or service provides those benefits.

Not all prospects will be interested in all the benefits that your product offers. For example, your product may offer superior styling, quality, and convenience. If you know that a prospect doesn't care about styling, you would stress the quality and convenience features of your product.

Detailed Presentation. A direct selling situation lets you present your product or service in more detail than an advertisement. You have the prospect's attention and the time needed to explain your product thoroughly.

Naturally, direct selling does not apply to many products and services. Perhaps the price is too low to justify the time, or the audience is too scattered and too large to permit talking with each individual customer. These customers can only be reached through advertising.

Media Selection

The principles of direct selling can guide your development of a marketing message. The selection of a suitable channel, or medium, for the message depends upon the nature of your market and the complexity of your message.

The table below describes some key features of the various marketing channels that could be available for your product or service. Advertising has been broken down into two categories as follows:

□ Media advertising such as radio, TV, newspapers, and magazines

□ Direct advertising such as mailings, handbills, and telephone solicitation

The third promotional channel, direct selling, has been included as a basis for comparison.

	Audience	Message	Cost Per 1,000	Expected Sales Return
MEDIA ADVERTISING	Large, scattered	Brief, universal	$2–$15	1%
DIRECT ADVERTISING	Medium, selective	Intermediate	$100–$1,000	1%–10%
DIRECT SELLING	Small	Detailed	??	10%–?

Audience Comparison

Compare the three approaches briefly. The first column compares the audience. Media advertising, where the audience is scattered, is ordinarily most useful for products and services that are sold to the public.

In direct advertising, the advertiser has somewhat limited control over a specific audience. For example, the audience for a radio commercial is limited to the show's listeners. With a direct mail or telephone campaign, the advertiser has greater selectivity. The mailer can be addressed to particular persons whose income, occupation, or special interests indicate a desire for the product or service.

Finally, for direct selling, the audience is usually known. The seller's only contact is with parties who have a known need or desire for the product or service.

Message Capability

The second column compares the message capability of each of the three types. Media advertising messages must be brief—perhaps 30 seconds of broadcast time or a few inches of print. Even if more space and more time are available, there is a limit to how much the audience is willing to hear or read.

In a direct mail or telephone campaign, the selected audience is usually more interested in the particular product or service and has time available to digest a more detailed message.

Finally, in direct selling, the seller has the advantage of being able to make a detailed presentation of the product or service and address it specifically to the needs of a particular customer.

Cost

The third column describes the cost per thousand persons reached, generally referred to as the "CPM." For example, a newspaper advertisement that cost $50 and reached 10,000 persons would have a CPM as follows:

CPM = Cost/Thousands of Persons
CPM = $50/10
CPM = $5.00

A direct mail campaign, with its more selective audience, would have a somewhat higher cost, perhaps $100 to $1,000 per thousand, as shown in the table. This would include the cost of mailer preparation, envelopes, postage, purchased mailing lists, and so on.

In direct selling, costs can vary widely. In fact, the sky is the limit! Perhaps a delivery driver is the salesperson. At each delivery point, the driver makes a quick sales presentation. The cost is virtually nothing. At the opposite extreme, when selling a high-priced service or product to industrial or commercial accounts, transportation costs, living expenses, commissions, and salaries must all be considered. For a salesperson in New York to make a single call in Los Angeles, the cost could be $500-$1,000 or more.

Sales Return

The final column shows the expected sales return. For media advertising, less than 1 percent of the entire audience can be expected to buy. Frequently, even a small fraction of 1 percent will more than justify the cost of the advertisement. In a direct mail or telephone solicitation, a somewhat higher return is expected, perhaps 1–10 percent. In direct selling, where the cost of each call is higher, a somewhat higher rate of return must be expected, usually 10 percent or more.

Direct Mailing Costs

The cost per thousand of direct mailers is generally higher than that of media advertising. Among the costs involved are the following:

- □ Preparation of copy
- □ Photography, artwork, typesetting
- □ Printing
- □ Envelopes
- □ Postage
- □ Cost of purchased lists

In some areas, there are businesses that will handle the entire job from start to finish at a fixed cost. Or it may be more economical to purchase mailing lists, hire printers or art services as needed, and do the rest of the job yourself.

Advertising Media

A wide variety of advertising media is available. Each has specific applications to various businesses. The marketer must understand the advantages and disadvantages of different types of media. We will examine some and see how they apply to small businesses.

- □ **Television.** This is the biggest and most expensive advertising medium. A single network television spot can cost tens or even hundreds of thousands of dollars. Yet brief (10-30 seconds) spots on local television channels can often be a wise buy for certain small businesses.

- □ **Magazines.** While the national news magazines are usually far outside the budget of small businesses, local magazines, regional editions of national magazines, and special interest magazines with somewhat small circulations often fall within the budget capability of small businesses.

Good advertising copy must be appropriate to the marketplace, the chosen media, and the expectations of the managers who are paying the advertising costs.

Evaluating Advertising Media

In choosing the appropriate advertising media, you should ask the firm (magazine, newspaper, radio station, etc.) you are considering using for a "media kit." This is an information packet that describes the demographics of the firms's readership or subscribers. These demographics should identify what type of customer reads that newspaper or magazine, listens to that radio station, or watches that television station. In addition, the media kit should include something about what these consumers like to do and how they spend their money. You need to match your customer profile with the demographics of the advertising media, to select the best advertising media for your business.

The following chart from *Business Age Magazine*, Vol. 2, No. 8, August 1988, summarizes the advantages and disadvantages of various advertising media:

Medium	Advantages	Disadvantages
Network TV	Powerful image/awareness generator Wide market reach Good sponsorship/control opportunities	High total costs Poor targeting Limited time frame
Cable TV	Powerful image/awareness generator Low cost per thousand Target market programming	Limited reach Very low ratings Deficient coverage in some markets
Radio	Cost effective for repeat spots Some target selection by programming Good support medium	No visual capability Sometimes used as "background" noise
Newspapers	High local market penetration Some targeting by section Direct response capabilities Message and announcement can be current or immediate	Weak/no color Size = degree of impact Higher cost for special positioning
Newspaper (Free standing insert)	Low cost Good for coupons and mail order Good local market coverage Good for catalog-type advertising	"Clutter" problem Low targeting capability "Discount" image
Magazines	Moderate to good targeting potential Good image awareness capability Good direct response capability Longer message life	Costly for repeats Limited formats Inefficient lower income targeting
Direct Mail	Highly targetable Good awareness and sale conversion Unlimited format options "Private" medium	High cost/1000 High up front testing costs Potential "junk" image
Telemarketing	Effective with existing customers Instant customer feedback Highly personable Easy to implement	High cost of lists Format limitations Poor image No demonstration ability

In evaluating any individual advertising medium, you will normally want to know three factors:

☐ Cost
☐ Audience size
☐ Audience quality

Each of these factors is closely interrelated. Let's take a closer look at what is meant by audience quality.

Audience Quality
To a seller, a quality audience consists of those people who are most likely to buy the product. It does not mean rich versus poor or educated versus

uneducated. To the seller of janitorial supplies, a magazine with a high percentage of janitors among its readers is a quality magazine. Why bother with magazines that reach polo players, yachtspersons, or gourmets? Conversely, the furrier would have little interest in advertising in a janitors' magazine.

The question to ask in evaluating the quality of a particular medium is whether or not its audience is representative of your market. The local suburban weekly may have a higher cost per thousand readers than the metropolitan daily, yet offer a higher quality audience for the local retailer. The suburb, not the entire metropolitan area, is the retailer's primary market.

To the seller of blue jeans, the local rock station offers a higher quality audience than the adult-oriented radio news show, despite relative audience size or audience income.

Audience Demographics

In selecting an advertising medium, it is frequently wise to examine the demographics of the audience. The demographics are an analysis of the audience according to social and economic factors. For example, the table below shows the demographics for two radio stations serving the same geographic area.

Demographics

	Station A	Station B
Age		
Under 18	43%	6%
18–25	27	7
26–35	13	23
36–50	8	42
Over 50	9	22
Income		
0–5,000	64%	5%
5,001–10,000	16	8
10,001–20,000	11	27
Over 20,000	9	60
Education		
High School Graduate	42%	12%
College Graduate	12	65
Graduate School	3	23
Occupation		
Student	51%	5%
Unemployed (non-stud.)	10	1
Clerical	7	8
Skilled	8	7
Unskilled	6	7
Technical	7	27
Managerial	6	26
Professional	5	19
Sex		
Male	46%	73%
Female	54	27

The audience of station A is considerably younger, has a lower income, less education, and fewer job skills than audience B. Nevertheless, the more youthful audience A might be a higher quality audience for certain products such as records, contemporary clothing, or fast foods.

To the seller of higher-priced items such as expensive automobiles, home furnishings, or real estate, audience B would be far more interesting.

Effective Cost-Per-Thousand (CPM)

In measuring the cost per thousand of a particular advertising medium, you are usually better advised to determine an effective CPM—in other words, the cost per thousand people reached who are representative of your target population.

To determine an effective CPM, divide the cost of the advertising by the effective audience—that portion of the total audience that is likely to be interested in your product—not the entire audience.

Effective CPM = Cost / Effective Audience (in thousands)

For example, assume that you have defined your market as persons with incomes over $25,000. You are considering advertising in one of two magazines, whose audience demographics (by income) are described below.

		X	Y
Cost		$ 100	$ 150
Total Readers		10,000	15,000
CPM		10	10
Reader Income	0–$10,000	25%	5%
	10,000– 25,000	45%	15%
	Over $25,000	30%	80%

Each magazine has the same CPM, based upon total number of readers:

X: $100 / 10,000 = $10 CPM

Y: $150 / 15,000 = $10 CPM

However, you are only interested in readers with incomes over $25,000. Therefore, the number of potential buyers you would reach through each magazine must be calculated as follows:

X: 10,000 × .30 = 3,000

Y: 15,000 × .80 = 12,000

You can now calculate an effective CPM based upon the number of readers of each magazine that fall within your market.

Magazine	Cost	Effective Readers	Effective CPM
X	$100	3,000	$33.33
Y	$150	12,000	$12.50

Although both magazines have the same CPM based upon total readership, the effective CPM of magazine Y, based upon the total number of readers within the market, is far less expensive.

Advertising Costs vs. Sales Generated

The expected sales generated from media advertising is generally small, usually less than 1%. However, since audiences are large, even a small fraction of 1% often justifies the cost of the advertisement. Consider the example of a local radio advertisement with a $5.00 CPM. If one out of 100 listeners bought the product, the advertiser would realize 10 sales (1,000 × ($5.00/ 10) per sale. While this would obviously be unsatisfactory for selling a $0.50 product, it could be a bargain when selling a higher priced product with sufficient gross profit margin to justify the expenditure.

Direct Promotion

In those businesses where media advertising is impractical, it is often economical to promote through direct mail, telephone solicitation, or some other medium. The first advantage of these promotions is the availability of a far more selective audience.

The cost per thousand mailers is generally from $100 to $1000 per thousand persons reached. However, the return expected from a direct mailing is usually higher than that expected from advertising since the original audience should have a higher degree of interest. For example, a ski equipment advertisement in the local newspaper would be read by thousands of people who hate the snow and the cold! For less money, you might be able to make a direct mailing to all skiers in your area. The more selective your audience, the higher the rate of return you can expect.

Direct Mail Message

The direct mail message may be brief or somewhat detailed. In the simplest case, with a mailer similar to a handbill, preparation costs may be no more than a few cents each. The piece could be self-sealing so that there is no need for an envelope. Addressing costs could be three or four cents each and postage, using lower mail classes, can be reduced to pennies.

Publicity

Another form of promotion is **publicity**. Publicity is information about your product or company that is not a direct message from you to the potential customer: it is usually reported by an independent party. You do not directly pay for publicity, but its value to you in terms of sales can be dramatic. An example of publicity is the weekly food column in the newspaper. If you own a restaurant, you do not pay for a restaurant review, but information about your business, food, and service is reported to the public. Publicity can be either good or bad and you have little control over what is reported. The review that raves about the quality service at your restaurant can double sales overnight. A bad review about how unpleasant it was to dine at your restaurant can cause the few remaining customers you have to never come back. Finally, although your business might be recognized in the media for community involvement, this recognition does not necessarily convey any specific message to any of your target market segment, and might not generate any sales for the business.

There are several basic observations about publicity that should be made at once:

Publicity is free advertising. At the minimum it makes many people aware of your existence and your enterprise. At the maximum it promotes many sales directly and has often been directly responsible for major marketing triumphs (like Robert Ringer's book, *Winning Through Intimidation* and Gary Dahl's *Pet Rocks* of a few years ago). Even between those extremes favorable publicity generates sales leads and paves the way for direct sales efforts in other ways.

For our purposes here, publicity is defined simply as public information about you, your enterprise, or what you do or sell. It appears in newspapers, periodicals, on radio and TV, and in any other medium that reaches the general public, although there are some exceptions to this that we shall discuss later.

Sometimes publicity comes about spontaneously, as a by-product of something else, but useful publicity is most often the result of your specific efforts.

Publicity is free, at least in the sense that you do not pay directly for it (although it may sometimes cost a great deal of money to get the "free" publicity!). However, while that is an advantage, the cost or lack of cost is incidental. What is significant is that good publicity can be and often is far more effective than paid advertising. In fact, publicity has sometimes been truly priceless, producing results that could not have been achieved through paid advertising of any magnitude.

The Press Release

Since by its nature publicity is most frequently information in print via newspapers and other periodicals, it is not surprising that the news release (also called press release, publicity release, and simply "release") is by far the most commonly used tool of publicity or public relations (PR) specialists. Probably some 90 percent of all releases are promptly discarded with hardly a glance when received.

That's not a condemnation of the release as a useful tool of PR. It is simply the consequence of hasty, careless, and perhaps unenlightened release-writing practices. And it is due, in some part, to thoughtlessness in sending releases out to inappropriate destinations. Good releases, mailed to suitable recipients, are picked up and used as intended.

Releases are sent to editors in the hope that the editors will use the release or some part of it in their publications or broadcasts (in the case of radio and TV newsrooms). There are at least three reasons for releases often being spurned by editors:

1. Some releases are pure hype, thinly disguised commercial advertising, offering no news or information of value to the editor and his or her audience.

2. Some releases are adequate in their content and writing, but are sent to inappropriate prospects or sent at the wrong times.

3. Some releases are scheduled by editors for use but are unfortunately shouldered aside at the last moment by more important material that competes with the release.

Release Writing Style. Writing a release properly is as important as writing advertising copy properly, and the basic rules are the same: Write the material out at length, including all the information, in the first draft. Then rewrite, organizing the material for the most effective presentation. Then rewrite at least once more, editing heavily to eliminate all unnecessary verbiage. A cliche of the writing trade is that all good writing is rewriting. Most experienced professionals believe that firmly, and expect to rewrite at least once. But most rewrite again and again before they release their copy. And truly professional writers are not entirely satisfied with their copy even then, but always ponder whether they ought to do at least one more edit and rewrite.

By then the release should tell the story, get to the point as directly as possible, and then stop. And, like advertising copy, it should have a lead with some opening grabber or hook that can be summarized in the headline and expanded on in the body copy, preferably in the opening sentence. That headline and/or first sentence or two may very well determine whether the editor reads further before deciding to be interested—or not to be interested—in the release.

Other Sources of Print Publicity
One way to overcome that inherent disadvantage of limited readership is to gain exposure in other, more widely circulated, periodicals. That is the purpose of the press release, of course. But, the press release is not the only way to make an appearance in newspapers and magazines. There are at least these other ways to make those other PR appearances:

- ☐ Contributing articles to periodicals
- ☐ Writing letters for the Letters to the Editor feature
- ☐ Writing a book
- ☐ Contributions (letters) to regular columnists and feature writers
- ☐ Getting yourself or your venture written about

The Press Kit
Something called a press kit or media kit is a must for serious PR activity. This is a prepackaged kit of publicity materials you would normally make available to the media as a core element of every PR activity such as a press conference or any event—conference, convention, seminar, demonstration, or other—that is to be covered by the press. Such kits are also often mailed out to anyone inquiring into your activities or seeking information about your activities.

In any case, the kit normally includes two types of material: standard materials that are normally included in all your press kits, and materials that have been especially developed for the occasion. Among the kinds of items normally found in press kits are any or all of the following, as appropriate:

- ☐ Photographs (of yourself or whatever you wish to publicize)
- ☐ Releases
- ☐ Brochures
- ☐ Biographical data
- ☐ Prepared statements/"white papers"
- ☐ Reprints of articles/news items by or about you/whatever you are publicizing
- ☐ Catalog sheets/specification sheets

☐ Broadside
☐ Circulars/flyers
☐ Release (permission to quote/reproduce, not a press release!)

New Product Columns

Photographs are also invaluable for another kind of publicity. Many periodicals have new-product columns that describe new products, with photographs where appropriate, and usually with prices and where or how-to-order information. Sending photos and product information—the news release is suitable for this, but you can send a simple typed statement using the release format—will get you a great deal of valuable free advertising in these columns.

This way many periodicals have specialists who will actually try out new products and write reviews of them, sometimes rather lengthy reviews. Where this is a practice and is appropriate to your product, you may send a sample of your product to the appropriate columnist. (Major items, items that are too costly to give away freely—for example, computers and automobiles—are generally loaned to columnists, to be returned at some future time.) Computer products, especially software programs, are usually offered to computer periodicals for review, for example, as are new books and many other items. Be sure when you send photographs or products that they are properly identified; do not depend on the enclosed release or statement for this because it may become separated from the photograph. The only sure and safe way of doing this is to attach a description of the item to the photograph cemented or taped to the back. It also does no harm to send more than one photograph of the item if you have more than one useful view. In fact, for some items it is necessary to show more than one view.

Radio and TV Appearances

Getting on radio and TV to talk about or to demonstrate your product is excellent PR, but it is not easy to do. As in other cases of seeking PR opportunities, it requires some work.

In searching out opportunities in the electronic media, you must do your research first:

☐ Seek out the programs, radio and TV, of interest
☐ Call the studios and find who the producers are
☐ Send the producers releases or complete press kits
☐ Follow up with telephone calls
☐ Persist and persevere. Don't get discouraged, for persistence and perseverance are the keys to success in this area.

Principles of Selling

A person-to-person sales approach is the third approach to promotions, **personal selling**. The advantage of this approach is that it allows for two-way communication between your representative and your potential customer.

The role of personal selling in the marketing mix varies extensively by company size, industry, and product line or service. Large consumer-oriented organizations rely on advertising and sales promotion to reach the broad customer base. Small industrialized companies emphasize personal selling to reach narrow market segments. Still others use a combination of a company sales force and manufacturer reps.

Basically, personal selling involves a flexible, two-way conversation between buyer and seller. The sales rep has all kinds of resources at his or her disposal to convince the potential customer to buy. For example, the sales rep can use a standard company pitch or deviate to meet the individual concerns and needs of the particular prospect. The sales rep can rely on facts about the product or invoke powers of persuasion and selling techniques to achieve the desired results.

Objectives of personal selling depend on instructions from the company, but the most common are to provide the buyer with product and promotional material; to gather information on competitive activities; and to provide a service or repair function and to physically deliver or demonstrate the product.

In addition, the sales force will be directed by management to carry out different kinds of sales strategies, such as selling a proper mix of items in the product line; concentrating on key accounts; prospecting for new accounts; reducing credit losses and training wholesale or retail personnel.

Defining the Salesperson's Job

It used to be a widely held assumption that a good salesperson could sell anything. Today, this notion has largely been dispelled. This is because organizations have specific sales requirements and position descriptions based on their particular products and the way they do business. It is usually up to the sales manager to determine the traits, level of experience, and education needed to fill the sales rep positions. These could include degree of persuasiveness, self-confidence, ambition, interpersonal relation skills, knowledge of the business environment, persistence, utilization of time, and more. If the job description includes adjustments for damaged goods or customer claims, the sales manager may want an individual who is firm and objective, yet tactful. If the salesperson will be required to carry heavy samples, then physical strength, energy, and stamina will be necessary. Typically, the representative will be required to follow five steps:

1. Make contact with the prospect
2. Deliver the presentation
3. Handle any objections that might arise
4. Close the sale
5. Provide follow-up services and support

Defining the Market

Clearly identifying the targeted customer market is just as important to the function of personal selling as it is to advertising and the entire marketing effort. To identify profitable sales potential by segment and by account, sales management compiles lists of customers that are either heavy, light, or former buyers. In addition, they provide the sales force with lists of prospects who they would like to serve or who could benefit from the purchase of the product or service. Salespeople rank their lists of customers in order of their potential profitable sales volume. Based on this list, the salesperson plans travel and selling time and charts the best travel routes. The most effective salespeople know as much as possible about prospects before they call.

Training Sales Representatives

This task takes on increasing importance as competition heightens, buyers become more sophisticated, and the market more complex and diverse. Generally, the sales training program addresses four key areas:

1. The company—its history, product, manufacturing process, policies, prices, promotional efforts, service, credit, and delivery.

2. The market—who buys the product, where, and when.

3. Sales techniques—how to communicate knowledge of the company, its products, and benefits.

4. Personal management—routing, processing of orders, using expense accounts, filling out call reports, relationship with other reps and sales management, feedback on competitors and compensation.

Companies develop their own sales training methods, but most commonly they consist of lectures, conferences, and group discussions on the one hand, and field training on the other.

Although personal selling generally results in more sales directly related to promotional efforts, it is a very expensive form of promotion. Another disadvantage is that it can limit the size of your potential target market segment. Some types of direct selling include the "canned" presentation where a sales representative recites a memorized sales pitch to the customer. Although this allows you more control over what message the customer receives, it does not allow for an open channel of communication like the "feature vs. benefit" approach, and often puts-off potential customers. In feature vs. benefit selling, your representative spends time asking the customer what his or her wants and needs are. The representative then attempts to show the customer how your company can satisfy those wants and needs better than any competitor. This type of sales approach usually leaves the customer feeling satisfied with his or her decision. If there are any misunderstandings or reservations, your salesperson can handle them before closing the sale. Feature vs. benefit direct selling is also an excellent opportunity for you to gain valuable insight into the wants and needs of your target market, to track changes in customer demand, and to collect good feedback on the performance of your business. Deciding what type of direct sales approach to choose determines what type of sales force you must hire. These decisions follow very closely your decision on distribution. You have the choice of hiring a captive direct sales force or using independent sales representatives who represent your company as well as other companies. If you choose independent representatives, your expenses will most likely be lower, but you have less control over the representation of your company and products. If that sales representative is unprofessional or chooses to emphasize another product that will earn him or her a higher income, the sales and reputation of your business could suffer. With a captive direct sales force, you will have increased expenses, such as Social Security, pensions, and medical insurance. Your choice of compensation includes salary, commission, or some combination. In motivating your salespeople, remember that people respond to recognition, money, advancement, status, security, working environment, and pride in a worthwhile job.

The selling principles of a successful direct selling effort are equally valid in shaping a message to larger audiences. Therefore, to understand the basics of the sales message, we will begin by analyzing the direct selling situation. Later we will relate these principles to developing the message for other marketing channels.

Three Major Steps
A direct selling situation usually has three major steps as follows:

☐ **Qualifying the prospect.** Determining the prospect's needs and wants so that the salesperson can then explain the product or service in terms that will show how its features provide those benefits.

☐ **Presenting the product.** Describing the product and its features in terms of the benefits that the prospect seeks.

☐ **Closing the sale.** Securing the prospect's commitment to buy your product or service.

Qualifying. In the first step, qualifying the prospect, you (as the salesperson) want to learn why the prospect needs or wants your product or service. Perhaps you sell sewing machines. A prospect has seen your ad for a low-priced model and has arrived at your shop. Naturally, you have a variety of models and you want to find out which model is best suited to the customer's needs. By simply taking the order for the lowest price model, you might be doing a disservice both to yourself and the customer. If the customer simply wants a machine to hem dresses or patch jeans, perhaps the lowest priced model is entirely adequate. If the customer plans to make clothing for a family, a higher priced machine might be better suited to the customer and more profitable for you.

Asking Questions. How can you find out which machine is best suited to the customer's needs? By asking questions such as:

☐ "How do you plan to use the machine?"
☐ "How often do you sew?"
☐ "What type of sewing do you do?"

These questions help you learn more about the customer's needs and wants.

Indirect Questions. Qualifying questions should be indirect questions, usually beginning with words such as why, what, when, and how. These questions usually cannot be answered with a simple "Yes" or "No." They require more complete answers that reveal buying motives.

You can learn about your customer by asking about competition. This is particularly helpful when selling high-ticket consumer goods or when selling to commercial and industrial customers.

If a person is buying a replacement for something he or she already owns, you can ask questions about the product he or she now owns. "What kind of refrigerator do you now own, Mr. Baker?" When Mr. Baker tells you that he now owns an Electromat X99, you might ask other questions such as:

□ "Is that the 12-cubic-foot or 15-cubic-foot model?"
□ "Is it equipped with automatic defrost?"
□ "Does it have automatic ice-making?"

The answers to these questions will help you lead into features of your more expensive refrigerators such as larger capacity, automatic defrost, and an automatic ice-maker.

Presentation. The second step in direct selling is presenting the product. An effective presentation often depends upon the information received in the first stage, qualifying the prospect. This permits you (as the salesperson) to explain the features of your product and its advantages, so that your prospect clearly understands its benefits. Qualifying information lets you direct your explanation to those specific benefits in which the particular prospect has expressed an interest.

Transition to Close. The presentation is followed by the primary objective—closing the sale. This is most effective if introduced as a smooth transition from the presentation. Sometimes it's easy. The prospect, absolutely convinced of the advantages of the product and the benefits that it offers, will come right out and buy it. More frequently, it's up to the salesperson to bring up the closing question.

Trial Closes. An easy way to do this is through trial closes. A trial close is a question that is asked to determine the prospect's readiness to buy. The following is an example of such a question:

"Are you satisfied that our product will help you reduce your maintenance costs?"

If the answer is negative, you can reemphasize how your product reduces maintenance costs or you can ask the prospect to be more specific about the cause of his or her doubt.

Seeking Agreement. If the prospect agrees with the salesperson on a series of points, it becomes difficult to say no when the salesperson asks for the order. However, the prospect who disagrees on a number of points probably will defend this position by also saying no when the salesperson asks for the order.

The salesperson should seek agreement on several points such as:

□ "Don't you think the self-defrosting feature of this refrigerator is a real convenience, Mr. Baker?"

□ "You probably need a larger refrigerator than your present one, don't you?"

The salesperson probably knows the points to which the prospect will agree. The idea is to summarize them and ask them consecutively to establish a pattern of agreement, one that will make it difficult for the prospect to say no when the salesperson asks for the order.

Benefit Summary. Another effective transition is a statement that summarizes product benefits, such as the following:

> Ms. Andrews, I think you'll find that the Brand X washer has everything you're looking for. A partial load cycle saves you water, energy, and money. Temperature controls protect your fabrics. And Brand X's reputation for quality assures you that this machine will operate dependably for a long time with little or no maintenance.

Closing the Sale. Now let us look at the most vital factor in the selling process—closing the sale. All previous steps have been taken with one purpose in mind—to close the sale, to get the prospect to buy.

Unfortunately, many salespeople fall apart at this stage. The salesperson is afraid that a negative response will end communication with the prospect forever. Having maintained a sociable communications level up to this point, the salesperson resists the possibility of rejection. This is a perfectly natural reaction for many people.

Various Techniques. A variety of techniques can be used to close the sale. The best approach often depends upon the salesperson's individual selling style, the prospect, the product or service that is offered, and the salesperson's earlier success in convincing the prospect of the advantages of the product and the benefits that it offers.

Direct Close. The direct close assumes that the prospect is ready to buy. In closing, the salesperson asks a direct question such as the following:

- □ "We can deliver your sofa next week. What is the address that we should ship to?"
- □ "You want this in green, don't you?"
- □ "Will this be cash or charge?"
- □ "Would you like to put this on a budget plan?"

Assumptive Close. The assumptive close is a modification of the direct close. The salesperson assumes that the prospect is ready to buy, but asks less direct questions, such as:

- □ "Which color do you prefer, red or green?"
- □ "Which model do you prefer, the standard or the deluxe?"
- □ "Shall I call an electrician to arrange the installation?"

Dealing with Delay. Not all closing attempts are immediately successful. The prospect may delay, unable to make a decision. If so, the salesperson should ask the reason for the delay. The reason will often help the salesperson plan the next course of action in reestablishing the presentation of the product or service.

For example, the prospect might say: "I think I'll stick with my present machine a while longer." If you properly qualified the prospect earlier, you might respond: "But didn't you say that repair costs were running awfully high? Isn't it worth a few dollars to know that you will save on maintenance costs, and not have to worry about a breakdown at a critical time?"

Dealing with Objections. A prospect may express some objection, real or imaginary, to your product. An objection should never be considered a barrier to a sale. Once you know about it, it is no longer a barrier, simply a hurdle that must be cleared.

A prospect may say, "Your price is too high." First, try to find out how much too high. Perhaps it can be reduced. Or the objection might be a signal to reemphasize more features of the product that offset any apparent price disadvantage.

Open-Ended Close. In the open-ended close, the salesperson asks open-ended questions that imply readiness to buy, such as:

- □ "How soon will you need the sofa?"
- □ "When should I arrange for installation?"

The prospect's answer to these questions leads to an easy close. If the prospect needs the sofa in three weeks, the salesperson can respond, "Then I'll need an order right away to assure you of delivery on time."

Action Close. The salesperson takes some positive step toward clinching the order, such as:

- □ "I'll write up the order right now. As soon as you sign it, we can deliver."
- □ "I'll call the warehouse and see if they can ship immediately."

Urgency Close. The salesperson advises the prospect of some compelling reason for ordering immediately:

- □ "That's a pretty tight schedule. I'll have to get an answer from you very quickly if we are to be able to meet it."
- □ "That item has been very popular and right now our inventory is running pretty low."
- □ "Our special price on this product ends the 15th of the month."

Choosing the Closing Technique. The choice of closing techniques will depend upon you, your selling style, your customer, and the facts. Despite the technique that you choose for your business, the most important thing to remember is that you pursue some closing technique and don't avoid this critical step.

Developing Selling Skills. Some people seem born with natural powers of persuasion. At an early age, they can easily convince a person of the value of some product or service. However, not all people have these inherent skills.

These skills must be developed, and the way to develop them is by a logical, well-considered, planned selling system of qualifying, presenting, and closing.

These skills can be learned. With planning, practice, and diligent pursuit, almost anyone can sell.

The ability to sell is particularly critical in small businesses where the owner is often called upon to conduct the entire selling effort personally. Even if the owner does not sell personally, the sales force must be trained, supervised, and directed.

Selling Skills and Other Marketing Techniques. Any marketing technique that you use must incorporate many of the same selling concepts that were explained in the direct selling situation.

Consider how the basic principles of qualifying and product presentation apply to the development of an advertising message. You cannot qualify the prospect directly by asking questions—unless you can afford a costly marketing research effort. Instead, you must make certain qualifying assumptions about your prospects. What are their needs and wants? What benefits do they seek?

These answers then determine the benefits that you will stress in your product message. The message must explain your product in terms of these benefits, for example:

☐ "Our insulation will save you money."
☐ "Won-Kote latex paint is easy to apply and lasts longer."
☐ "Our trained technicians will repair your television set and back it up with a 12-month warranty to put an end to your maintenance worries."

Closing. An advertising message seldom has a specific "close," but it should have an objective. This objective should be expressed in terms that incorporate the concepts of the closing techniques of a direct selling situation, for example:

☐ "Don't you owe it to yourself to look at our new line of washers before your present one fails?"
☐ "Buy now while the special price offer lasts."
☐ "Call today for a free estimate, before winter sets in. Our estimator will show you how much you can save with all- weather insulation protection."

Sales Promotion

The final promotional technique is a catch-all category called **sales promotions**. It includes all other types of promotions like videotape presentations, contests, premiums, coupons, trading stamps, displays, and sampling.

Sales promotion refers to that wide range of activities that supports and helps supplement advertising and personal selling. While 15 to 20 years ago advertising accounted for the lion's share of the marketer's budget, sales promotion has become a top priority. Why has sales promotion emerged as such a dominant force in the marketing communications system? Here are some reasons:

1. It fulfilled management's need for quick short-term results. While advertising takes time to build and show results, which were often unclear in any case, the return on sales promotion could be quickly seen. Sales promotion is viewed as a "short-term incentive to purchase."

2. It helped alleviate the pressure on the sales force. With management expecting quick returns, the pressure was on the sales force to deliver. It naturally requested and received assistance in terms of more trade incentives that tended to manipulate the product price. These included off-invoice allowances, volume, stocking and display allowances, trade coupons, and rebates.

3. It helped lure financially-strapped consumers. In tough economic times such as the most recent recession, consumers reluctant to part with hard-to-come-by income were lured into purchasing by various promotion techniques, such as coupons.

Sales promotion directed at distributors often features price cuts that can legitimately be considered part of marketing's pricing policy or distribution efforts. Others, such as user case histories, product catalog and trade show exhibits, are normally thought of as part of the selling function. Promotions aimed at the ultimate buyers are a mixture of price cuts (sampling, two-for-one, and cents off) and modifications in the product (cereal plus a premium).

A major function of sales promotion is to develop buyer awareness and influence attitudes through trial use. This explains why sales promotions are frequently used with the introduction of new products. Trial use helps to promote the advantages of the product to the customer. Some products have to be used, felt, seen, tasted, and smelled before their real value becomes apparent. Advertising alone cannot accomplish this goal.

In addition, sales promotions serve as attention-getting devices and increase readership of advertisements. It has been shown that ads featuring coupons, contests, or premiums get higher readership.

Finally, sales promotions provide marketing with one means of differentiating its product from the competition's. For instance, unique premiums or contests set the company's product apart from the competition's in the eyes of the consumer.

Sales promotions offer marketers a variety of benefits: they enhance the effectiveness of the major media; they are controllable in that they can be started and stopped easily; they are demographically and geographically selective; they offer a predictable controlled cost and their benefits can be easily measured.

Finally, it is important that you understand that success does not depend solely on how you promote your business, but also on the promotional message. For example, advertising children's cereal on TV Saturday morning is probably quite effective. However, the same advertisement would most likely be a complete waste of money if run during Monday Night Football.

Your Plan

Your overall marketing strategy is a combination of the elements you have just studied:

- [ ] Your PRODUCT
- [ ] Your PRICE
- [ ] Your PROMOTION

Your product, whether it be goods or services, is the basic reason you are in business. Your product must be oriented to the audience, or market segment, you expect to attract. To that end, your product must be the items or services which that audience demands, and be offered at a competitive price which that audience can be expected to pay. And, to get your message across to that audience, you must promote your product in terms that relate to that audience.

The three elements are closely interrelated, and a change in any one of them necessitates a review of how you are handling the other two. No one of the three can be considered independently. Your total marketing strategy is a careful balance of all three.

Most Critical Element

Of all the elements required to make a business successful, none is more critical than marketing. The greatest product and service ideas are of little value unless their story is told in the marketplace.

Your marketing effort is the foundation of all other aspects of your business. Marketing attracts the sales dollars that cover the costs of doing business while providing the profit upon which to build the future of your business.

Consumer Orientation

Successful marketing strategies are based upon knowledge of customer needs and wants. Your product or service line should be determined by the purchasing interests of your market. After all, it is easier to sell what people want to buy.

Establishment of the best price to charge for your product hinges upon the determination of customer reaction to various possible prices. There is no one and only price to seek for most products or services. Instead, there is a range of possible prices. As the price becomes higher, you can expect sales to decline. Therefore, you must try to select that price that offers the most profitable combination of sales volume and unit contribution.

Similarly, your choice of a marketing message should stress the benefits that your product or service offers customers. And your choice of marketing channels to convey your message must consider which channels provide the most efficient and effective means of reaching your intended audience.

Application to Your Business

The principles of marketing presented here, applied to your business, can guide you in the development of a customer-oriented marketing strategy that can dramatically improve your business's chances of continuing success.

Setting the Advertising Budget

Logical and systematic processes for setting the advertising budget include:

1. **Past or predicted sales approach.** Advertising dollars are calculated as a percentage of sales.

2. **Market share approach.** Advertising budget is based on achieving a certain market share objective. Caution must be exercised here because there is no positive correlation between profit-related figures and market share.

3. **Competitive parity approach.** This method encourages matching the competition's advertising budget either dollar for dollar or by some ratio, say, 90 percent.

4. **Objective task approach.** In this approach specific advertising objectives are defined and then the tasks and associated costs required to accomplish the objectives are determined.

5. **Affordability method.** Some managers first earmark money for bills and then use what is left for advertising. They view advertising as a luxury, as if it had little relationship to sales. This situation can become a "Catch 22." Without the proper level of effective advertising, their vitality decreases and they can "afford" less and less.

The age of accountability is also influencing the budgeting process for advertising. Management is trying to review past events, including sales, and analyze what impact the advertising strategy had on these trends. There is an outcry for more advertising and media research to measure the effectiveness of specific advertising campaigns. Various sales incentives have been poured into ads that not only help in closing a sale but also provide feedback on the advertisement. For example, coupons and contests placed in ads have given valuable data for deciding future budgets.

In summary, in formulating a budget, marketers should consider these salient variables: past advertising-sales patterns, the competition's advertising (both amount and quality), the company objectives for marketing and advertising, economic forces, the research methods for judging advertising successes or failures, and the other steps in the media plan. These other steps are interrelated and will affect the budget, tasks, and strategies that are formulated. For instance, a certain advertising message or type of media will influence how many dollars might be spent for advertising. If management wanted to increase the number of television commercials while maintaining advertising levels for other media, a significant increase in ad dollars would be needed.

Advertising budgeting is a complicated process, and several staff meetings and discussions with in-house executives and the advertising agency may be needed before a budget is arrived at that is right for the company.

A good media plan should be prepared well ahead of the time required to place specific campaign messages. The media plan might be considered the core of the advertising campaign. It provides a disciplined approach for strategy formulation. A good media plan helps to prevent the common mistakes made in developing advertising strategy.

A good media plan should contain clear statements of advertising objectives, such as:

1. **Reach.** The number of individuals, groups, households, or organizations that are exposed to either an ad or a group of advertisements, as in an advertising campaign.

2. **Frequency or intensity.** The number of times the advertising message is to be given within a certain period.

3. **Target audience.** Where the media plan should be targeted and the amount of geographic coverage desired. Is local, regional, or national coverage preferred?

4. **Continuity and scheduling.** Whether to have constant advertising exposure or to give greater weight to a particular season or the end of the budgeted year (the seasonal nature of the business will partly determine the pattern of scheduling).

5. **Creative preferences and copy requirements.** A preference for certain colors; visual, sound, or message effects; product demonstrations; or complex messages limits the type of media that can be used.

Defining these five objectives helps to formulate where the advertising should carry the company. Actual media selection determines how these objectives are to be achieved.

The key rules are that objectives should be specific, clear, and free of general cliches or platitudes. It is meaningless for marketers to say, for instance, that the advertising will increase sales (really a marketing objective) by changing consumer habits (a general and difficult task). Also, the objectives should be stated in a communicative context, with use of such communication terms as "goodwill," "awareness," "knowledge," "preference," "attitude," "recall," "conviction," and "liking." Most sophisticated marketers try to measure the current situation (pretest) and then, through the advertising campaign, to improve the levels of awareness, preference, attitudes, social concern, and the like.

The function of marketing research and testing of advertisements serves as a control to see how well desired advertising objectives are being met. Lastly, advertising objectives serve as a starting point for selecting media and deciding which ones to emphasize in the media plan. Without these objectives, the marketer may wander aimlessly and end up using media with little logic, poor continuity, or a lack of marketing mission or purpose.

10

Managing and Developing the Sales Activities

As noted earlier, it is marketing's responsibility to develop the plan of actions (strategies) that will accomplish the goals that higher management has set for the company. Once the marketing plan has been developed and agreed upon, it is the responsibility of sales management to develop and carry out the tactics (the skillful methods to gain an end) and train a sales force in these tactics that will be used to implement the marketing plan in contact with the customer(s).

Managing the Sales Force

The sales manager has total responsibility for designing and administering the sales force. (This statement and following principles apply also to the service and support managers' roles.) Thus he or she, aided by support staff and working with the marketing group, will be required to follow five steps:

1. Recruit, select, and train sales representatives
2. Design and apportion the sales territory, based on such factors as number and size of existing and potential customers, time required per sales call, frequency of calls by type of customer, experience of sales representatives (reps) and regional managers, the degree to which the territory has been developed, and the strength of the competition
3. Determine sales force compensation
4. Supervise sales reps and regional managers
5. Evaluate and control sales performance

A sales manager does not work in a vacuum. A good deal of the sales manager's success or failure will depend on how well he or she works with other personnel both inside and outside of marketing, including the relationship with marketing management, marketing research, advertising, and individual product managers. For example, the sales manager must rely on marketing management to communicate all details of the finalized marketing plan, specific objectives and strategies, and should be required by marketing to participate in and contribute to the creation of that plan. If this participation does not occur, sales management will not feel an "ownership" interest in the plan and sales reps may concentrate on promoting the wrong elements of the marketing mix. They may choose to focus on price when the company's objective is to establish the company's reputation for quality and service.

The sales manager has a two-way relationship with the marketing research manager. Although the nature of their jobs may lead to infrequent meetings, the sales manager must provide research with feedback on the competition and on how individual segments of the market view current products. The marketing research manager should incorporate this data with other market intelligence, analyze the total, and inform the sales manager who the best sales prospects might be, in terms of geographic and demographic segments.

The sales manager also will want to coordinate the sales unit's efforts with advertising and sales promotion to ensure that they do not work at cross purposes. The sales manager, with marketing management, must also work with and understand:

- □ Finance—credit, sales contribution to profits, and pricing
- □ Personnel—recruitment, training, and compensation measures
- □ Production—to assure adequate supplies of the product, delivery schedules, and quality control
- □ Research and development—to provide feedback from customers on what they expect in terms of performance of existing and new products

Note: The research and development relationship can be very sensitive because salespeople are known to "sell futures." That is, if they are told prematurely of a coming product that will meet the prospect's needs, they will tend to sell that product since it is the easier product to sell. This action can have very harmful consequences to the complete marketing and sales tactic as well as to customer relations.

It is the responsibility of the sales force to convince the prospect that the product represented is the best product to satisfy the prospect's needs, and that no other product on the market will satisfy those needs as well for the price. In this manner the sales force produces sales and contributes to the financial success of the company—meeting the company sales goals and providing that all-important cash flow.

Marketers must sympathize with the common career-related complaints and concerns of sales personnel. As in other professions, salespeople experience periodic problems and job dissatisfaction. In dealing with a sales force, the marketer should think about the particular challenges of selling. Although all the following traits may not be typical of one organization, they illustrate the breadth of concerns in this area.

Salespersons' Requirements

The selling process requires sales personnel to deal with management functions while still being effective in the sales presentation. To succeed, they must know how to plan, organize, coordinate, control, and follow through. This requires daily, weekly, monthly, and even yearly tactical decisions. They must make many choices in budgeting, managing time, interdepartmental networking, and so on. Decisions must sometimes be spontaneous. No matter how well they plan, uncontrollable circumstances abruptly surface, usually from the home office or customers.

In addition, salespeople must work with and through other people. They must interact with their peers and other departments in the company. Supportive backup help and committee selling are often mandatory. A cooperative intracompany network system is vital to the accomplishment of these interactions.

The sales force, working with their customers, has to go through many people in the customer organization before finding the decision makers. This can be tedious.

Listing the steps in a sales presentation is easy. But the continuous successful application of these steps by sales personnel is difficult. Salespeople must orchestrate the various steps to each selling situation by meeting the specific needs, problems, and benefits of the prospect. Selling demands an uncanny knack of being able to flow with the situation while still meeting certain selling objectives. Most salespeople cannot control their environment. Instead they must learn to adapt to interruptions, various personalities, different physical surroundings, uneven group dynamics, changing policies, and the like. They must therefore modify and customize their sales presentation to fit the environment.

Salespeople must identify and address the prospect's unmet needs and problems. They must therefore be good listeners and highly sensitive to both obvious and subtle clues. They must sometimes exercise interpersonal and technical product skills. This requires, usually, extensive training in both sales processes and product knowledge.

A sales force may need a continuous diet of training and updating to stay abreast of the latest product innovations and specifications. Salespeople also may need schooling on particular complex topics relevant to the industry it serves. Some sales personnel get "burned out" because of the steady schooling requirements. They may feel they are on a treadmill with no end in sight.

The physical requirements of some selling careers can be stringent. Certain sales jobs require constant travel, lifting of supplies and equipment, and much standing, walking, waiting, and driving. Many sales people are away from the office for relatively long periods of time, and some see this as a strong advantage. Still, the exhaustion and isolation of traveling can cause problems with job expectations, moral support, and career growth. Salespeople may feel left out of office politics. Lack of communication or few home office visits may create self-doubt. They may believe that the periodic sales meetings and conferences are too infrequent.

It should be noted that many companies rely on their personal sales staff more than on any other marketing group. The marketing budget is often geared toward this group. Therefore, top executives may have high expectations or tight controls over the performance level of the sales force. They may desire specific numbers and accountability for achieving certain sales revenues. The sales staff will therefore have to balance the revenue side with the costs side of doing business. Sometimes the two can be contradictory. Furthermore, salespeople must deal with other intracompany peers who are evaluated with different criteria. Sometimes short-run conflict surfaces over buyers' needs and an intracompany departmental objective; for example, liberal credit terms desired by a buyer versus the seller's finance department's tight credit restrictions for improving cash flow. This short-run conflict creates additional in-house pressures on the sales force.

Following is a list of prime causes for career dissatisfaction among salespeople:

1. Inadequate or complete lack of information from the home office or management
2. A laissez-faire approach that keeps salespeople in the dark on their career development
3. Little opportunity to grow professionally
4. Little responsibility and control over job content
5. Few opportunities to offer suggestions or make recommendations about improving marketing strategy, especially within their territory
6. Lack of respect for personal selling within the organization

Type Categories of Sales Personnel

The interests and abilities required from the sales staff should coincide with the requirements of the sale. Different types of sales positions and selling tasks are interrelated and interdependent. Sales positions include industrial, retail, door-to-door, wholesale, missionary, telephone, manufacturer representative/ agent, and national account manager. Some of these positions call for order takers, while others need order getters.

An order taker mainly processes orders and helps complete the sale. This person might arrange the displays, stock items, fill out forms, respond to correspondence or phone calls, and answer simple questions. Order takers may even merely serve to carry out sales that were already closed by order getters.

Order getters use professional selling approaches as described earlier. They must be creative and analytical, carefully identifying customer problems, needs, and concerns. They assume an advisory approach in their relationship with prospects. The tasks of generating viable customer leads, making in-depth presentations, and closing the sale with proper postsale servicing are vital responsibilities. Instead of dealing with routine tasks, order getters must constantly make creative pitches to ever-changing markets. As a corollary, they often have to pursue additional training, possess a technical skill or certain aptitude, and/or work with all levels of executives. With the current complexities and challenges of the marketplace, more and more selling situations seem to require the order-getting approach.

Tactics Enhancement

To enhance its sales tactics, a company must identify the type of selling tasks and approaches that seem most appropriate for it. This clarification has extensive implications for decisions on staffing, training, compensation, motivation, and type and degree of support to give the sales force. The complexities of these decisions are magnified if the salespeople are to be pure order getters. More time and investment are required to sustain this group successfully. They need the mental and physical tools to grow and prosper. They may also require all types of backup support to ensure powerful, creative, and fruitful sales.

The company must avoid the common mistake of putting order takers into a selling environment that really requires order getters. For example, an electrical distributor decided to penetrate the industrial market by using retail/wholesale salesclerks who were mere order takers. These salespeople had problems dealing with purchasing executives who sought sophisticated answers for potentially large transactions. The experiment did not succeed because the owner was afraid to invest in the development of a new type of creative sales personnel. He was also reluctant to train the current staff or give them field support. His industrial market is still nonexistent.

The degree of corporate emphasis and budgeting bias for personal selling should depend on specific variables. These variables will dictate the relative thrust and type of personal selling tactics to be employed. Interestingly, in few firms management has a bias toward a certain type of personal selling, such as door-to-door selling. It is preferred because the situation requires strong involvement by the sales force.

The sale of complex, customized, and expensive products often requires the personal touch of a salesperson who explains the products and closes the sale.

The type of goods sold sometimes dictates how much emphasis should be put on personal selling tactics. In intermediate markets, creative selling is critical for fixed assets, including raw or fabricated materials, installations, capital goods, and accessory equipment. Buyers for these goods want to negotiate and explore issues on capital budgeting, product applications, servicing, and trade-in variations. In the consumer sector, specialty or shopping goods will frequently need sound sales tactics to prompt consumer actions. With some intermediate products, many technical questions on product performance, pricing, and servicing must be answered on a personal basis. Usually, the sales personnel are the ones who then complete the deal. Without them, these types of products could not be marketed.

An emphasis on personal selling may be more efficient when the geographic market is highly concentrated. Everything else being equal, the incremental travel-related expenditures are somewhat modest compared with the potential benefits of personal visits with good prospects. Also, sometimes promotional media are unavailable or inefficient, and personal selling is the best option for promotion.

Many marketers have a few key accounts that are critical to their bottom line. VIP treatment is required to keep these large customers satisfied. Personal selling and regular visits may be the absolute minimum. Many marketers have even organized in-house accounts or the national account management (NAM) concept. (The NAM structure will be explored later in this section.)

As a rule, a sales force is needed to close the sale of a high-priced item. Buyers are reluctant to say yes until someone personally explains/shows the wisdom of making the purchase.

Short channels of distribution allow easier direct contact with purchasers. Eliminating most middlemen enables the marketer to pinpoint selling opportunities to various prospects while keeping track of the physical movement of goods. Alternatively, a powerful sales force may be needed to push the product through a channel.

Intense and strong competitive forces often motivate selling tactics. Top management focuses its attention on the sales force when competition increases. As one company expands, its sales force increases, and competing marketers usually decide to add to their sales force in turn. It then becomes a tough struggle to maintain just the status quo and counteract the competitor's efforts. In fact, for many small businesses the personal selling approach may be the only way to offset the competition presented by large retail chains.

Last—and maybe most important of all—many purchasers in all types of segments and markets are becoming more sophisticated. In certain economic sectors, consumers have learned to expect personalized explanations and service, and will not tolerate anything less.

When making allocation decisions on the amount to spend on personal selling versus other marketing activities, the company should appreciate the type of products, competition, and customers involved. Most companies use a combination of promotional tactics.

Motivating the Sales Force

Managers must identify potential problem areas where the sales force may need motivation. Listed are some complaints or areas of indifference that create major managerial challenges in motivating the sales force:

- □ Too much paperwork
- □ Excessive goodwill/missionary work
- □ Handling unfounded complaints (any complaint must be addressed, but not necessarily by the sales force)
- □ Gathering data for marketing research
- □ Unnecessary travel
- □ Collecting dead credit accounts
- □ Slow payments on bonus or commission
- □ Many staff meetings
- □ Old/dead products (product life is constantly getting shorter)
- □ Long lead time between sales effort and sales
- □ Weak product mix to sell
- □ High-priced items
- □ Poor territory design
- □ Requirement to always push new products
- □ Cold canvasing new prospects

Some sales management tools for monitoring the sales force include:

- □ Administratively support, then give more selling time
- □ Contests/sweepstakes
- □ Special one-time cash rewards

☐ Prizes such as special status or recognition awards
☐ Management by objectives
☐ Special bonus awards for hard selling situations (new account sales)
☐ Participative product development by sales force (feedback to R&D)
☐ Involvement of sales force in planning meetings/workshops
☐ Clear policies and procedures on credits/collections
☐ Fair compensation structure that rewards harder sales tactics
☐ Reasonable time payment on commission
☐ Careful planning of travel itinerary
☐ Participative role of sales force in planning sales meetings
☐ Analysis of territorial design for fairness
☐ Offer promotional opportunities

Using Compensation to Motivate

Since the sales force requires a great amount of self-motivation, management must find the right inspirational blend of compensation incentives and support. The following questions serve as a handy checklist for planning and designing a motivating pay structure for sales personnel:

☐ Does everyone understand the structure and know what is expected?
☐ Do salespeople have continuous input into fine-tuning of the pay structure?
☐ Does the compensation program tie in with the desired strategic organizational and marketing objectives of top management?
☐ What relationship does actual pay have to the sales quotas?
☐ How well are talented sales personnel rewarded? Is there a good positive correlation between pay and performance?
☐ Is the plan understandable and fair to both management and salespeople?
☐ Does the plan penalize sales personnel for things beyond their control?
☐ How do the pay levels compare with those of the competition? Are they adequate to keep good people, including entry-level people, oldtimers, and high achievers?
☐ What type of supporting efforts are needed, such as automotive, expense accounts, fringe benefits, stock options, professional association dues, club memberships, and travel amenities?
☐ Does the system offer financial security and enough incentive?
☐ Does actual pay coincide with the conclusions of the performance appraisal analysis?
☐ When inflation is prevalent, do salespeople actually earn the extra income or do they merely ride the inflationary coattails?
☐ Does the system offer rewards for doing the harder or less desirable tasks (opening new accounts, missionary work, or selling harder product lines)?
☐ Does the plan adjust to the conditions of the marketplace?
☐ What are the general advantages/disadvantages of the compensation program?

- ☐ Are the incentives realistic enough so the sales force has a fair chance of achieving them?
- ☐ Does the pay plan avoid high pressure or overloading of customers?
- ☐ What type of vested retirement package is included to prevent good, experienced sales personnel from leaving and taking good accounts with them?
- ☐ When was the last time the organization's sales compensation program was carefully studied?

Expense account policy for the sales force must be clear and fair. An expense plan could include:

- ☐ Nonreimbursement for expenses
- ☐ Unlimited coverage for selling-related costs with no maximum amount
- ☐ Flat allowances for certain selling expenses
- ☐ A range of allowable amounts for various categories

Each of these have pros and cons while being applicable to different situations. The company must decide on the one that best fits its organizational structure and can help meet its objectives under the constraints of financial strengths and weaknesses. The expense plan also must tie in well with the company compensation plan while motivating salespeople and giving the company managerial/operating controls.

Consider these minimum guidelines when selecting a policy:

- ☐ The reimbursed amount should reflect actual expenditures incurred.
- ☐ Expenses allowed should reflect the different geographic costs of doing business.
- ☐ Expenses should be reimbursed as soon as possible, if credit accounts are not available.
- ☐ The plan should be consistent and equitable for all sales personnel.
- ☐ The plan should be easily understood and easy to administer.
- ☐ Salespeople should not have to limit their efforts owing to inadequate reimbursement levels.
- ☐ The amounts should coincide with the type of customers and markets being served.
- ☐ The plan should be competitive with industry standards and what the competition is doing.
- ☐ Padding of expenses should be watched for and discouraged.

If company policy is to not reimburse the sales force's expenses (such as for manufacturer representatives), the compensation structure should reflect this. Otherwise the sales force will not be motivated to push the firm's goods or even work for it.

Using Sales Quotas

When using sales quotas, management must make salespeople feel like winners instead of losers. This rule is essential to the productivity and morale of the sales staff. In their book, *In Search of Excellence,* Thomas Peters and Robert Waterman clearly dramatized the importance of this winning perception among salespeople. To paraphrase: Excellent companies design systems that make people feel like winners because targets, quotas, and goals are set (often by people like themselves) to allow this to happen. For instance, IBM ensures that 70 to 80 percent of its salespeople meet yearly quotas, while in a competing company only 40 percent of the sales force meet them. Thus at least 60 percent of the salespeople in the competing company think of themselves as losers.

Sales quotas can indeed be a winning tool. Here are some tips for their successful use:

- ☐ Make sure they are realistic.
- ☐ Make sure they are equitably and objectively determined.
- ☐ Allow for modifications whenever profound changes occur either in a certain territory or within the total industry.
- ☐ Avoid complicated quotas that no one understands.
- ☐ Consider a quarterly or semi-annual review to observe progress.
- ☐ Make sure there is acceptance and agreement between the sales force and management.
- ☐ Utilize systematic research and analysis to help formulate quotas.
- ☐ Ensure that the sales quotas match company and marketing objectives.
- ☐ Give support to help salespeople meet quotas.
- ☐ Tie in the sales quotas to actual results to evaluate and reward the sales force.

Sales Territories Construction

To achieve optimal sales strategies, management must carefully construct sales territories. It is the executive's responsibility to ensure proper territorial design for maximum sales force efficiency. Otherwise, territories may lack adequate sales coverage or have too much. The time spent by salespeople in their territories must be well worth the dollar sales return.

How can the allocation of sales force personnel enhance the territory design and improve company strategies? What factors should be considered when deploying sales personnel? How will the proposed structure help meet bottom line objectives? These questions do not have easy answers. But, a search for answers may improve a company's territory management. The following methods help in finding answers:

1. **Market account analysis.** An attempt must be made to measure the market potential of and previous sales levels in each territory. The special expertise of salespeople and their unique relationships with accounts are considerations, as is the length of cooperative relationships with accounts. An essential factor is that the territory design serve the customer and achieve satisfaction. The company especially wants to give ample time and resources to major customers. A common mistake is to design a territory that is too big for adequate time for follow-up or repeat calls on key accounts, and for new prospect calls or new product pro-

motion. The first consideration of territorial design, just like the other parts of the sales/marketing strategy, is customers and how well they might be served.

2. **Cost factors.** The cost of serving different territories must be studied. Will the distribution and logistical costs of supporting the sales force be justified in terms of profit contributions to the organization? The "Survey of Selling Costs" (published annually in *Sales and Marketing Management* magazine) is a good starting source for attempting to estimate initial costs for new territories or to set control procedures.

3. **Workload.** The size of the territory must be analyzed to explore the amount of work needed to handle the accounts. Travel time, call plans, calling frequencies, and amount of time spent in actual selling should be quantified. Geographic areas must be reasonable so that the sales force can handle its accounts without being on the road constantly or having too few planning or selling opportunities.

4. **Territory potential.** Sales personnel must believe that the size of their territory offers them a decent sales performance level. Realistically, territories are seldom designed so that everyone has equal potential. Too many variables, such as geographic uniqueness and idiosyncrasies, make equality impractical. The best territories are often used as a carrot and given to the best performers or assigned to those who have "paid their dues." The central objective, however, is to ensure that the firm obtains good coverage and full market potential.

5. **Competitive forces.** Often new or tougher competition forces the company to rethink its territories. The competition may be quite aggressive and seek the company's accounts in certain markets. This threat may necessitate plan modifications, creating a need for more support, realignment, or smaller territories. The firm should not go overboard in reacting to the competition, but should alter its tactics for better territorial management. This situation becomes more demanding in no-growth markets, where the company has to fight to hold its same market share. Alternatively, the company has the opportunity to change a territory in order to benefit from weak competition in certain markets.

6. **Product mix.** The products may be complex and heterogeneous. To truly serve customers, individual salespeople may have to specialize in the applications, specifications, and attributes of a single product line. This requirement will result in the sales force crossing over into each other's territories.

7. **Capabilities of salespeople.** Some salespeople may have an uncanny ability and aptitude to take on additional accounts or territories. Sometimes a firm finds advantages through consolidation of territories. Not only does consolidation enhance productivity in these cases, but it may motivate professionals to raise their own career goals.

8. **Selling/administrative time management.** Most salespeople probably spend more time on paperwork, travel, tracking orders, waiting, indirect sales activity, and administrative tasks than on actual selling. And most

sales require several repeat calls (some estimate four to six) before the deal is clinched. Management must see that the sales force devotes as much time as possible to actual selling. Time management becomes an integral aspect of territory planning. Travel time, routing, call reports, warehousing/distribution, and field support systems with adequate numbers of sales branches are elements that should influence both time and territorial decisions.

More companies are using computers or in-house models to compose their territories. Computer programs can provide quantitative answers to the traveling/territorial sales problem. Also, some models have surfaced that manipulate data and prescribe action (some are GEOLINE, CALLPLAN, TOURPLAN, ALLOCATE, and DETAILER).

Note: For more information on these models, refer to James Comer, "The Computer: Personal Selling and Sales Management," *Journal of Marketing* (July 1975), pp. 27–33 and David Hughes, "Computerized Sales Management," *Harvard Business Review* (March–April 1983), pp. 102–112).

Sales Training

An organized and formal sales training program helps to convert both new and established salespeople into a productive force. The following are the necessary steps in preparing a sales training program:

1. Assess training needs.
2. Formulate the educational requirements and behavioral objectives of the training sessions.
3. Decide who should do the training.
4. Select the appropriate facilities and location.
5. Decide what should be covered.
6. Decide on the best pedagogical (teaching methodology) mix.
7. Follow up to judge the impact.

Using Sales Representatives

For wider market coverage and penetration at reasonable costs, possible use of an outside sales force should be explored. Using an outside sales force can provide a variety of benefits:

- ☐ Reduces fixed costs and administrative demands
- ☐ Makes costs more predictable: no sale, no expenses
- ☐ Helps overcome cash flow problems
- ☐ Gives immediate market access and penetration
- ☐ Allows sharing of advertising and promotional costs
- ☐ Provides experienced sales force
- ☐ Lowers cost of training
- ☐ Offers wide variety of markets
- ☐ May increase frequency of calls per customer

□ Offers industry market intelligence

There may also be negative implications to using an outside sales force:

□ Divides loyalty among different principals
□ Agent carries many items
□ Agent may sell competing goods
□ Agent could be mere order taker
□ Harder to train, monitor, motivate, and control agents
□ Agent may lack in-depth product knowledge
□ Customer may not be sure if deal should be made with reps or principals
□ Potential communication problem

National Account Management (NAM)

The national account management structure is a consideration if key customers require extra care and service. All marketers have their criteria for grouping customers as national accounts. The most common requirements, however, are the following:

□ Orders exceed some minimum sales volume (most popular criterion).
□ Purchasing operation is centralized.
□ Many departments and levels of management are involved in making purchasing decisions.
□ Individual transactions are substantial.

A company that wants to start this organizational structure or improve its current NAM program should recognize and apply these essential tactics:

1. Develop a good policy and procedures manual for planning and implementing the NAM program.
2. Carefully decide on the criteria that make customers eligible for this special relationship.
3. Create comprehensive job descriptions and qualifications to help in recruiting, selecting, and training national account managers.
4. Make sure other professional personnel respect these managers and give their support.
5. Use the NAM position as a favorable career move with good opportunities for growth and financial rewards.
6. Let the customer know its business is so valued that a special high-level person has been assigned to the account and a long-term happy relationship will be a major objective.
7. Decide who should have authority over national account managers.
8. Provide continuous training and support to national account managers, including teaching essential skills in negotiating, selling, product/technological applications, relationship building, and the like.
9. Make sure that top executives are committed to and supportive of the NAM structure (the best way is to monitor the cost/benefits to illustrate results).

Tracking Sales Tactics

Periodic audits of personal selling tactics are beneficial. A sales audit helps in making decisions about some of the issues, such as territory design. Selling tactics are a good place to start trying to enhance marketing strategies. Unlike audits in other marketing areas, sales audits yield contributions that are quickly realized and often tangible to top management.

The audit is begun by examining certain information sources. The most productive sources include sales reports, call reports, sales invoices, internal market research reports, expense reports, routing schedules, account analysis forms, and time logs. This examination should provide answers to these types of questions that could positively influence the sales tactics:

☐ What is the relationship between incremental selling expenses and increased revenues?
☐ Who are the most productive salespeople?
☐ How much time is actually spent on selling?
☐ Which geographic areas need to be better served?
☐ Is there a better way to organize the sales force?
☐ How many calls are required on the average to make a sale?
☐ Would a prescribed routing pattern help secure better coverage?
☐ What are the positive and negative trends in relation to profits? Sales? Expenses? Sales penetration?

Sales Promotion Targeting

Sales and marketing management should always aim to encourage better results through sales promotion techniques. Through the years, sales promotion has been an afterthought to the planning and development of marketing strategy. It often consists of a concoction of techniques aimed at increasing sales. Some are successful; others are dismal failures.

Today a spontaneous, random approach is not suitable in this exceptionally competitive milieu. Firms that succeed are those that create professional and sophisticated promotion techniques. Considering that sales promotion for U.S. companies grows about 12 percent a year in expenditures and is currently over a $50 billion undertaking, executives cannot afford a capricious approach to this tactic.

Sales promotion can be described as nonpersonal presentations that supplement and complement personal selling and advertising. By its nature, it is nonrecurring and used only for a limited time. Management often expects the promotion to induce immediate action in the form of consumer sales or encouragement of channel members to respond to this extra sales push. However, management must realize that to accomplish immediate consumer response, the promotion must be specifically designed for that purpose.

The most common types of sales promotion include contests or sweepstakes; coupons; samples; rebates; bonus packs; deals (merchandise, service, price); stamps; in-packs, on-packs, and near-packs; trade coupons; trade allowances; premiums (gifts or surprises with purchased product); games; fixtures; trade shows or fairs; and refund offers. Marketers have learned that many of these techniques can be combined or altered to give a host of strategic alternatives. The key is deciding the best combinations for achieving the organization's objectives (whether those objectives are direct sales, name recognition of company or product, etc.) while appealing to members of the targeted marketplace.

Listed are types of sales promotions and circumstances in which they are effective:

1. Many consumers who have never tried certain products might be motivated to do so by sales promotion tactics. For example, a free sample, a bonus pack, or a money-off incentive induces prospects to test the product at little financial risk. Such techniques may be even more effective than advertising or personal selling promises. These sometimes appear to the consumer as empty and glib puffery. Getting consumers to try products, especially new products, is one of the biggest strategic applications of sales promotion.

2. A promotion that includes such tools as coupons, rebates, stamps, contests, and refund offers is well remembered by the marketplace. These added incentives create extra interest and excitement among the promotional audience. Consumer awareness and recall level for advertising is enhanced when various sales promotion techniques are incorporated in the message. These may serve to distinguish the ad from all the other competing advertisements.

3. A carefully designed program can sometimes counteract an adverse economy. Coupons, rebates, bonus packs, refund offers, and trade allowances furnish strong monetary incentives to consumers during a recession. In good economic times, premiums, contests, trading stamps, fashion shows, and fairs are popular. Consumers are in a more lighthearted mood and are attracted to the excitement generated by these promotional techniques.

4. Vigorous trade incentives are sometimes needed to motivate middlemen to do extra work on existing or new products or to stick to practices that are ingrained within the industry. (Special price allowances, display allowances, extra samples, and attractive fixtures are examples of trade sales promotion techniques.) In the drug industry, for example, doctors are given free drug samples, and druggists are provided one free case when they order a certain minimum quantity. Ideally, to really motivate middlemen, a sales promotion program should be periodic rather than continuous. Otherwise the motivation incentive is lost. In some industries that is easier said than done.

5. Periodically a sales promotion method is adopted by one company because the competition has done something similar. The company may find that sales or market share is decreasing due to a new competitive sales promotion program. It then starts a similar or better program to combat the differential advantage. Since sales promotion is a short-run tool, competitive retaliation is common. Such retaliation is likely if perishable goods, high market share, excessive capacity, or large fixed costs

are at stake. Trading stamps, rebates, games, and contests are prime techniques in searching for an advantage over rivals.

6. Greater flexibility in pricing strategy may be feasible with sales promotion tools that emphasize money-off benefits. Once a price itself is lowered, consumers are reluctant to accept a price increase when a change must be made. Price-cutting promotionals, however, are usually perceived by consumers as a short-term opportunity. They understand that the lower price is only for a limited time. Consumers have learned that they must either take immediate advantage of the price break or pay the normal price later. Price-off allowances, especially rebates, give marketers greater control over pricing. Also, if the government ever springs another wage/price freeze, the marketers will not be locked into the lower price.

7. Certain sales promotion devices, such as coupons, can be used to measure advertising or personal selling effectiveness. Through formal control procedures, the company observes the rate of response to some type of advertising or personal selling stimulus. Coded coupons have been extremely popular to evaluate advertising media decisions.

Sales Promotion Trends

Managers must understand trends now prevalent in sales promotion. Knowing these trends may encourage managers, from company management to local sales management, to think philosophically about how they might get more mileage out of their sales promotion tactics:

1. Management's attitude toward sales promotion has become more positive; sales promotion is now considered more than a weak stepchild to advertising.

2. Support for sales promotion is receiving increased emphasis in modern marketing/sales strategy.

3. To overcome clutter and "me-tooism," more firms are using a combination of methods within the same sales promotional effort. For example, a sweepstake may be added to a coupon offer to improve the redemption rate.

4. Middlemen in the channel have become more sophisticated and are demanding better sales promotion offers.

5. Advanced technology and electronic equipment have given rise to better monitoring systems for evaluating the impact of specific sales promotion techniques.

6. Top management desires systematic procedures for quantifying the actual return on a sales promotion effort; closer examination of incremental revenue versus incremental sales promotion cost is expected.

7. More specialists and organizations have surfaced to provide help and advice for performing the sales promotion function. Many advertising

agencies have organized special departments to provide a host of services in sales promotion.

8. The creativity and variety of merchandise and premiums have expanded to cultivate the interests and fancy of dealers and consumers.

9. The attitude of sales personnel toward sales promotion programs has become more positive. They perceive sales promotion as a competitive weapon for securing a more favorable customer or dealer reaction to their sales presentation.

Major Problems of Sales Promotions

When designing a sales promotion strategy, sales and marketing managers should be particularly sensitive to common problems. Major problems encountered with sales promotions are as follows:

1. Underestimation of consumer response rates, especially with money-off promotions, and thus exceeding budget expectations.

2. Fraud, misredemption, and questions on the purchase or use of the products and their accompanying sales promotion incentives.

3. Methods of distribution of the sales promotion package to consumers, middlemen, or other interested parties (electronic distribution may soon become as popular as newspapers, magazines, and direct mail for placing the offering in the hands of consumers).

4. Too low a face-value money-off incentive, which generates few incremental trials or a low redemption rate.

5. Apathy to or negative attitudes about the sales promotion idea from intraorganization marketing personnel or middlemen.

6. Retaliation by competition, which induces an expensive sales promotion war in the marketplace.

7. Creation of evolutionary conditioning, so that the trade and consumers expect and demand sales promotion incentives.

8. Administrative work connected with proof of purchase.

9. Postsales promotion rebound, in which the trade and consumers must work down their inventory (are future sales sacrificed at additional sales promotion costs?).

10. Cheapening of the image of the product or service it is associated with if sales-promotion or price-reduction techniques are overused.

11. Special sales promotion incentives that detract from the promotion efforts of advertising and personal selling.

With so many potential problems, a good sales promotion program takes time and systematic planning. A last-hour defensive program in reaction to a competitor's action can be costly.

An ongoing, thorough audit and research process for sales promotion is a prerequisite to creating meaningful sales promotion strategies. Sales promotion strategies must be carefully interwoven with the other parts of the total marketing strategy. Sales promotion objectives are usually defined as specific and measurable goals such as the following:

1. Between September and the end of December, increase trial use of our new cosmetic product line by the Northeast teenage market by 20 percent.

2. Reduce distributor inventory stock of electronic motors by 10 percent within the next fiscal year.

3. Increase market penetration (dealer inventory building) by 5 percent with new appliance retailers within the next six months.

4. Motivate independent manufacturer representatives to increase sales by 7 percent in their territories.

5. With the next direct mailing advertising, increase the number of consumer inquiries by 25 percent.

6. Increase the repurchase rate of 5 percent for our national senior citizen market.

7. Maintain current market share of 40 percent for our leading brand by matching all competitive sales promotion allowances.

8. During the Christmas season, build retail traffic by 10 percent with special events.

A sales promotion program must be pretested to see how well it will be received by the trade or consumers. A poorly designed program can be costly and can also alienate the trade or consumers. A random survey or experiment could be undertaken to predict the impact of a proposed concept, especially if the concept is a national program or a major expenditure. One warning, however: Pretesting must be done quickly but objectively, lest the competition find out and enter the marketplace first with a similar program.

The sales promotion program must gain the support of the various parties who are either involved with it or influenced by it.

Logistics, Timing, Duration, and Responsibility

The logistics, timing, and duration of the sales promotion program must be coordinated. One person should have authority and responsibility over the sales promotion function.

Frequently these variables are judged secondary. A beautiful idea fails because a firm may have been either too early or too late with the project. Adequate lead time is needed to produce and distribute the materials necessary for the program. Also, transportation and warehousing bottlenecks create problems in getting the right sales promotion materials to the best locations. At times, physical distribution personnel and field salespeople must provide major supportive efforts in getting the sales promotion program started successfully. Their reactions are most beneficial in scheduling the time parameters of the promotion program.

Finally, timing and the length of various sales promotion programs should be evaluated. The optimal times for running different programs within the sales promotion strategy must be determined. It may be a grave mistake, for example, to run two different programs back to back. The second program could have negligible results if consumers or dealers still have a large inventory of the product. The duration of various programs should be timed to take advantage of, or compensate for, the company's media plan. The two could complement each other, or a certain program could be run during slack advertising periods.

Personal selling activities may also influence the timing and duration of different sales promotion programs. For example, a concept may be initiated that will increase customer inquiries, which would then give the sales force a solid prospect list. This tactic could be planned for a slow sales period. Sales personnel may appreciate having this list rather than having to canvas cold in the field.

In summary, given the basic types of sales promotion techniques, there are over 823 million sales promotion combinations and variations that can be offered in the marketplace. A company thus has ample opportunities to be creative and aggressive in formulating its unique strategy. Still, despite the strategy or strategies used, the plan for their use must be a joint effort between the marketing and sales groups. Without that cooperation, the sales group will feel little or no obligation to follow or support such strategies. The realized results will be far from full potential.

Planning

If you don't know where you're going, you will end up somewhere else. Think about that—it makes real sense!

Suppose you live in Boston and decide to drive to San Francisco. Would you use a map? Of course! What would happen if you didn't? It would be a very long, hard trip. And if you didn't know your geography, you probably would not make it to California, never mind San Francisco.

Starting or running a business without proper planning is like driving from Boston to San Francisco without a map. Planning will show you your destination and the best road to get there. Good planning also will prepare you for plan changes (detours) en route.

Planning Can Be Difficult

The key to profitable organizational growth is the planning function. Yet, it is common for business managers at all levels to confuse the different types of planning. The lack of clarity is not inconsequential. Rather, it can cause executives from all the different company departments to formulate the wrong conclusions on how they should go about contributing to the planning process.

Although planning is critical to your success, it is often overlooked in favor of intuition or "gut feeling," especially in the marketing management environment. There are other obstacles that hinder planning:

- ☐ Lack of know-how: It is sometimes difficult to know how to plan and what to plan for
- ☐ Fear of the unknown: It is hard enough dealing with the problems of today without worrying about what's going to happen in the future
- ☐ Inexactness: The best set plans have a funny way of not working out exactly the way they are supposed to.

These obstacles are very real. Still, they must be overcome if you are to be successful. While we may find it difficult to face the future, heading into it without direction is much worse.

Corporate Planning System

Planning provides a means to an end. Many challenges and problems can occur during the planning process. Management should prepare for problems during the planning process. The following are typical problem areas:

1. **Unavailability of complete and perfect information.** Decisions must be made on the best information obtainable, especially if you are operating with time and cost constraints.

2. **Impossibility of predicting future events.** Errors will often occur in forecasting sales, market growth opportunities, expenditures, and so on.

3. **Lack of commitment by top or middle level executives.** The perception of merely going through the motions may make plans useless or superficial.

4. **Need to balance time, costs, and personnel priorities.** Daily tasks and expenses must be met while planning is also being done.

5. **Need to coordinate creativity with realism.** Good planning should not discourage creativity and sound risk taking. Unrealistic objectives, goals, and expectations are catastrophic to morale. Such actions can make the planning process become a feared and dreaded undertaking. Managers should realize that planning does not prevent all mistakes, and the plan should not be perceived as threatening.

6. **Conflict between strategic and operational decisions.** Marketing people are expected to make decisions for short-term opportunities while still contributing to the long-term strategic plan. Given limited allocated resources, the two may not always coincide, and juggling the demands of both may become a tedious task. Overemphasis on either strategic or operating decisions can adversely influence the organization.

The two main types of planning are strategic and marketing. Strategic planning is the complete corporate system for planning growth. It is composed of individual (strategic) plans for each of the company's major departments or units, such as finance, manufacturing, marketing, sales, service, and personnel. Marketing planning centers on the annual or longer-term plan compiled by that department and related functions, such as advertising distribution and new product development. It is also a subset of the complete strategic plan. A 1980 study by the Marketing Science Institute (Cambridge, Mass.), entitled "Top Management Views Of The Marketing Function," found that because marketing is regarded as the critical strategic function in most of the surveyed companies, many respondents said that it is impossible to make a clear distinction between marketing strategy and total corporate strategy.

The overriding importance attached to marketing planning in the total corporate planning system is exemplified by these comments reported in the study:

> We have taken a very aggressive growth position in our industry. Marketing is the key in the planning system. The un-

dergirding of our resolve to move aggressively was a marketing judgment. Marketing is the key input. . . .

Marketing is change. Good marketing strategy brings out good technology, good manufacturing facilities, and so on. We have found that good marketing is the glue that holds things together. Marketing is the key to the whole business. . . .

When I talk about marketing planning, I am talking about the very fundamentals of business and strategic planning, the basic selection of markets and products which is the fundamental strategic choice which the firm has to make. . . .

To me 80 percent of corporate strategy is marketing strategy and that is the guts of any business plan—how you win or lose in the marketplace based on your marketing decisions. . . .

Strategic Planning: A Major Managerial Responsibility

Because there is so much confusion on the subject, it may be helpful to state first what strategic planning is not. It is not the application of a scientific method. It is more than forecasting, which is basically projecting the past into the future. It is not making decisions in the future; the only time you can make a decision is in the present. Strategic planning is not an elimination of risk.

Then what is strategic planning? It is a commitment by management to look into the futurities of markets to decide which products or services should be aggressively promoted, which ones maintained, and which ones abandoned; to decide which businesses should be acquired and which sold; and to establish priorities in the direction of new product development.

When looking ahead five to ten years, management has to ask many questions and then estimate the probability of each answer becoming a reality. What technological advances are envisioned? What amount of federal and state government regulations will be in force? What direction will competition take? What business (or businesses) is the corporation in now? What business (or businesses) should the corporation be in five years from now? Ten years? If the corporation were to distribute 100 units of new money, how should it be allocated over the next three, five, and ten years? What should be the optimum location, size, and type of production facilities for the corporation in five years? Ten years?

An outcome of this strategic planning process is the development of a companywide statement of mission or purpose. Surprisingly, many managers responsible for planning would be hard put to answer the "What business is my company in?" question accurately. Not so surprisingly, the plans they create are either rejected, revised, or filed indefinitely. Often, fault for not making clear a firm's business rests with top management, not individual departmental managers.

The way to head off this type of problem and start the planning process off smoothly is for management to issue a "statement of mission." This document about the company's identity defines what the company does and why it exists. It gives the company planners a direction. The mission can be portrayed in terms of one or several marketing-related factors, such as products manufactured, services rendered, and customers serviced within a geographic area. It can be as simple as "XYZ company supplies automotive parts to retail outlets in the Northeast." In addition, the mission statement can be valuable in showing how the company intends to change directions. For example, a magazine publishing company recently cited its mission as "to expand the scope of our business by developing the capability to transmit information electronically."

There are four key elements of the strategic planning process:

1. Identification of the business
2. Situation analysis
3. Selection of strategies
4. Establishment of controls

A strategic plan should include major components pertinent to both the environment and the resources of the firm. Any good strategic plan should consist of these minimum basics:

1. **Corporate mission.** What business are we in? What business should we be in?

2. **Competitive threats and opportunities.** What are the current and future long-term strengths and weaknesses of the competition? Who might be our future competition? What can be done to improve our future competitive position?

3. **Environmental conditions.** How will changing economic, political, technological, cultural, and social conditions affect the business? Will the future climate be positive or negative for our business?

4. **Company resources and cultural climate.** What are the strengths and weaknesses of the organization? Does the company have the resources and commitment to meet future challenges and opportunities?

5. **Long-term company objectives and strategies.** After recognizing our resources and limitations, how can our strengths be matched with future business opportunities? What should be our long-term objectives? What type of strategies would be most effective?

Decision areas to be considered include acquisitions, mergers, divestments, overseas expansion, and vertical or horizontal integration.

The usefulness of the strategic plan depends on the information provided by marketing. Strategic planning is a demanding task that requires pertinent information to maximize opportunities and minimize risks. Marketers are in an excellent position to keep top managers abreast of competition, emerging industries, and new technology.

The limitations of strategic planning must be understood. A strategic plan is not a guarantee of future success. Mistakes can still be made, and tough decisions will be needed to overcome them, especially decisions to write off millions of dollars.

In developing the strategic plan, upper management must look closely at the future. For instance, it is predicted that during the decade of the 1990s, 25 percent of today's work force will be working out of their homes. That, at least, is the estimate of people involved in communications. The reasons? One is the cost of energy, another is advanced technology. How can it happen? They say there will be no need for these employees to go to their companies' offices because all their communication needs will be serviced by electronic mail, word processors, and other forms of computer magic. They will be able to talk to their contemporaries face to face just by punching a button on the communications console (personal computer) in their homes. Instantaneously, the person they ask for will appear on a screen similar to today's television set.

In 1980 the number of robots sold was equal to 50 percent of all robot sales during all past years. Some robot manufacturers were sold out by March. General Electric was using ten industrial robots in 1978. By 1979 it had 26, and 26 more were "hired" for 1980. By the end of 1989, General Electric expected to have a robot force numbering over 1,000.

A new generation of robots that "see," "feel," and even "think" is emerging from the laboratories. Some automation experts say that these smart robots could replace 65–70 percent of today's work force. Today, robots can pick out selected parts that come down a conveyor belt at random. They can even determine which items are defective. If the number of defectives increases above a preset amount, they can signal another robot that is in charge of manufacturing and tell it its quality control is lousy.

Another wonder from the electronic world is voice mail. You can call a person who is not in and dictate your message into the phone. When the person you called returns, he or she just pushes a button and receives your message.

Other changes are profoundly affecting every industry. The constantly rising price of petroleum is already jeopardizing the plastics industry, and it is becoming too expensive to grow trees for paper manufacturing. Douglas firs, for example, are now being put to more profitable use in the chemicals industry.

These are just a few examples of why there is such a great need for corporations to envision what their markets will be five and ten years from now. Every corporation that wants to stay alive has to make decisions today about what has to be done each year to put that company in the best possible competitive situation during these years of drastic changes. It is now the consensus of many that the business world will change more during the 1990s than it did during the 1960s, 1970s and 1980s combined.

That is not to say that corporations didn't use strategic planning in the past. The former chairman of IBM, Thomas Watson, Jr., said to his management some years back, "We don't want to be in this punch card business all our life. We should get into the computer business. That's where all the action is going to be." At that time, IBM had little or no experience in the computer industry, so Watson decided the company's immediate need was to establish the largest data bank in existence on computers.

Letters went out to all IBM salespeople telling them to immediately send the home office a list of all computers in their territories, including the names of the owner/user companies and their industries; the brand names, model numbers, and ages of the computers; the names of people who use the computers and the purposes of the use; and in what areas the computers did not perform adequately.

Being typical salespeople, the field staff submitted information on a few computers and then went back to selling punch cards. When Watson realized what was happening, he sent out a second letter, reminding the salespeople that they are frequently transferred and stating that if a new person coming into a territory found one unreported computer, the previous salesperson would be fired. Within a short period, Watson had his research.

IBM compiled the data and determined what computers were serving what industries and the various ages of the equipment. Watson and his people then looked for areas where the competition was not fulfilling the needs of the different industries. After they found the untapped segments, Watson called in his engineers and told them to design computers that would fill the voids.

After the engineers had completed their mission, Watson called together his salespeople to introduce them to the new IBM line of computers. When they returned to the field, not only did they have all the information on the new line of computers, but they also had day-to-day itineraries on what companies to call on and all the other background information from the extensive data bank.

Across the country, IBM sales personnel went into various companies and said, "Hi, I'm John Smith from IBM. It's my understanding that you have computer #XYZ, and it's five years old. It currently handles your payroll, but is inadequate for all the other needs you have in this department." Customers were amazed at the extent of IBM's market research, but that's not all that impressed them. Before they could catch their breath, the IBM people displayed their new computers. Not only could the IBM computers do more than anything else on the market, they were substantially less expensive. The rest of the story is history.

Inevitably, some future events will catch us off guard, confronting us with perplexing or frustrating new realities. Consider the following scenarios, with their likely impact on marketing:

□ Hunger is eliminated as food production and distribution improve. International tensions subside. Armed conflict becomes much less likely, and a golden age of commerce dawns.

□ Product liability throws a monkey wrench into business. Flawed and tampered-with products become more common, provoking an increase in lawsuits. In their wake, insurance rates soar, and many manufacturers can no longer afford coverage. The American insurance industry collapses. Lawsuits, however, continue to plague companies that are no longer insured. Product after product becomes too risky to market.

□ True artificial intelligence is developed. "Thinking" computers and robots become colleagues of creative humans. Vast new technologies, products, and wealth result.

□ Loan defaults trigger worldwide financial collapse. Global marketing withers. Firms that survive struggle to serve limited national and local markets.

☐ The trillion dollar Star Wars shield is successfully deployed. America reigns supreme in the military electronics and aerospace industries. Japan, having devoted its resources to civilian industries, dominates in computers, microchips, software, biotechnology, shipbuilding, construction, and banking.

☐ Drugs in the American workplace become as pervasive as alcohol in East European industry. The quality of American products continues to deteriorate. Nobody seems capable of doing anything quite right. Japan, Germany, Korea, and other nations increase their industrial might.

☐ The Eastern European countries evolve into democratic or free-market states. Copy machines and networked microcomputers put these citizens in touch with one another. The disentegrated KGB no longer controls the flow of information and can no longer control the people. A worldwide golden age of commerce and culture ensues.

☐ A science-fiction miracle comes to pass. Radio astronomers detect information-laden signals from an extraterrestrial civilization. The alien knowledge enables us to transform our technology and industry, and improve the lives of all the world's citizens.

☐ The environment is severely contaminated. A devastating nuclear or biotechnological accident poisons an entire region, such as the farm belt. Local businesses fold, and companies elsewhere suffer financial repercussions. Atomic war, or course, would literally vaporize markets—and marketing.

☐ A planetary change in consciousness occurs because of the worldwide communications explosion. In his classic book *Lives of the Cell*, Lewis Thomas writes, "We pass thoughts around, from mind to mind, so compulsively and with such speed that the brains of mankind often appear, functionally, to be undergoing fusion." French philosopher Teilhard de Chardin and others have speculated on the emergence of a kind of global mind. Farfetched? Sure. Impossible? Who knows. The impact on marketing? Again, who knows.

Top Management Must Set the Tone for Planning

Before market planning can commence, it is imperative that top management create an environment that is conducive to planning. The following factors should be priority considerations:

☐ **The style and role of the chief executive or president.** The head of the company sets the tone for planning. He or she has (or should have) the clearest vision of where the company should be going, its purpose, and whether expectations can be met. He or she may have a range of options in mind, but has yet to reveal the substance of these plans.

☐ **The size and complexity of the organization.** A somewhat small company that markets only one of several products will not need a long, complicated plan since it should have the ability to react quickly to changing conditions. On the other hand, a large company with varied product lines and many layers of management will have to detail objectives and strategies for each line and prepare organizational procedures that will enable the firm to cut through the bureaucracy.

- [ ] **The need to train managers in planning.** Both marketing and non-marketing executives will often show a tendency to react to short-term pressures rather than view conditions in terms of the company's capacity for long-term growth. Thus, it may be necessary to have managers participate in either in-house or outside training sessions.

- [ ] **The structure of the plan and planning procedures.** The plan must be sufficiently flexible to allow for changes in corporate and marketing goals. While it must take a realistic view of the company's current and potential resources, it should also provide managers with the leeway to take risks. Market research should provide the basis for planned actions, but managers should be permitted to make certain decisions not grounded in raw data.

- [ ] **Communication of the importance of planning to the entire executive team.** Top management should make clear that planning is a critical managerial function, one on which executives will be evaluated for advancement opportunities and career growth.

- [ ] **The need for confidentiality.** Strategic marketing plans consist of all kinds of proprietary information, including product development plans, pricing, market share strategies, and customer targets. Naturally, should this information find its way into the hands of a competitor, it could undermine the entire planning effort. So, managers must be reminded to keep plans under wraps.

Strive for Knowledge and Flexibility

In the past, the future has always surprised us. In this period of chaos, surprise seems more certain than ever. Hundreds of things could happen in the next few years. No one of them may be probable, but some improbability or other will almost certainly occur.

How can you prepare for such a future? These three suggestions may be some small help:

1. **Don't put too much faith in your predictions and plans.** They're bound to be wrong, at least in part. Michael McCracken, President of Informetrica Ltd., Ottawa, Ont., warns of the "Future Fatal Flaw." By that he means an overconfidence in our ability to predict and control coming events. Smugness about our foresight can blind us to developments and hamper our ability to react.

2. **Keep well-informed.** Track trends, and watch for deviations. Events are moving very quickly, and it's easy to be caught off base. Aim to be

among the first to spot discontinuities or fresh developments. Alter your marketing plans accordingly.

For example, Videotex used to look like a great way to sell a variety of consumer products. The medium seems to have fizzled in the U.S., but it's catching on like wildfire in France. Or, CD-ROMs, a form of laser disk, seem to be a winning new medium for selling information such as stock market quotes, demographic data, and engineering specifications. Or, a competing form of technology could knock CD-ROMs out of the running.

3. **Above all, be flexible.** Predict and plan tentatively, warily. Use your plans to prime your thinking and condition your reflexes, not to prescribe action cast in concrete. Reassess your marketing strategies and tactics often, at least once every six months.

In the year 2000, the same as today, marketers will look for needs and try to fill them, hopefully making a profit in the process. They will look for those needs and fill them differently, however, thanks to revolutionary changes in technology, world trade, and demographics. Whatever the outcome, the marketing game will not lack for challenge then or in the years to come.

Strategic Plans Require Periodic Review, Update, and Modification
Because of the long time parameters involved in the strategic plan, several changes will be needed. Since completely accurate forecasting of future events is not possible, managers must often make new decisions in light of new developments. Even the best plans must be altered to reflect dynamic and ongoing changes in the marketplace.

Differing Goals of Strategic and Marketing Planning
The goals of strategic and marketing planning run a parallel course: both exercises are charged with anticipating change in the marketplace or business environment, setting objectives to deal with change, formulating strategies for carrying out objectives, and instituting action programs to see that strategies are implemented at the operational level.

Of primary significance to the nonmarketing manager is the fact that his/her role in the strategic planning process will differ markedly from his/her role in the marketing planning procedure. In the strategic planning process, the nonmarketing executive will eventually be asked to formulate a plan for his or her department for incorporation into the strategic plan, But if the same executive is also charged with setting total corporate strategy, he or she will likely have some responsibility for evaluating the marketing plan. Here, the following key point, as stated by a top corporate executive, takes on special meaning:

"Marketing strategy is best formulated when it reflects overall organizational strategy and strategic direction. Then it can become a strategic partner with other organizational functions, such as finance, human resources, and R&D, so that they reinforce each other for the best organizational advantage."

The planning process, both strategic and marketing, sets the objectives and goals the company aims to achieve in a specific time period.

Objectives answer the question: What are you trying to achieve? Listed are some typical objectives:

☐ To establish a product, product line, or brand in the marketplace
☐ To rejuvenate a failing product
☐ To introduce a new product

Goals are the specifics of the objectives. Here is an example of a typical goal tied to an objective: Introduce a new product and dominate the market while achieving maximum sales. Time to achieve: one year. Now the question is: Does introduction mean to distribute it among 500 major retail outlets or at only one? Is maximum sales $100,000 in six months and $1 million in one year? What are the figures that demonstrate introduction? What exactly do the words in your objectives mean? How about dominating the market? Is dominating the market having a market share of 100, 90, or 50 percent? When the market is fragmented, you may dominate the market by taking a 25 percent share (or less). Note that objectives can be broken down into smaller intermediate units within the total time period specified. These shorter term objectives are also goals. Thus maximum sales may be defined at the end of the period indicated (one year) as well as at shorter intervals, say six months. The same can be done to define dominating the market.

Professor George A. Steiner, an expert in strategic planning, recommends the following ten criteria to help in developing objectives:

1. **Suitability.** Your objectives must support the enterprise's basic purposes and help to move the company in that direction.

2. **Measurability over time.** Objectives should state clearly what is expected to happen and when so that you can measure them as you proceed.

3. **Feasibility.** Your objectives must be feasible. If they cannot be fulfilled, they motivate no one. Be certain that they are realistic and practical even if they are not easy and require considerable effort.

4. **Acceptability.** The objectives you set must be acceptable to the people in your organization or to those who may allocate resources to carry out your marketing plan. If your objectives are not acceptable, you will not receive the necessary funds. If someone besides yourself is working on the marketing plan and the objectives are not acceptable, you cannot expect to receive the same cooperation.

5. **Flexibility.** Your objectives should be modifiable in the event of unforeseen contingencies and environmental changes. This does not mean that they should not be fixed, only that, if necessary, they can be adapted to environmental changes.

6. **Motivation.** Objectives should motivate those who must work to reach them. If your objectives are too easy or so difficult that they are impossible to achieve, they will not be motivating. It does help, however, to have difficult but achievable, precisely defined objectives to challenge those who work to reach them.

7. **Understandability.** Your objectives should be stated in clear, simple language that can be understood by all. If they are not clear, they may be misunderstood and some individuals may unintentionally be working against them. You may also alienate those who allocate resources and capital. In fact, your plan may be stopped midway through execution simply because your objectives were not clear to everyone.

8. **Commitment.** When objectives are set, especially by more than one person, it must be made certain that everyone working on the development, planning, selling, and execution of the marketing plan is committed to those objectives.

9. **People participation.** Professor Steiner points out that the best results are obtained when those who are responsible for achieving the objectives take some part in setting them. Thus it is important to consult with all who might participate in any way with the execution of the plan. If other staff members are committed to your objectives from the start, you will have much less trouble keeping them on track throughout the implementation of your plan.

10. **Linkage.** Naturally the objectives should be linked with the basic purposes of your organization, but they must also be linked with the objectives of other collateral organizations in your firm. They must be consistent with and meet top management objectives. It's no good, for example, to set objectives that involve high sales if this runs counter to top management's overall philosophy at the time of securing market share. Therefore, ensure that the objectives you set are linked to other aspects within and without your organization that may be important.

Finally, planning is the most important part of starting and running a successful business. It is a fact—if you don't know where you are going, you will end up somewhere else.

In the following portion of this section we will explore the core of business planning—the marketing plan. All other activities of a business are in some way dependent on a workable, successful marketing strategy and methodology. In some situations the marketing effort is less pronounced than others, but if your business does not attract customers, your business will not exist long. By developing a solid marketing plan you can have greater assurance of success in your business.

Why the Marketing Plan Merits Special Attention

As was noted earlier, top executives consider the marketing plan crucial to the company's ability to grow. This is because (1) the marketing plan deals with the customer, what that customer needs, what the customer wants, how the customer purchases, how much the customer is willing to pay, how the customer can be influenced, how the customer influences, and how the customer changes; and (2) the marketing plan deals with the forces of change in the business environment—competitive, economic, political, social, technological, etc. The marketing plan, then, provides the framework through which the company studies trends and projects the future so that its products or services meet the needs of its customers despite outside influences.

More specifically, the marketing plan enables the company and its management staff to:

- ☐ Foster communication and cooperation between marketing and other departments and units

- ☐ Anticipate problems and clearly identify opportunities

- ☐ Set standards of responsibility, performance evaluation and progress for company products, services, and personnel

- ☐ Provide for a better understanding of alternative courses of action, which in turn simplifies decision making

- ☐ Establish priorities, both in the allocation of resources and the formulation of corporate goals and strategies

- ☐ Formulate assumptions on which decisions are based

- ☐ Identify competitive forces and suggest countermeasures

- ☐ Spot misdirected policies in time to take corrective action

Short- and Long-Term Marketing Plans

There are two basic types of marketing plans—(1) strategic or long-term plans and (2) annual or short-term marketing plans. Both types of plans have almost the same components but they differ in purpose, scope, and time frame. The strategic or long-term plan sets the pace for marketing strategy and activities several years down the road. It is intended to help in the general formulation of corporate strategy and establishes priorities in terms of the firm's general objectives. The plan normally becomes a part of the general business plan. The annual or short-term marketing plan (which usually conforms to the firm's fiscal year) is an operational plan designed to implement or carry out the priorities of the long-term plan in carefully-determined stages. The annual plan is generally lengthy and detailed; the strategic plan may be a somewhat brief document. For purposes of this discussion, we will consider the **strategic marketing plan** since it is central to the company's opportunity for growth and because it has special significance to nonmarketing executives.

Hidden Traps in Marketing Planning

Like almost all other major corporate undertakings, the marketing plan can be misused unless responsible executives from top management take the proper precautions. Managers who contribute to the planning or evaluation process should be mindful of the following pitfalls:

1. Failure to inform all managers/personnel affected by the plan of its content, direction, or recommendations.

2. A rigid planning format that discourages creative thinking.

3. Preoccupation with current developments in the marketplace to the exclusion of the long-range considerations of the business.

4. Inaccurate, out-of-date, or incomplete market research data that can lead to misguided objectives and strategy.

5. Lack of sufficient time to draw up the plan thus leading to gaps in information and possibly overlooked opportunities or problems.

6. Failure to insist that all departments provide marketing with relevant data according to the marketing plan's schedule.

7. The view that the marketing plan is a theoretical document that bears no relationship to the practical demands of the marketplace.

Most companies that take marketing planning seriously make sure that the plan is set down in writing and reviewed periodically by top management. In addition, because the marketplace is characterized by sudden and often sweeping change, constant review of the strategic marketing plan is a necessity.

Things to Avoid

A good example of what happens when a company does not continually look into the future is the financial plight of the Singer Company. Very few companies enjoyed a greater consumer franchise. Whenever you think of sewing machines, what name comes to mind? Singer, of course.

Singer had never done any market research, and its executives were not bothered by the fact that there were no trade associations to collect market data. They thought gathering this sort of information would be valuable only to the competition.

As stated in the November 5, 1979 issue of *Fortune* magazine, Singer sewing machine sales started to decline in the United States, but because sales were still up in Europe, Singer did not foresee any problem. Even when sales declined one year in Europe, the company called it an aberration. It was not until sales declined the second year in Europe that Singer executives began to consider that maybe women's life-styles were changing. They commissioned a research study, and the facts were devastating. The downward trend was so strong that it showed only 18 percent of females 16–24 years of age would own sewing machines in 1985, compared with 46 percent in 1970. The drop in 25–29 year olds was even more dramatic, with only an estimated 31 percent owning machines in 1985, compared with 79 percent in 1970.

Also, you can have foresight and still fail. Bell Laboratories invented the transistor but couldn't find an application. It took Japanese visitors from the Sony Corporation to notice how American teenagers struggled with their huge portable radios. They went back to Japan and used the transistor to develop the first small portable radio, introduced it in the United States, and overnight became No. 1.

The following is a list of the ten most common marketing mistakes made by businesses throughout the world. These are not listed in any order of importance—they are all important.

□ **Failure to understand and appreciate trends in the marketplace.** Consumer life-styles and the accompanying competitive forces change frequently and quickly. Marketing inertia results in obsolete marketing programs.

□ **Lack of a continuous and efficient marketing intelligence system.** Both commercial and nonprofit firms need to gather pertinent primary and secondary information. A company cannot afford to ignore feedback from key sources. The excuse of being too small, too inexperienced, or not wealthy enough to accomplish this does not suffice. The cost of information gathering need not be large.

□ **Failure to understand buyer behavior differences among market segments.** Marketing personnel should know the various factors that cause consumers, including industrial buyers, to behave in a certain manner when buying and consuming goods or services. Consumer behavior is a complex phenomenon. Only by attempting to understand it can marketers develop an effective marketing program.

□ **Indifference to sound budgeting techniques.** Marketing managers often do not plan or control the budgeting process; instead they spend on a day-to-day basis. Therefore specific marketing objectives are not matched with cash outflow. This problem is very common with advertising expenditures.

□ **Poor integration between strategic marketing planning and short-term marketing plans.** Quite often executives are unable or are not encouraged to see the impact of their day-to-day decisions on the long-term vitality of the organization. Although an evaluation and reward system is difficult to design and implement, it encourages marketers to think strategically. Marketers must move beyond the mere question of how to sell the product. A company cannot afford to sacrifice long-term opportunities for short-term gains.

□ **Lack of coordination of product offerings with market targets and the organization's own capabilities.** Many product considerations must be recognized by management. For instance, products can quickly become obsolete, and therefore a line up of new products in the organizational pipeline is a necessity. Marginal products are a cash drain and may waste excessive time and corporate resources.

□ **Indifference to market realities and company objectives with regard to pricing.** If top management ignores the challenges and complexities of setting pricing policies, procedures, and individual prices, the company becomes:

1. Too cost oriented
2. Too stagnant to capitalize on a changing environment
3. Indifferent about competitive prices
4. Lazy about regularly reviewing and analyzing prices (the responsibility of chief marketing executives).

□ **Indifference to the interface between physical distribution of products or services and channel management.** When a company can't get the right goods to the right place at the right time, it may alienate interested parties, customers, or channel members. Today's marketers must recognize that their profits and survival depend on cooperation with the middlemen or suppliers who are partners in moving their goods or services through the channels of distribution.

☐ **Failure to plan, coordinate, and evaluate a total organizational communication program.** To do a good job of promoting a product or service, marketers must appreciate the sales devices that work. Balance is needed among the advertising, personal selling, sales promotion, and public relations functions. All must be cohesive and persuasive to get different market targets to buy the product.

☐ **Neglect in answering a vital question: What makes an effective marketing person in our industry?** Many managers are unable to identify the key traits needed to market their firm's products and services successfully. They don't know how to match the person with the job requirements and challenges. An experienced and successful marketer is aware of the common marketing blunders and knows exactly what an organization must do to develop a good marketing program. However, if top management has not defined its own preferences for the marketing department, bitterness, misunderstandings, and lack of commitment may become prevalent. This last mistake could be the most significant of all—it has been the direct cause of the slow deterioration of many businesses.

Actions for Managing Mistakes

Following is a short list of suggestions of actions and attitudes to take to help avoid and handle the above mistakes.

☐ Recognize the limitations of marketing—it cannot create demand or perform overnight miracles.

☐ Keep a sense of humor—by staying loose, marketers can retain their objectivity and seek solutions to their misfortunes.

☐ Analyze why mistakes were made, to avoid making the same ones again. (Remember, analyze to determine the "why," not to find a scapegoat or "point a finger.")

☐ Remember that bad news travels fast, while daily decisions and successes may be forgotten.

☐ Communicate and listen across channels of communication—openness and honesty often result in a forgiving climate.

☐ Recognize that a competitor may want top management in other firms to think its own marketers erred, thus opening an opportunity for the competitor.

☐ Don't allow "management by crisis" in trying to overcome blunders; it can breed additional mistakes.

☐ Don't forget that one mistake can result in a vicious circle ending in more mistakes.

☐ Don't forget that a failure can be relative—it is not always absolute. An example is the introduction of Coca-Cola Classic.

☐ Don't threaten marketers or create a hostile environment if an error is made. It will inevitably cause more mistakes.

The Marketing Plan: A Blueprint for Organizational Growth

Companies that are static in nature, those that continue to market the same products in the same way without regard to the changing business environment, eventually falter and collapse. The executives who run these companies are usually caught up with day-to-day operational considerations, and delay any long-term plans for growth, if those plans exist at all. The primary concern is short-term profit, and the guiding corporate philosophy is to take as much cash out of the business as is possible. Eventually, the company's infrastructure begins to decay and executives begin leaving the company.

Fortunately, this bleak scenario is not as prevalent as it once was. The contemporary manager is generally more sensitive to developments occurring outside plant or office doors, events that frequently have a profound impact on company profitability, both in the short- and long-term. Rapidly emerging technology, the cyclical nature of the economy, foreign and domestic competition, changing customer behavior and expectations, and unpredictable legislative and political events are all major factors that can disrupt even the best-managed companies. Thus the exercise of planning for change has emerged as a primary business procedure.

Marketing Plan Topics and Contents

Marketing plans vary from company to company in terms of length, complexity, and subjects addressed. However, marketing planners are judged not on the basis of the number of pages they produce, but on the quality and insight of their thinking. In fact, review of marketing plans is greatly facilitated if they are kept relatively short and to the point. While top management will want to see the basic data upon which recommendations and conclusions are based, these can be provided as appendixes or supporting documentation.

Format for a Marketing Plan

With marketing plans, as with business plans, there are many different ways of presenting the information. It can be a brief verbal presentation to an informal gathering or a formally presented written document. It is suggested for reasons of reference and continuity of marketing activities toward a defined goal that the plan should be written and contain as much of the following material as is applicable.

The marketing plan provides expanded details of the expected revenue dynamics of the business. A typical plan will contain most of the following:

   I. Executive Summary
   II. Table of Contents
   III. Introduction

The Executive Summary—the marketing plan in brief. Normally prepared by the marketing director and staff, this summary is intended to let management know what the major factors are in marketing the particular product(s) or service(s). It contains the substance of the proposed marketing plan and identifies any major departures from previous marketing practice or procedure. Finally, the summary outlines primary changes that are occurring in the business environment.

The Introduction—a brief statement explaining the marketing mission and how it supports the corporate mission statement. (This is sometimes included in the executive summary.)

The Situational or Environmental Analysis—an examination of the company's current position in terms of product grouping, customers, and competitors.

Basically, the purpose of the situation analysis is to answer the question, "Where do we stand now?" This section *briefly* describes the recent history of the firms's products or services and sales or revenue, profiles its customers, and examines its competitors.

Products/Services and Sales

The marketing manager's job is to ensure that products are depicted in terms of such characteristics as appearance, content, and name. It is also essential that the product or service be described in terms of stage in the product life cycle, market position (leader or follower), and market share. The picture can hardly be complete without the inclusion of a product's sales history in terms of dollars and units and a comparison of actual sales performance with previously set sales objectives. Sales may further be broken down by geographic region, field territory, type of distributor, and by profiles of end-users or customer segments. Much, if not all, of this information is available as "secondary" market research data.

Customer Profiles

As was stated, a cardinal rule of strategic and marketing planning is "know thy customer." One could hardly be in a position to plan strategy for growth, new products, pricing policies, or market penetration without an in-depth knowledge of the current and potential customers. Customer profiling will not be a difficult chore if markets have been properly segmented, before the planning process, into the major categories—demographic, geographic, usage rate, benefit identification, and psychographic.

Competitor Analysis

In the past, many companies gave this section of the marketing plan short shrift. But now, the intensity of foreign and domestic competition has made this an area of central importance. The questions that should be addressed are:

1. Who are your competitors, by name, size, and industry?
2. What are their sales levels and trends?
3. What are their actual and potential shares of the market?
4. What are their strengths and weaknesses (including product quality, distribution channels, and management personnel)?
5. What are their strategies and priorities?
6. What are their current and future objectives?
7. What are their profit figures?
8. What are their current financial positions?
9. What damage have they inflicted on us in the past?
10. What threats do they pose for the future?

The Opportunity Analysis—a review of the company's capability to take advantage of new opportunities in the marketplace and minimize or avoid problems.

If properly done, the marketing plan's exploration of products, sales history, customers, and competitors should have uncovered both growth opportunities and problems. Opportunities, for example, could include unsuspected strengthening of demand in a particular market segment, a competitor's servicing problems, or the emergence of a new end-use for a product. Among the potential problems that may have appeared are weakness in a particular sales territory, a potentially threatening new product offering by a competitor, and a shift in customer attitudes toward a particular product or class of products.

The opportunity analysis, then, answers the question, "What market factors are in our favor and should be exploited and what obstacles must we overcome for our plan to work?" But to deal successfully with opportunities and problems, management must consider the wide range of external and internal factors that bear on the firm's capacity to respond. Among the external factors are:

- □ **The economy.** What are current and projected economic conditions? Consider all the major factors—interest rates, inflation, personal income, disposable income, GNP figures, etc. Most attention should be focused on those indicators that have special relevance to your industry or line of business. Thus, furniture manufacturers would be especially interested in housing starts; rubber and steel manufacturers would be looking at automobile sales.

- □ **Technology.** Technological advancements lead not only to improved products, but also to new ways to meet customer needs. Companies must consider not only how automation, for example, can be used to deliver a better product, but also how it can be used to improve operational efficiencies in the office and factory.

☐ **Socio-cultural influences.** The 1990 Census confirmed that vast changes are occurring in society. Some of the areas marketers would want to study for possible opportunities include increases in numbers of working women and single men, the shrinking of the family unit, the graying of the population, the growing importance of minority and ethnic groups as marketing factors, and distinctive buying habits based on regional characteristics of shifts in the population.

☐ **Government/Legal.** Are Congress, the regulatory agencies, and state legislatures likely to have a greater or lesser impact on our business? Are we exposed to legal action by customers or competitors? Could we have product liability problems?

Here are some internal factors that will affect the firm's capacity to take advantage of opportunities and correct problems:

☐ **Mission.** Is pursuit of the firm's marketing opportunities consistent with its corporate strategic plan? Marketing activities should not extend beyond the boundaries established by the company's stated purpose.

☐ **Marketing resources.** Development of a new or better product or service does not guarantee success. Marketing personnel must be tuned in to what's going on in the business and customer environments. All elements of the marketing mix—advertising, distribution, customer service, etc.—must be in a position to contribute to the total effort.

☐ **Production and technological resources.** Management must assess the production unit's capability to meet expected customer demand and R&D's expertise to meet the challenge of competitive innovations.

☐ **Financial resources.** Funds must be made available to underwrite marketing, production, and the personnel needed to seize opportunities or deal with problems. For example, entry into some markets may pose insurmountable financial barriers. Other apparent opportunities, though attractive, may not yield sufficient profit to meet the hurdle rate set by senior management.

☐ **Organizational structure.** The ability to react to sudden opportunities may very well hinge on organizational flexibility. A company that is decentralized and that has delegated decision making to the lowest feasible management level is in a much better position to take timely action. Top management control of all decision-making apparatus can cripple the company's ability to take maximum advantage of emerging marketplace opportunities.

The Trend Analysis—a look at emerging trends and projections that are used in the formulation of marketing objectives.

This section of the marketing plan involves plotting sets of trends, each pertaining to sales, profits, and return on investment.

One set is a projection of future performance based on past results and other information (customer and competitor behavior, for example) and on continuation of present marketing methods and policies. One way of making this projection entails five steps:

1. Project industry sales over the planning period.

2. Project company sales. Company sales for the period could be derived from projected industry sales and by using your anticipated market share figures.

3. Estimate company revenue, costs, and profits. Expected prices multiplied by expected unit sales yields the revenue figure. Profit, of course, is the difference between revenue and the costs associated with producing and marketing the product(s).

4. Project required investment. What level of investment would be necessary to support the projected marketing program and anticipated sales volume?

5. Estimate return on investment (ROI). Profit divided by net investment yields ROI, generally regarded as the ultimate indication of success.

Remember, the difference between where management is going and where it wants to go is called the planning gap. To close the gap, management must revise objectives and calculate a new set of sales, profit, and return on investment trends.

The Development of Objectives—identifies the direction in which the company should be headed.

Marketing objectives answer the question, "Where should we be headed?" They are formulated with general corporate objectives and goals in mind and pertain to sales, profits, market share, products, distribution, etc. Here are some examples:

□ Achieve total sales revenue of $XX million over the next three-year period.

□ Ensure that product line A accounts for at least 25 percent of the total sales over that period.

□ Increase market share of product Y in territory X to 30 percent from the current 10 percent.

□ Earn net profits of $YY million over the planning period.

□ Develop and launch new product G and attain sales of $Z million over the period.

□ Add nine new distributors of product X and boost sales by 15,000 units within three years.

Note that each objective is measurable, designed to accomplish one result, set against a deadline, realistic, and given to a particular manager to be held accountable for its achievement.

Again, as with the plan itself, the objectives are not cast in concrete. At any point in the planning cycle, top management may have to decide whether it wants to sacrifice the attainment of short-term objectives to realize the greater benefits of meeting long-term targets. Snags in the marketing plan may, and probably, will develop. That doesn't mean that the executive team should give up on the plan. Serious flaws, on the other hand, may require that the entire plan be reconstructed.

The Development of Strategy—specific courses of action used by the company to attain objectives.

Without follow-through, objectives are just so much wishful thinking. Strategy, sometimes referred to as an action program, is designed to answer the question, "How do we attain our objectives?" For simplicity's sake, marketing strategy can be broken down into three groupings: evaluating market opportunities, evaluating the product line, and evaluating the market share/market growth potential.

Evaluating Market Opportunities

Here there are four basic areas to examine: existing products/existing markets, existing products/new markets, new products/existing markets, and new products/new markets.

☐ **Existing products/existing markets.** This strategy dictates that the company keep doing what it has been doing but strive to do it better. The focus is on cost reduction and improved efficiency in all areas. For instance, manufacturing will be expected to boost productivity and trim waste. Finance will seek new investment opportunities and improved payment policies. Personnel will attempt to reduce turnover, streamline the screening process, and devise more equitable wage policies. Marketing is the most critical area—the one with the most options: attract new customers, convince traditional buyers to increase orders, enlarge the sales force, realign territories, increase advertising and promotion, and alter pricing policies. Also, the firm can do much to improve existing products such as adding new models and features, and boosting quality and service.

☐ **Existing products/new markets.** If the firm finds growth in existing markets stymied, it can capitalize on the strength of its product by seeking new markets. What is usually called for includes changes in packaging, promotion, advertising, and distribution channels. There are three important management considerations: the necessary market research data must be compiled, the market must be properly segmented, and the sales force must be retrained to deal with new customers.

☐ **New products/existing markets.** Management may be able to capitalize on the company's reputation through the introduction of a new line. What's more, early planning of new products is essential since existing items are prone to obsolescence. Here, strategy entails properly using marketing expertise and building research and development, and production capabilities.

☐ **New products/new markets.** This is the most risky strategy both to devise and to implement. But it is the only recourse for a company whose products have declined and whose markets are saturated. Here, management should seek new markets with plenty of room for growth, not dominated by large competitors and largely shielded from fluctuating economic or political conditions. Look for industries with a high potential value-added, so that management can more easily pass along inevitably rising costs.

A company should not limit itself to one market-opportunity plan. Strategy could include a combination of several options:

1. Emphasize existing products in existing markets to realize short-term improvements in return on investment and cash flow, maintain dividends, and continue to project the company's image.
2. Plan to sell existing products to overseas markets.
3. Expand the product line to eventually increase sales, return on investment, dividends, and profits.

Evaluating the Product Line

Another method of generating strategies is based on the recognition that different competitive approaches may be indicated by considering the product's place in its life cycle. This idea assumes that products evolve through four common stages: introduction, growth, maturity, and decline. The best strategy for dealing with the product will change as it moves through the life cycle. Thus, during the introduction stage, management will want to focus resources on advertising and promotion and add staff. In the growth stage, the emphasis is on market expansion, reducing prices to discourage the competition and broaden distribution. During the maturity stage, strategic moves would include sales incentives for the field and improved customer service. When a product is declining, the strategy called for is to spend little on promotion, reduce inventory, and cut personnel. The ideal situation is to have a new product in the introduction stage as another moves into decline.

Evaluating Market Share/Market Growth Potential

Growth potential cannot be measured with any degree of certainty. Thus, devising strategy for a product or market is a tricky business at best. Many companies have come to use the growth-share matrix developed a few years ago by the Boston Consulting Group (shown below), to put the various pieces of the marketing puzzle into proper perspective.

Growth-Share Market

	High	Low
High	Stars	Question Marks
Market Potential/ Cash Needed		
Low	Cash Cows	Dogs

The following is a description of each factor in the matrix and a review of what "current thinking" says the best strategy ought to be:

1. **Cash cows (high share of a low-growth market).** These are profitable products that earn more cash that can be used. The strategy here is to invest only to maintain cash flow, not for growth. Opportunities for expansion will come from other product lines. Concentrate on improving operational efficiency. Reduce R&D expenditures. Conventional wisdom dictates raising prices while still maintaining market share.

2. **Stars (high share of a high-growth market).** These are growing, usually profitable products in markets with plenty of room for expansion. However, such products consume heavy amounts of cash, needed to maintain their dominant market position. If dominance can be continued until market growth slows, these products become major contributors of cash and profits. Premature attempts to take cash can stifle growth and result in loss of market-share dominance.

3. **Dogs (low share of a low-growth market).** These products neither generate nor require significant amounts of cash. Whatever funds they manage to generate must be reinvested to maintain market share. The strategy here is to get out as much cash as possible before the product has to be scrubbed. Scrubbing, of course, requires a planned obsolescence strategy to avoid alienating the customer base.

4. **Question marks (low share of a high-growth market).** Having high potential for growth, these products require large amounts of cash in their struggle to obtain a dominant position and they are usually risky. The strategy: Decide whether the product is more likely to become a star or a dog. Then either invest aggressively or divest.

In all cases, marketing, in consultation with top management and sales management, must decide the best course of action to achieve objectives and then put it in writing as part of the marketing plan. Generally, it's better to have several proposed strategies, each as detailed as possible, but to the point. The strategies should include timetables for making critical decisions, a description of outside factors that could have a positive or negative impact on the strategy, a general statement concerning required resources, anticipated problems and solutions, and a forecast of how close the strategy will come to meeting objectives within the time horizon set by the plan.

Marketing Tactics—managers should be aware that besides the overall strategic blueprints of the marketing plan, action programs must be called into play. Some of the most common marketing tactics include:

□ **Product-oriented action programs.** These programs are designed to alter a company's product (service) or product mix in a beneficial way. The three major action options are modifying, deleting, or adding products. Symptoms that may prompt such action include chronic or seasonal excess production capacity, insufficient product breadth to exploit sales force contacts efficiently, persistent sales or profit decline, technological developments that threaten competitive position, or a disproportionately high percentage of total profits from a few products.

□ **Distribution-oriented action programs.** These center on the need to select distribution channels to reach new customers effectively, modify existing channels to reach and serve the needs of existing customers, or assist and monitor distributors to assure top-flight performance.

□ **Promotion-oriented action programs.** Enhanced promotional efforts may be needed to push or pull a product through the distribution system. Products are "pushed" when the promotion is directed at a middleman and "pulled" when aimed at the ultimate consumer or user. Usually this is not an either/or matter but one of relative emphasis. Among the factors that make up the promotional mix are personal selling and non-personal selling (advertising, publicity, point-of-sale displays, trade shows, and demonstrations, for example). The objective of a promotional message is not to describe the product in great detail but to convince potential buyers that it will satisfy their needs.

□ **Pricing-oriented action programs.** These are action programs to achieve the price-related objectives of the marketing plan and should be designed with a realistic picture of the competition's pricing practices. Included are list prices, transaction prices and volume, contract or bid prices, allowances, rebates and discounts, escalator clause terms, credit terms, advertising and promotional allowances, shipping and delivery charges, post-sale services, and guarantees and warranties.

□ **Sales tactics.** These are the method(s) you use or intend to use to sell your products or services. Will you use your sales force, sales representatives, distributors, or retailers? What role will advertising, promotion, and public relations play? Compare your established margins and commissions to those of your competitors. Describe any special policies regarding discounts and exclusive distribution rights. Show the company's normal sales terms. What percentage of sales are made for cash or credit? What discounts are offered for rapid payment?

Monitoring and Control—the procedures set down by the company to track the plan's performance.

An integral, yet often downplayed, portion of the marketing plan is the section that establishes policy and control procedure. Surprisingly, many companies do not know the profitability of individual products, they cannot identify weak products, they lose sight of or ignore predetermined objectives, and they shift strategies for no good reason.

Still, if the marketing plan to this point has been properly prepared, deficiencies are less likely to develop. If objectives have been expressed as measurable targets, then performance can be readily seen. Anyhow, marketing should be called upon to provide periodic reports, both financial and nonfinancial, on how the plan is progressing.

The Development of Contingency Plans—these allow the company to change course quickly and with a minimum of damage in the event that assumptions prove incorrect.

Contingency plans outline the company's response should key assumptions concerning the economy, the competition, the marketplace, and other factors not be borne out by subsequent events. The failure of assumptions to occur could pose serious problems for the firm and necessitate a rapid response from management.

The following techniques can help management anticipate and deal with contingent events:

1. Identify developments that could have a major impact.

2. Estimate the likelihood of occurrence for each development.

3. Establish "trigger points" for events on your list that have both a potential major impact and a high probability of occurrence. A "trigger point" is the signal or indication that a major event has occurred.

4. Develop a simple strategy for coping with events. For example, an 8 percent inflation rate may trigger the need to raise prices.

Appendixes—Supporting documents, tables, statistics, and advertising samples that support critical statements in the plan.

Always remember that the structure and basic components of a marketing plan are not written in stone. Since it serves its main purpose, identifying business opportunities that will put the company in a position to grow, the plan can be altered to suit the organization's particular needs and style.

The marketing planning process closely resembles the planning process nonmarketing managers employ either to assess the capabilities of their units or to help plan the strategic direction of the company. As the procedure's starting point, the situation analysis bears a close relationship to the familiar department audit. It's based on the premise that before a manager can set objectives and map out a plan for development or growth, he or she must have a thorough knowledge of what marketing has done and what it can do in the future.

Unless marketing is to be left to the vagaries of ad hoc decision making, the marketing plan is essential. Its components should be well-integrated and its objectives and strategy effectively coordinated with the many other areas of the company that the plan affects so significantly.

Developing the Annual Marketing Plan

The annual marketing plan should be developed after the strategic plan has been or is nearly completed. Marketing people can use the strategic plan or its preliminary ideas, handed down by top management, to formulate their annual marketing plan. This top-down approach is useful in defining short-term marketing tactics, the required budgets, and the annual goals and quotas. In preparing the annual plan, marketers should ask and answer the following vital questions: Where have we been? Where are we now? Where do we want to go? How do we get there?

A good annual marketing plan should contain certain elements. Although the planning process varies among organizations (some taking a highly structured approach, others setting up only general guidelines), the final plan should include identification and analysis of the following elements:

□ Brief marketing and sales history

□ Short assessment of where the company, division, or product stands in the marketplace

□ Specific and measurable marketing objectives and goals, including an ordering of priorities

□ Target markets and customer analysis

□ Marketing strategy and tactics (courses of action in product/service mix, pricing, promotional activities, physical distribution interface, and channel management)

□ Implementation steps (timetable, budgets, quotas, and assignment of various tasks to different marketing people) **Note:** This is one of the most overlooked aspects of marketing planning; a major oversight that ruins the entire annual planning process.

□ A formalized way to evaluate how well the plan has worked at the end of the operating period.

Objective controls are needed to find whether the company has been successful in establishing a marketing plan. These controls should relate to the marketing objectives that were developed in the plan. The controls would consist of evaluation of specific results such as (1) profit, sales, and/or cost breakdowns by different marketing units, (2) job tasks actually completed, (3) consumer- and market-related achievements (such as a decrease in number of customer complaints, product recalls, or achieved market share), and (4) overall contributions to the organization. The transmission of the control reports should be timely and accurate.

Planners should understand and use common techniques and aids for creating the plans. A few popular and/or helpful planning aids and techniques related to marketing are briefly highlighted in the following section.

Planning Aids in Marketing

Portfolio Analysis. Examination of composition and value of business units/products and their relationship to current and future profits, risks, and growth opportunities. Originally a financial tool by which management searched for the best mix of current and future securities. Three planning portfolio marketing analysis tools are (1) market growth/relative market matrix (also known as product portfolio matrix), (2) industry attractiveness/company strength matrix, and (3) directional policy matrix.

Brainstorming Sessions. A formalized "think tank" approach that encourages free thinking and promotion of new ideas or novel concepts. Strategic and operational ideas are evaluated later.

Market Research and Marketing Intelligence System. A systematic process of compiling and analyzing pertinent data related to marketing activities (including experimentation, surveying, and test marketing).

Product Life Cycle. Investigation of products' sales, profits, customers, competitors, market potential, and marketing strategy from beginning to end.

Profit Impact of Marketing Strategies (PIMS). Ongoing study that analyzes various environmental, company, and marketing variables on profitability and return on investment (ROI).

Marketing Simulation Models. Creation of complex models that resemble the real process, system, or marketplace.

Forecasting Techniques. Use of different quantitative and qualitative methods for predicting future events for both sales and company-related concerns.

Business Screen. Combination of interplay between financial concerns (e.g., cash flow, ROI, capital budgeting, financial objectives) and strategic marketing opportunities and risks.

Checklists and Published Forms. Use of criteria or questions that need to be performed or considered before and/or during the planning process.

A Short List of Do's and Don'ts of Marketing Planning

- ☐ Include all facts, assumptions, and pertinent data, but be concise.
- ☐ Set timetables, budget figures, and specific goals/tasks for planners.
- ☐ Encourage candid comments and feedback on proposed plans.
- ☐ Emphasize the learning opportunities during the planning process.
- ☐ Consider yearly bottom-line objectives with long-term implications.
- ☐ Integrate marketing strategy into the strategic plan.
- ☐ Encourage a management information system that incorporates environmental, market, and competitive information.
- ☐ Don't be afraid to make strategy revisions if the desired financial and marketing results are not met.
- ☐ Don't be overly concerned with petty details and create a nightmare in paperwork.
- ☐ Don't use the plan as a "straitjacket" or "club" for marketers.
- ☐ Don't forget some type of mechanism to evaluate current and future plans.

Market Planning

Marketing is something that must pervade the entire company. It is the responsibility of everybody in the company. Everyone employed by the company should be taught about the product or service their company sells. Designers need to go out and meet customers face-to-face.

Marketing studies make us feel secure about the marketplace. Studies tend to circumscribe our imagination. They limit the fact that we create market opportunity. For example, in the 1970s Mr. Hewlett of Hewlett-Packard Co. was advised, after a six month market study, that the pocket calculator market was very limited and not large enough to be sufficiently profitable to warrant their company's interest. Mr. Hewlett chose to go ahead with the project. Based on the success of the market created and its profitability, a new company division was formed. The market has since been found to be large enough not only to support that division on an ongoing basis, but also other competing companies who later entered that market.

Studies give you one answer. But they don't help you understand what is going on underneath the surface to create opportunity and change.

Marketing in its very fundamental sense means building relationships with customers, not with statistics.

Today the entrepreneur has the advantage. It's easier for a small business to service the smaller market niches of today and to be close to the customer than it is for large corporations. Big firms have been set up to service mass markets. Changing over is a hard task.

In an entrepreneurial company, decisions are made and implemented by a small team of people.

By finding a market segment (niche) and dominating it, you can create your reputation and identity. Then you can expand. Today, the way to get big is to think small.

You need to do a new kind of qualitative marketing to get in touch with your customer. Determining what keeps the customer coming back to buy the same product requires some fundamental rethinking about how to maintain consumer loyalty.

One key to that process is to look at analogies. Consider lawyers and doctors. We don't change our doctors and lawyers very often. That's because we have a certain relationship with those people and it encourages loyalty. We have to learn how to create that feeling as part of a product relationship.

Another technique is looking at the infrastructure of a marketplace, isolating 50 to 100 important people, talking to them, getting their endorsement. This core of people forms your reference system. Through word of mouth, they'll establish your reputation.

If you were selling a new drug to treat heart ailments, you might want to start by pinpointing certain leading cardiologists, people known as gurus in the business. Those people tend to work in certain teaching hospitals. Try to get a few of these eminent specialists on your advisory board. Then you might find the most influential older drug companies, and try to build distribution alliances with them.

Don't start out by spending a lot on advertising. Begin with a narrow reference structure and educate the people in it about your product.

Market-driven companies need to incorporate the customer into product design. That means getting more and more members of an organization in contact with the customer—manufacturing and design people, as well as sales and marketing staff. You can, for example, have customers sitting in on your internal committee meetings. Or have your manufacturing, R&D, and marketing people call on customers as a team on a regular basis, and then write reports on their findings together.

These changes have to become a part of the culture of the company, so they're not an event but a regular process.

Do a lot of internal training. You don't want to bring in outside people, because you need to develop more of a mentoring process. And everyone must be involved.

The goal really is to train people to think differently. You have to train them to react quickly and to be willing to make mistakes. That could involve special projects where, for example, you divide different employees into groups. Then tell each group to develop a marketing plan, and bring them back to debate their findings.

Today you must establish market relations: to build relationships in defined marketplaces, extending beyond the media to all influential players.

About 100 years ago, society underwent a transformation when we converted to mass-market manufacturing: everything was done on a uniform basis. Eventually, that erupted into societal movements of the sixties and seventies, in which individuals, pitted against institutions, cried out for an end to uniformity.

Technology has created tools of diversity that allow you to produce a solution for ever-narrower segments of society. This ability to reach ever more targeted groups is feeding into larger societal pressure for less uniformity and more choice. Issues addressed by production strategy today include the processes and technology that will be issued; the requirements for materials, equipment, facilities, and staff; where facilities will be located; and the cost of achieving sales goals.

We have to recognize that the future is uncertain, that we'll need to do more creative planning to deal with an unpredictable world.

Planning the Introduction of a New Product or Service

At the heart of your product introduction strategy must be a positioning strategy. Your company must develop a style of marketing compatible with this new era of rapid change—you must start with a new approach that has been called "dynamic positioning."

With this approach, positioning evolves gradually, like a person's personality. It has three interlocking stages—product positioning, market positioning, and corporate positioning. These stages create a whole that is much bigger than their individual parts.

Stage One: You must decide how you want your product or service to fit in the market. Should you build a reputation for low cost? Or for high quality? Will you try to sell to all companies?

Stage Two: Now your product must gain recognition in the market. It has to win credibility with customers. You need to understand the network of retailers, distributors, analysts, and journalists who control opinion. If you can win the hearts and minds of the most important 10 percent of the people in an industry, your company's market positioning is assured.

Stage Three: You must not position your products, but your company. This is done primarily through financial success. If the company's profits slip, its image becomes tarnished. Then the company must start over at product positioning and rebuild its place in the market.

Stage one may necessitate a formal R&D strategy. A formal R&D strategy is needed when a firm is in an environment characterized by rapid, frequent technological advances; when a firm is in a highly competitive environment in which a new or refined product introduction is a major determinant of market success; and when new product development is expensive and requires long lead times.

Marketing Scope and Distribution

Market scope may be local, regional, national, or international. Distribution may be direct to consumers or retailers or it may require a wholesaler, distributor, or broker. Describe your company's market scope and your channels of distribution. To what degree do you depend on middlemen?

Innovation—Risk vs. Reward

Here is a short list of market questions for a new product survey:

1. Can potential buyers who would need and want the new offering be identified?
2. How many potential buyers are there? Can all of them be contacted? If not, will a random sample be possible?
3. Do buyers know what their plans are without trying the new concept? Do they have specific intentions?
4. Will buyers overstate their buying intentions?
5. Will the competitive and economic environment change from the date of the survey to actual commercialization of the new product?

Caution: Be careful when the brand manager or someone else is excited simply because a survey shows favorable buyer expectations and planned purchases for the new product.

A new product or service should be carefully tested and evaluated before selling begins. In the highly competitive marketplace, marketing people sometimes rush the product development process. For many reasons—such as to beat competition, motivate the sales force, satisfy channel members, impress top management, or beat the "market window"—marketers may prematurely take a faulty product to consumers. Quite often this hasty action results in damage to the company's image and reduced sales of the company's other products.

Countless numbers of well-known companies have fallen into the trap of rushing a product into the marketplace before it was perfected. Sometimes salespeople are already taking orders before the lab people have perfected the product, in fact, sometimes before the product is even technologically feasible.

Rewards reaped by innovators may not necessarily be shared by followers who adopt similar marketing practices. Many companies have hesitated to introduce a new product only to see the competition go ahead with it. So their competitors are the first in the market and receive the publicity, accolades, and lion's share of the market.

A proposed new product can cannibalize sales of existing products. Osborne, which had to declare Chapter 11 bankruptcy, learned the importance of this rule when it was planning to introduce a new executive portable computer. Although the new computer was not meant to compete against the original Osborne 1 computer, customers and dealers decided to postpone purchases of the Osborne 1 when they heard a new product was in the pipeline. The marketing miscalculations created bad cash flow problems for a company already overleveraged.

Management must always appreciate the impact that a new product may have on existing products. For example, a new product that is poorly received can hurt sales of the firm's established products. This situation is amplified when the company markets both new and older products under one brand name.

The company must have assurance of adequate supplies and raw materials before deciding to market a new product. The logistics of receiving the raw materials and supplies and of shipping the finished goods are also crucial in the product development process. Strategic logistical planning becomes especially important in high sales volume industries. We can easily imagine the huge amounts of chicken needed for the introduction of Chicken McNuggets.

Management must think strategically when developing new products, services, or technological innovations. Managers in every organization must find out the impact that a new concept will have on (1) the other components within the organization and (2) the well-being of the firm in the years to come. For the most part, new offerings are not created overnight, and there is plenty of time to evaluate how the product will affect future company well-being. There have been cases in which one new concept either caused the organization to fail or saved it from extinction. The odds for a successful outcome are improved when the new offering has a nice corporate fit (synergism) with the other products and resources of the firm.

Marketers can capitalize on the experience-cost curve effect. Costs may be kept low by these types of favorable factors:

- [ ] Economies of scale
- [ ] Ready access to distribution channels
- [ ] Built-in customer loyalty
- [ ] An established sales and promotional network (e.g., routes, sales force, and point-of-purchase displays)
- [ ] Availability of physical distribution facilities and infrastructure
- [ ] Technical plus managerial expertise within the product/market fit

A new concept can still be successful even if it is completely new to the firm and lacks synergistic advantage. The innovative or technological breakthrough may fill a nice void in the marketplace. However, the potential profits can be dramatic and the risks less when that new offering fits the firm like a glove and meets the general purpose of the business.

Once a new product or service is introduced, the company must set quantitative and financial objectives for it. Often a new product or service does not fulfill the expectations and excitement of its sponsors. A tough decision must then be made as to how long to leave the new offering in the market and what criteria will determine its success.

To help answer difficult questions, managers must formulate expected financial objectives. These may include return on investment (the most common one for new offerings), market share, unit profit contribution, and contribution to cash flow.

Executives should also identify nonnumerical criteria that can be used to evaluate the new offering (for example, image, educational value, middlemen reaction, and completion of a product line). An organization that has not formulated and does not periodically evaluate its criteria for defining success or failure for a new offering has a weak product development system.

The aesthetics and marketability of the package should be considered when designing the new product. A package can enhance sales of a new product. Consumer product marketers have appreciated the importance of careful package design for years. Lately, marketers in the home computer industry have also begun to acknowledge this critical rule. They are now designing attractive, furniture-compatible computers. A good package may be the difference between success and failure for a new product.

A new product sometimes needs different concepts and designs to appeal to various channel markets. The assumption that only one type of package is needed can be erroneous. For example, attractive point-of-purchase racks, displays, and packages may be needed for sale of new cosmetics in self-service retail outlets. In specialty shops and full-service department stores, however, a different, more sophisticated packaging approach can be used.

The power and impact of product positioning and advertising strategy should not be underestimated when introducing new offerings. The promotional strategy for new products or services must develop a distinctive positive image in the minds of consumers. The company wants its market targets to mentally rank the new product or service first in the buying process. For instance, some brand marketers of beer, jeans, perfume, and cigarettes privately admit that their new offering does not differ from products of the competition. Nevertheless, they try to sell a positive image, partly through product positioning, that will enhance new sales.

Decisions behind product positioning should be dictated by prior marketing research and competitive analysis. Voids and unmet consumer needs in specific market sectors will often be found. This vacuum provides opportunities to position the product in this sector.

No matter how strong the attributes are for a new product or service, a poor promotion program will cause failure in the positioning process. To ensure some success, marketers should stick to the following minimum rules:

1. Present uniqueness and benefits of the new offering to consumers.
2. To avoid confusing consumers, don't mention too many benefits.
3. Position the product clearly and concisely.
4. Set sights on a specific and identifiable market target.
5. Repeat and reinforce the new offering's name or brand frequently.
6. Pretest the message and the accompanying people, props, devices, and the like.
7. Develop a consistent and total theme in the advertising.
8. Avoid trying too much with too few advertising dollars.
9. Constantly monitor the impact of the advertising approach.
10. Be prepared with a contingency advertising program in case positioning problems occur.

Product marketers must understand two important concepts: the consumer adoption process and diffusion of innovations. Consumer adoption is defined as a decision-making process in which an individual passes from hearing about a new offering to buying it on a regular basis. According to Everett Rogers in his book *Diffusion of Innovations*, a person normally goes through five stages: (1) awareness, (2) interest, (3) evaluation, (4) trial, and (5) adoption.

The different rates of acceptance have resulted in identification of five adopter categories: (1) innovators, (2) early adopters, (3) early majority, (4) late majority, and (5) laggards. Knowing who the innovators or early adopters are for a particular product line helps in targeting the promotion when the new offering is introduced.

The following elements partly dictate the speed of consumer acceptance of new offerings:

1. **Relative benefits and advantages.** When prospective buyers can easily obtain major pluses from the new offering, they are more likely to buy it immediately. An industrial purchasing manager will be quite excited when the benefits far outweigh the costs of the new office equipment.

2. **Complexity.** Consumers are slow to adopt an offering that is difficult to understand. The are often indifferent to the technical attributes and marvels of the product. They want to visualize how the innovations will meet their needs and solve their problems. Marketers should not be enamored with the technical aspects of their products while ignoring the task of simplifying its complex features.

3. **Compatibility with current lifestyle or operations.** The new offering should not upset the normal lifestyle or operations of prospective buyers. We are indeed creatures of habit. Although there are cases when an upheaval is desired, the diffusion process will usually take much longer in this case, if it does take place.

4. **Transparency.** The major advantages of a new concept should be easily observable. When buyers can quickly notice the positive opportunities presented by the innovation, they are more likely to buy it regularly. Consumer confusion about the features will slow down the diffusion process. Sales personnel must be able to show exactly how the new product will help consumers.

5. **Degree of risk.** When the new offering presents a high financial, physical, social, or personal risk, consumers may be slow or hesitant to try to adopt it. Marketers must try to minimize the risk or to share in the amount of risk taken by consumers. High risk factors or strong doubt may require marketers to offer a scaled-down version or smaller quantities. Consumers may be willing to take a risk if they can invest a smaller amount of money. Industrial marketers of capital goods frequently build smaller prototypes or allow organizational buyers to try the new item at little cost to them. One robotic manufacturer/distributor is starting to charge a nominal "rental" fee. Prospective buyers can try out the programmable robots in the manufacturing process, to see if the robots do help productivity.

6. **Degree of support among opinion leaders and influencers.** When a new offering has the strong support of respected leaders in a certain marketplace, the acceptance rate is notably increased. Marketers must therefore identify and convince opinion leaders and influencers about the virtues of the new offering.

Before a new offering is introduced into the marketplace, its marketing plan should be well thought out. Ironically, an organization may spend months or years on the engineering and production of a product, and then spend just a few days on developing marketing strategy and tactics. A last-minute, poorly developed strategic marketing plan can often doom even the best concepts taken from engineering, research and development, and/or production. A marketing game plan must be interwoven throughout the later stages of development of a particular product or service.

To avoid new product or service mistakes, marketers should know common reasons for failure. The most common reasons for failure of a new product or service in the marketplace are:

□ Poor market analysis
□ Market target too small
□ Technical product/service defects
□ Costs higher than anticipated
□ Poor positioning
□ Lack of worthwhile differentiation strategy
□ Inadequate management support
□ Insufficient marketing effort
□ Lack of channel support
□ Unrealistic forecasts in sales, profits, or return on investment
□ Strong competitive reaction
□ Bad timing
□ Lack of understanding of the buying process
□ No real benefit to consumers
□ Lack of required organizational resources

Many of these reasons are interrelated and interdependent. No one can perfectly predict future failures and successes, but management can use the diagnostic approach of studying reasons for previous failures.

Actions for developing new offerings. Make sure the new offering ties in with management's desired image and mission of the organization. Follow these steps when developing new offerings:

□ Study the new product's fit with the needs and preferences of the market.

□ Integrate the internal, financial, and technological strengths with the new product plans.

□ Transfer technology and innovation into the operations of the firm; if needed, develop a prototype.

□ Establish concrete financial and marketing objectives for the new offering.

□ Make alternative sales and costs forecasts and analyze possible break-even points.

□ Use various capital budgeting techniques to analyze the wisdom of the innovation objectively.

□ Integrate and monitor the innovative process with a sound marketing intelligence system.

☐ Formalize and integrate the reward system and other executive perks with performance goals for new offerings.

☐ Encourage a continuous flow and movement of new products or services for strategic growth and organizational vitality.

☐ Don't forget to file for patent or copyright protection, if needed.

☐ Don't neglect continued marketing of current "bread and butter" products while developing the new offering.

☐ Don't ignore the legal, social, or political implications of the new product.

☐ Don't allow competition to dictate the developmental process; avoid me-tooism.

☐ Don't allow the new offering to cause severe cash flow problems that put the organization in bad financial straits.

☐ Don't forget essential after-sale service requirements.

☐ Don't allow day-to-day downside sales revenue or short-run pressure to result in premature withdrawal of the product.

☐ Don't allow personnel to become subjectively or emotionally involved with the new concept.

☐ Don't permit professional marketers to believe the new offering is a win-no-win situation in which their career is on the line (such an environment will uphold artificial, weak offerings).

☐ Don't forget that employees at all levels of the organization must feel committed to making product/service development a success.

Presentation Outline

When making the formal presentation of your marketing plan, whether it be the strategic plan, the annual plan, or a product marketing plan, the following general procedure will help make it a positive, upbeat, and successful presentation. Remember, this is general—the details and methodology of presentation should be as dynamic as possible—sell your audience on the plan.

I. **Introduction.** Here you cover the information in your executive summary, including the opportunity and why it exists, the money to be made, the money that's needed, and some brief financial information, such as return on investment, to support the extent of the opportunity as you see it.

II. **Why You Will Succeed.** Here you cover your situational analysis and environmental scanning and the research you did to support it. You should conclude the section with problems and opportunities as well as the project's goals and objectives.

III. **Strategy and Tactics.** Here you cover the strategy you are going to follow as well as the tactics used to carry out the strategy. The main message of this section is the competitive differential advantage that you have over your competition—that unique difference that will allow you to succeed where others may fail.

IV. **Forecast and Financial Information.** Here you cover your forecast, project development schedule, profit and loss statement, and financial ratios and data. This section will contain a detailed description of what you need and when you need it. Sometimes, because of the limited time available for presentation, you may have to cut down on this section and present only the main points. The important financial information, still, should always be available so that in the question-and-answer session that follows you can provide additional data.

V. **Conclusion.** Here you must restate the opportunity and why you will succeed with it, the money that is required, and the expected return on the investment.

12

The Global Marketplace—
Marketing's Future

We are entering an era of opportunity. If you now sell only to the American market, imagine not doubling, tripling, or quadrupling your sales potential, but multiplying it by a factor of 20. There are 4.5 billion consumers out there and millions of companies. America's 230 million people, for example, comprise only 5 percent of the increasingly accessible world market. That's the up side of globalization. On the down side, imagine multiplying your competitors by a factor of 20.

In his classic article "The Globalization of Markets," (*Harvard Business Review*, May–June 1983), Theodore Levitt foresaw "a new commercial reality—the explosive emergence of global markets for globally standardized products; gigantic world-scale markets of previously unimagined magnitudes."

The Roots of Global Business

Four key forces have promoted international trade for thousands of years:

☐ **Diversity of natural resources.** One land has spices or coffee; another, marble or lumber. Trade is natural.

☐ **Transportation.** Sailing ships, overland caravans, and now freighters, jets, trains, and trucks make the transfer of goods feasible.

☐ **Diversity of skills.** People of one land are skilled at making lace; people of another, ceramic tile or glass. Again, trade is natural.

☐ **Communications.** Writing and common commercial languages permit bargaining at a distance.

Today, transportation and communications are the factors exerting the greatest influences on world trade. Modern cargo ships and jet aircrafts can move just about anything anywhere in days or hours, so distance presents few economic barriers. New Zealand kiwi fruit is available worldwide. Fish remains fresh between Iceland and New York. Signed legal documents can be carried from one country to another within hours. Stock is exchanged globally 24 hours a day.

Commercial data that used to travel at the same speed as sailing ships now travel almost instantaneously via computer networks, communications satellites, and multinational TV broadcasts. These provide global opportunities for advertising, negotiation, and deal making.

Because of these changes, the U.S. market is no longer the special reserve of U.S. producers. And foreign markets are no longer too remote for even the smallest U.S. firms.

Global Trade and Beyond

Like the information age, global trade now is only about 10 percent of what it will be in the future. Here is how the forces promoting trade may affect it by the year 2000:

- □ **Diversity of natural resources.** There will be relatively little change here.

- □ **Transportation.** There will be more state-of-the-art cargo vessels and jet transports to accommodate greatly increased world commerce. Supersonic suborbital transports (space planes) may be a reality by the turn of the century. Overnight delivery services will reach most countries. Local delivery will be facilitated, in certain regions, by high-speed trains, robotic trucks, and short-range helicopters. There is even talk of the dirigible making a comeback (buoyed by helium this time); this could make it economically feasible to deliver goods in areas that lack finished roads or docks.

- □ **Diversity of skills.** Nations will specialize not in specific products or services, but in their approaches to producing goods and services. Some trends:
  - □ Germany—craftsmanship
  - □ Japan—reliability and economy
  - □ United States—innovation and entrepreneurship
  - □ Less developed countries (LDCs)—devotion to repetitive detail—in assembly work, inspection, and so on

- □ **Communications.** Sellers and buyers in advanced free nations will trade at the speed of light via personal computers, smart telephones, and TVs. Citizens of LDCs will follow close behind.

  English will be the world language, making global commerce all the easier for American marketers. Classes in English as a second language are now proliferating throughout the world. However, multi-lingual Americans marketers will be at an advantage in their markets.

By the year 2000, business will be not only global but extra-global. Space stations and modules lofted by the U.S., Japan, European nations, China, and private industry will be producing pharmaceuticals; crystals for computer chips; ultra-strong composite, bonded, and pure materials; and other commercial products. The dollar volume of space-based industry will, however, remain somewhat small until the mid-twenty-first century, with one exception—communications satellites, including TV transmitters, will continue to grow exponentially.

The Limits of Globalization

Local and regional markets will persist when nearness confers advantages, or when no value is added by distant sources. Thus, haircuts, fresh fruits and vegetables, and generic accounting services will continue to be supplied within localities or regions, while haircutting equipment, exotic fruits, and specialized accounting services will be marketed to the far corners of the globe.

What to Do Now

Now or in the future, you may find it profitable, if not imperative, to take the following steps:

1. **Redefine your company mission in global terms.** This may be a wise move even if your firm is very small and you wish to sell only in the U.S. According to Frederick E. Webster, Jr., professor of marketing at Dartmouth College, a firm must carefully define its "distinctive competence"—the sphere of expertise in which it, uniquely, excels. If you fail to concentrate on what you do best and what others cannot easily duplicate, you may lose out in tomorrow's international marketing battlefield.

   Bear in mind that you are unlikely to make a wise choice about where you wish to market unless you have first looked at the global picture. You need to know what foreign as well as domestic companies are doing, because thanks to ever-better transportation and communications links, foreign companies may be competing on your doorstep tomorrow.

   Now: Explore carefully to find where your unique competence lies or could lie. Some possibilities include:

   □ Finding an international market niche
   □ Becoming the lowest-cost supplier
   □ Adding value through extra services
   □ Maintaining an R&D lead
   □ Marketing value-added systems composed of products or components made by others
   □ Focusing on local needs that cannot easily be filled from afar

2. **Seek out foreign as well as domestic suppliers.** Your buying should be as global as your selling, maybe more so. By the year 2000, only the best, most economical ingredients, components, and services available will yield attractive offerings.

Don't let a misguided sense of national loyalty lead you to be non-competitive. If Canadian wood will allow you to reduce the cost of the furniture you make, buy it. If a Mexican artist can do the best design job on your brochure, hire him or her. Buy American only when American is better or equally good. This will force American producers to improve quality and service. In the long term, that is the only way we can compete in world markets.

Now: Begin sourcing foreign suppliers. Your trade association and the Department of Commerce can help you find them.

3. **Explore foreign markets.** For years, American marketers have focused most of their attention on America. Now is the time to look beyond our shores. There are two reasons for doing so—one offensive, one defensive.

If you sell to the world, and do so successfully, your future may be very bright. Atari's ST microcomputers are the best-selling PCs in parts of Europe, but they can scarcely be found in American computer outlets. What if Atari had gone after only the domestic market? Or consider if you could sell in the People's Republic of China on the same per capita scale as you do in the U.S., what would that do for your bottom line?

The defensive reason for exploring foreign markets is that foreign firms will continue to invade the American market in growing numbers, despite the swings in national currencies. Almost surely, they will take away some of your customers. Protect yourself by looking for new customers abroad.

Now: Use the Department of Commerce, both state and federal, and your trade association to look at foreign markets. For a personal look, combine a vacation with visits to potential partners or distributors in other countries.

4. **Develop standardized world-class products.** Laurence J. Farley, chief executive of Black & Decker, Towson, Maryland, has said the world is becoming homogenized. While there will still be plenty of national and ethnic differences in the year 2000, you may achieve nothing but increased costs if you cater to those differences. Instead, create products with universal appeal, like Toyotas, Levis, and Coca-Cola. Adapt to local preferences only when you must, or if you're trying to carve out a market niche.

Now: Think twice before opening up foreign plants or offices to serve local markets. You may achieve greater economies of scale by producing a uniform product in a single location, shipping it everywhere, and saving the "local" appeal for your advertising.

5. **Investigate relationships with foreign partners and agents.** If you want to sell successfully in the world market, you will need lots of knowledgeable help, unless you have the time to master foreign languages, customs, and laws. Seek out foreign-trade consultants. Explore relationships with exporters and importers. Think, too, about joint ventures and mergers with foreign companies.

Now: Start recruiting people who know the lay of the land. A 40-person packaging equipment company, for example, is already selling successfully in Puerto Rico and is currently seeking representation in Europe.

6. **Exploit the coming reaction to standardized mega-marketing.** While world-class products will be widely accepted, there will be a simultaneous demand for ethnic, regional, and personalized products and services. One-of-a-kind, handmade products and works of art will be sought after. So will locally grown vegetables and neighborhood delivery services. The milkman is already making a comeback.

Quasi-handmade items will be popular, too. One example includes the rough-hewn tables and chairs that are made for fast-food chains by Hunts Country Furniture, Wingdale, New York. Although mass produced, the pieces are finished off by individual craftspeople.

Now: If your company is in a position to take advantage of this countertrend, work on your reputation for quality and reliability.

7. **Target the Third World with first-rate products and services.** If you plan to sell abroad in the years ahead, don't rule out the less developed countries (LDCs). They will be an increasingly important market for all types of goods and services, from water pumps to engineering consultation, from all sizes of suppliers. The disposable income of LDC businesses and consumers will rise as more and more plants locate within their borders.

Now: Beware of the "poor-relation" attitude when marketing to LDCs. These nations have been a dumping ground for outdated models, used equipment, and second-string services. Observers believe this situation will change. Exposure to the mass media is rapidly building the sophistication of LDC consumers.

8. **Pay more attention to product quality and price.** Professor Lester C. Thurow of the Massachusetts Institute of Technology has pointed out that America enjoyed a 30-year period of "effortless superiority" after World War II. That period is over. Now we stand on a more equal footing with other nations.

George J. McNally, president of Borg-Warner Chemicals Inc., Parkersburg, West Virginia, predicts a "brutally competitive" period between now and year 2000. The world market, including the U.S., will demand two things: high quality and value.

Now: Get with your purchasing and production people to examine ways in which you might improve the quality or the price/value relationship of your product or service. If necessary, seek out new suppliers.

9. **Improve the quality of service offerings.** By the turn of the century, many services, from accounting to consulting, will be delivered by telephone or phone-connected computer workstations. Clients will be able to switch services simply by dialing a different number. Personal services such as catering or dance instruction will also be highly competitive, especially in metropolitan areas.

If you want to be part of the service industry in the years ahead, you will need to develop loyal customers by devoting great attention to personnel training, service scheduling, the physical environment that your customer sees (lighting, decor), and actual service delivery.

Now: How do the key elements of your service offerings stack up? Upgrading them will put you on the road to continued success in the year 2000. For example, increase your efficiency so that you can lower fees or prices, add convenience such as 24-hour availability, add more features.

10. **Protect local sales by adding special value to your products.** No matter what you sell in the U.S. in the years ahead, foreign competitors are likely to target your customers with a similar product at a lower price. If you can't, or choose not to compete on price, consider adding services that cannot easily be matched by competitors. For example, guarantee to send a repair person to the customer's premises within two hours of any reported malfunction in your service or product. Borg-Warner Chemicals builds customer loyalty by making a 20-person Design and Engineering Center available for free customer consultations. A maker of one-of-a-kind kites competes with foreign imports by giving free kite-flying lessons on Sundays.

    Now: Review your line. What explicit and implicit values do your products and your support services offer customers? Does your sales organization know how to sell those values? Train them now to help them build customer loyalty for the more competitive years ahead.

11. **Replace your products or services before competitors make them obsolete.** Pretend you are a hungry Japanese, German, French, or Korean businessperson. How would you take away your business? In the year 2000, marketers will have several times more competitors than they have today. With so many more eyes looking at your successes and trying to better them, survival may depend on your ability to rapidly upgrade or replace your offerings.

    Now: Look at your business as your competitor does. If you wait five to ten years to do so, you'll be too late.

12. **Develop a global sales force.** Unless you plan to team up with international sales organizations or foreign business partners, you'll need to hire sales managers and representatives who know how to reach non-U.S. markets. That means locating the right employment agencies and/or advertising for the people you need.

    Now: Begin developing qualifications for representatives to the markets you wish to crack. For example: "Must speak Spanish, have 5+ yrs. experience selling intangibles to South American executives. . . ."

What will be the most important development in marketing in the year 2000? According to Ernest Dichter of the Dichter Institute in Peekskill, New York, marketing will have more depth and dimension in many ways. It will be more international, more personal, and more diverse. On the one hand, we'll have global marketing, including direct marketing via TV. On the other, we're going to become much more aware of individual differences.

Traditional barriers will break down. Perfume will be sold in flower shops; flowers, in cosmetic departments; work clothes, in hardware stores; specialized tools, in fashion shops; travel services, in supermarkets. There will be bulk shopping services that deliver staple groceries, such as coffee, by truck. We'll go to the store only to shop for perishables and specialized items.

General repair shops will spring up. You'll be able to take in any gadget, from TV set to chain saw, and have it fixed. This is already happening in Moscow.

Appendixes

Appendix A

Example of a Start-Up
Business Marketing Plan

The following is an example marketing plan that was written for a high tech start-up. The plan was written for limited distribution to specific investor groups—primarily venture capitalists. The actual business of the venture has been changed to a fictitious business, but the format and general concepts of the plan are demonstrated.

Motor Imaging Technologies, Inc. Marketing Plan

(Rev. 2)

Prepared by:
The Marketing Dept.
Motor Imaging Technologies, Inc.
B. Thorough, Ph.D.
B. Good, Ph.D.

Contents

Corporate Mission

Motor Imaging Technologies, Inc. (MIT) is in the mechanical imaging business and is dedicated to exploring, developing, and exploiting noninvasive electromagnetic imaging technologies. The entry product will be targeting autovehicular imaging using multilead EMG sensing technology and state-of-the-art multidimensional computer display.

Corporate Objectives

Profit

To make a sufficient profit to supply the finances required to meet the other corporate objectives.

Customers

To supply our customers with products and services of the greatest possible value in our chosen business.

Growth

To grow at a rate which keeps MIT, Inc. the premier company in its market choice, and to provide its employees with opportunity for personal growth.

People

To assure that our people can benefit from the company's success; that their achievements are recognized; and that they are managed so that they can have personal satisfaction from their accomplishments. To hire and continue to hire the best people possible.

Management

To manage our company so that an equitable balance is struck between the needs for short-term financial performance and long- term product and customer growth. To allow individual freedom in attaining well-defined objectives.

Base 5500 Marketing Potential

The imaging technology being used is new and non-invasive and shows potential for expanded use in autobody scan applications as well as other industries in need of scanning methodologies.

Engine failure is the number one disabler in America, which makes this product a necessity in the mechanical community.

In America, someone suffers autovehicular damage every 32 seconds.

In 1986, engine and ignition failures disabled nearly one million motorists, almost as many as bodyrot, accidents, air intake, carburetor, and all other causes or damage combined.

Almost one in two vehicles suffer autovehicular failure.

Reference: The American Engine Association, *19XX Engine Facts*. The mechanical application market is growing at a compound annual growing rate of 11.0 percent per the years 19XX-19XX. The GNP is forecasted to grow at a rate of 305 percent during the same time period. The diagnostic segment is especially strong, and the penetration in the mechanical application field is relatively low. No new entries are foreseen in the mechanical application marketplace.

Marketing Objectives

It is the marketing group's objective to gain approximately 1 to 3 percent of the EMG market ($4 million to $20 million) within the first year of product introduction and increase that share at a rate greater than 32 percent per year until 30 to 40 percent of that market has been captured. At that time, the primary concentration will be on increasing product profit margin and cash flow rather than on market share.

Marketing Strategies

In order to maintain a conservative marketing analysis for BASE 5500, we have selected the current EMG market as a reference point. However, it should be understood that the BASE 5500 provides information way beyond the current EMG capabilities.

The primary competition existing for this product are the EMG-based products, which, by introduction of this product, may be rendered obsolete in the future. This product may also negatively impact the radio frequency imaging market as well as the magnetic field imaging (MFI) and ultrasound imaging markets. These markets will be affected to the extent that they address the practice of autovehicular imaging.

When the product is introduced and in production, it is expected that the company will experience a high growth period. This will be controlled by the sale of licensed production rights to meet geographic areas of demand throughout the U.S. and overseas markets.

Sales and distribution will be in the continental United States during the Beta testing period and most of the first year after product release. This allows us to track the product performance closely under field conditions. In addition, the anticipated domestic market is such that MIT, Inc. may be hard-pressed to keep up with that demand.

The marketing/sales force will be trained to act as the staff to train the Beta sites and ongoing site staffs in the proper use of the product.

Three to five Beta sites will be selected. These sites will be autovehicular training institutes and dealers. Two sites have been approved for the initial study—at LBJ Memorial Institute and at Althia Institute in Your City. Another site is under consideration in Arizona.

Target Market(s)

The market is the diagnostic specialty of the mechanical industry. This market is represented by:

Diagnostic practitioners
Diagnostic dealers
General mechanics
Institutes
    Service stations
    Repair/care units
Internal repair services
Technicians
    Towing services
    Emergency services

The first market area to be approached will be institutes and dealers, which are recognized as primary autovehicular training facilities within the U.S.

Market Phase I

Institutes in U.S.		6,281
Federal Institutes	322	
Non-Federal Institutes		5,959
Institutes, Special	5,517	
Engine Care Facilities (B)	178	
Engine Care Facilities (C)	74	
Institutes, Special/SD	190	

(References: Robert Weissber, ARA/NET Tues. 17 Jan. 19XX
Bruce Flaph, Standard Mechanical Library, Feb. 19XX.

Repairs
    General
    Diagnostic
        (to be researched—ARA Abridged Guide)

Market Phase II

Mechanics in U.S. market	81,788
Carburetor/Ignition Specialists	9,439
Emergency Repair Specialists	131
General Mechanics	31,888
Antique Specialists	448
Engine Specialists	39,882

Ref. Clark-O'Neill, Fisher-Stevens, Fairfax, New York

Market Areas (Geographic)

MIT, Inc. will concentrate initially on satisfying the domestic U.S. This will take an estimated three to five years. As this satisfaction occurs we will investigate the international markets for methods of penetration as well as profitability.

Domestic market penetration strategy is to concentrate marketing efforts in a region-by-region manner addressing the westernmost states first, then the eastern states, then moving on to the midwestern and southern areas.

Market Penetration Strategy

Advertising will be done by presentation of the product at selected mechanical conventions and trade shows:

American Engine Association (AEA)	Nov.
American College of Diagnostic (ACD)	Mar.
American Society of Mechanics (ASM)	May–June
American College Mechanics (ACM)	Apr.
American Academy of General Mechanics (AAGM)	Oct.
Emergency Repair Mechanical Show	Jan.

Advertising will also be done by print advertising in autovehicular and institute journals:
Journal of American College of Diagnostic
American Engine Journal
Fuel Ways
Ignition
Repair Diagnostic
Repair and Fixit Magazines

Other types of advertising to be done include:

Direct mail to the autovehicular community

Promotion of discounted software updates

On-line product technical support (telephone technical advice/operational troubleshooting)

Public relations (TV and radio news PSAs, mechanical science breakthrough announcements, press releases)

Further research into this penetration strategy is being done to identify the specific institutes, dealers, and trade shows to contact and attend.

Services and Products

Initially, MIT, Inc. will be a "systems integrator" (refer to Product Profile and Sketches). The company will produce software that will be loaded into a hardware configuration purchased from a vendor (i.e. Comput-Graphics and/or Sol Microsystems). The company will also contract with a manufacturer (Stateside) to produce the devices necessary for sensing the engine's signals.

These above stated elements will be brought together under the complete direction and control of MIT, Inc., and will remain in that control until it is found advisable to move that integration process outside MIT, Inc.

This strategy is practicable due to the software being developed on the Open Architecture System (DOSS), which causes the hardware used to be virtually transparent.

The initial product will have the following features: It will identify:

☐ Specific areas and volumes of wear, acute damage, and repair methodology. Areas include transference and subtransference determinations.

☐ Localization of areas and volumes of wear, acute damage and repair methodologies despite subtransference conduction delays or bundled cable blocks.

☐ Locations of accessory bypass pathways in ERC methods.

☐ Localization of sites of combustion complexes or sites of exhaustive reentry for use in mapping of hydrocarbon exposure for ecological purposes.

The product will have:
☐ Three to five minute sensor/screen refresh rate
☐ 55 sensor input device
☐ 55 sensor signal display and printout
☐ Multi-dimensional image generation at normal size image display orientation (to be determined):
☐ Interior and exterior views
☐ 1 mm segmentation
☐ Zoom to approx. 9X
☐ Full image rotation
☐ Panning
☐ Color print of screen image
☐ Sensed data recorded on removable hard disk
☐ (60 engine cycle sample requiring less than 1 MBytes)
☐ (Disk cartridge capable of 400 GBytes storage)

Free user training will be provided for each Beta unit.
Installation and training will be provided at a cost of $9000 per each production unit and option.

Product Improvements

Ongoing Product Development (1.5 to 2 years)
    Enhancements
        Damage mapping
        Repair methodology monitoring
        Emergency unit monitoring
    Software Version(s)
        Overrun application
        Fuel system application
        Digital display of latent damage and potential volume
        Stop time review

Product Profile

(To be supplied by Engineering)

System Integration

Comprehensive system integration diagram is currently on display at MIT, Inc. offices. Nonproprietary diagrams are included here.

MIT, Inc. Market Advantages

The major advantage MIT, Inc. has in the market is the fact that the company was founded by a highly respected group of mechanical practitioners from the autovehicular specialty. These people lend a great deal of credibility and long-term prestige to this company and its entry product(s).

Another advantage is the fact that this imaging product is a **Noninvasive** autovehicular device. This greatly reduces mechanical risk. Thus, it becomes much more attractive to the customer than those imaging products that are invasive.

A further advantage is that it is state-of-the-art equipment for alerting customers of potential engine failure dangers as well as for diagnosing the damage caused by an engine failure (i.e. latent mechanical stress).

MIT Inc. Market Disadvantages

The company has two primary market disadvantages: 1) a market that is currently satisfied with the status quo, 2) the company size dictates limited resources.

These disadvantages will be addressed in the following manner.

The market will be educated to the superiority of this product in relation to the EMG products now in use. This will be done by demonstration at major mechanical conventions and trade shows as well as strategically placing dealer test units in major autovehicular training institutes. Also, technical papers regarding the dealers' use of the product will be written by the practicing board members and published in the appropriate mechanical journals and presented at the appropriate conventions.

The company size and limited distribution resources will be overcome by establishing a strategic alliance(s) with established major mechanical system suppliers such as Morganstein, Howard Johnson, etc.

Pricing

It is expected that the pricing of the product will follow the general software industry pricing trend.

Initial Price is currently set at $40,000, which is based on current hardware costs of $15,000 to $24,000 providing a gross margin of 40 to 63 percent which is comparable to the general software industry.

Free user training will be provided for each Beta unit.

Installation and training will be provided at a cost of $9,000 per each production unit and option.

Advertising and Promotion Costs

15-20 percent of gross sales product revenue is normally spent on media by industrial firms. MIT, Inc. is targeting less than that since it is expected that a strategic alliance(s) will be established and we will not be required to bear the total cost of this burden.

Timetable and Schedule

Available at MIT, Inc. offices.

Financial Projections

The EMG unit sales growth for the next ten years is projected to grow at the rate of 10 percent per year. MIT, Inc. is targeting a growing yearly penetration of that market starting with 1 percent in year 19XX and continuing at 5, 10, and 15 percent during fiscal years 19XX, 19XX, and 19XX respectively. That being the case, MIT, Inc. expects its gross revenues for each of those years to be $3.67 million, $20.15 million, $43.45 million, and $71.10 million respectively.

Anticipated gross net profit is targeted to be in the range of 30 percent of gross sales or greater; $.29 million, $7.25 million, $17.38 million, and $28.44 million for years 19XX, 19XX, 19XX, and 19XX respectively.

Marketing expense is targeted at an average of 11 percent of projected gross sales and includes the following income statement items: marketing and delivery, salaries, fringes and taxes, and travel. The projected budget for this expense over years 19XX through 19XX is $1.1 million, $2.42 million, $4.35 million, and $7.11 million respectively. This is to cover the expense of convention and show attendance and display, journal and magazine advertising, direct mail advertising, and public relations activities of TV, radio, and press release announcements of our technological breakthroughs.

A more detailed breakdown of this expense item is provided on the following financial pages.

Financial Projections Details

(To be supplied by Accounting)

Marketing Research

Market research once begun will be an ongoing activity to discover new areas of application for the current product and new uses of the unique imaging technology. This ongoing research is part of the costs associated with Phase II financing and will consist of at least the following activities:

Profile Testing

Evaluation of market product usage to establish improvements.

Distribution

Evaluate alternative channels
    Strategic alliances
    Mechanical wholesalers
        McFerson—Los Angeles
        Bervin Burnswig—San Francisco
        Feldomier—Dallas

Pricing Study

Determine acceptable price for the market being addressed.
Areas to consider:
Procedure cost
    Full EMG analysis currently costs customer $700 to $900.
    Comparative procedure cost (being researched—B. Thorough)
        Mechanical Stress test
        Mechanical Echo test
        Radio Frequency test
        Running Dye Test

Usage Study

Extension of profile testing but related to the question of who is going to use the product rather than how it is used.

Phase III Research

Phase III research will address the question of who are the major competitors and competing products. A competitive fact book analysis will be made and will cover EMG and imaging products at a minimum.

Industry Analysis

The market being used for initial study is the current EMG market which is represented by the mechanical application market.

MIT, Inc. conservatively expects to gain 15 percent of the EMG-based market and to ship at least 80 units during the first year after product introduction and continue a minimum of 32 percent sales revenue growth rate through the first five years.

Sales Trends

The mechanical application market will grow 11.0 percent in revenue and 29.3 percent in units, compounded over five years.

Average system prices are decreasing as the industry moves toward the use of micro and personal computers.

Future Industry Trends

The forces motivating the user to purchase computer tools for mechanical applications are:

☐ Increasing liability insurance costs are causing mechanics to perform as many nonintrusion diagnostic techniques as possible.

☐ Sophisticated mechanical diagnostic equipment is becoming increasingly more complex, requiring computerization.

☐ There is a need to integrate many instruments to improve productivity and increase utilization of expensive instruments.

☐ There are shortages of mechanical technicians and journeymen with critical skills.

☐ Labor costs are increasing. In the years of the 19XX's, a drastic attention has been projected to focus toward repair and autovehicular-related progress.

Outside Influences Facing the Industry

Mechanical products are subject to the following restrictions and influences:

☐ Liability insurance

☐ Government regulators such as FCC and FTC

☐ Mechanical associations sales and criterion

☐ International Trade Policy (for out-of-country export)

☐ Political status of mechanical environment

☐ Insurance industry regulations

☐ Repaircare cost containment

☐ Third party pay regulators

These outside influences have generated the following recent activities:

☐ Liability insurance for mechanics has almost doubled making them more responsive to new, no-risk, noninvasive technologies, which provide early warning of an impending disaster.

☐ Mechanical products have relatively short lives.

☐ Institutes, mechanics, and suppliers are competing among themselves for available funds since insurance companies and the government have capped spending for repair programs.

☐ Monitoring of engine function in all repair customers is becoming an industry standard.

☐ The trend is toward using micro, board, and personal computers in mechanical applications.

Sales Management

General end user sales methodology will be finally determined during the Phase II marketing research. Options to be studied include strategic alliances, mechanical equipment distributors, direct sales force and others.

Once the methodology is determined the method of management can be addressed.

Appendix B

Competition and the Law

Some executives choose not to familiarize themselves with the law and agencies that govern business practices and, instead, leave it up to the attorneys to unravel or head off any legal difficulties. This, however, is the kind of attitude that can, and sometimes does, lead to disaster. The marketing operation in particular, through the unwise selection of policies, can put the company, and responsible executives, in dire legal straits. Here, for example, are some of the penalties that can be imposed on the company and its executives for violation of federal antitrust and consumer protection laws:

- ☐ The payment of triple damages for antitrust violations

- ☐ Jail sentences for executives responsible for illegal price fixing

- ☐ Fines of $10,000 per day for ignoring FTC orders to correct misleading or false advertising

- ☐ Loss of sales and market share due to public resentment over unfair advertising and sales promotion techniques

- ☐ Costly damages for product liability

It is important for executive decision makers to recognize that legal complications that can lead to such stiff penalties are avoidable provided that (1) managers have a basic knowledge of applicable laws and regulations, (2) they use this knowledge by raising questions about any problem areas in the marketing plan before it is approved, and (3) they inform top management of misguided marketing practices and advise consultation with legal and regulatory experts.

Naturally, it would be a nearly impossible feat for managers to plow through the thousands of pages of legal documents to become totally versed in antitrust and consumer protection law. Even then, the fine points of the law change with each new court case and decision. But managers should have a broad view of the legal ground rules and sufficient knowledge to recognize danger signals and seek the expert opinion of legal counsel. What follows is a brief, but pointed, review of the major laws and regulations that affect the marketing function.

The Antitrust Laws and Their Impact on Pricing, Distribution, and Competitive Relations

The basic purpose of the antitrust laws is to prevent anticompetitive business practices or those that may be "in restraint of trade." The first antitrust laws were generally intended to break up the huge trusts such as oil, sugar, and tobacco, and alleviate the growing public concern that too much economic and political power was concentrated in the hands of too few companies. But as the economy expanded and became more complex and marketing methods become more sophisticated, the reach of the laws extended to companies of all sizes and in a variety of industries.

The Sherman Act

Generally, this law bars agreements, combinations, and conspiracies in restraint of trade. Prohibitive practices include price-fixing, allocations of customers or territories, refusals to deal, unreasonable restraints, monopolization, and conspiracy to monopolize. Some of these practices are explained below:

□ Horizontal price-fixing exists when competitors fix prices, even when the objective is to stabilize or lower prices. There are many different situations that can be construed by the enforcement authorities as instances of price-fixing. When two or more competitors curtail production through factory closings or put limits on the hours of production, they can be accused of acting in concert to raise or stabilize prices. Red flag signals of price-fixing may arise when competitors have identical freight charges, bids, credit and warranty terms, discounts, or trade allowances. Competitors that often exchange price lists have been charged with price-fixing.

   Generally, follow-the-leader pricing is not illegal in itself. But it can be when the same firm always initiates the price change, competitors follow the price leader within a short time, there exists artificial standardization of the product, a history of price maintenance activity can be demonstrated, or a showing of price increases occurs when a surplus exists.

   Note: A company that makes pricing decisions on a purely unilateral basis is generally safe from price-fixing suits. However, enforcement officials may try to infer price-fixing by calling attention to the company's numerous contacts with competitors at trade association meetings, industry seminars, or joint research projects.

□ Vertical price-fixing may occur when a supplier and buyer of a product agree on the price which the buyer subsequently uses to resell the product. Such illegal arrangements can exist between wholesaler and retailer, manufacturer and distributor, franchisor and franchisee, or licensor and licensee. Courts have generally held that a supplier can influence resale price unilaterally by urging buyers to resell at a price suggested by the supplier, announcing that buyers who fail to adhere to the established price will be cut off, or terminating sales to those buyers subsequently found to have departed from the predetermined resale price, for example. A supplier can get into trouble by using methods other than refusal to deal, such as requesting buyers to report price variations or conditioning discounts on price compliance. This area of the law is confusing and requires guidance from legal counsel.

□ Group boycotts and concerted refusals to deal are illegal under the Sherman Act. Group boycotts can arise, for example, when a group of competitors tries to stop others from entering an industry by establishing artificially high requirements in terms of product standards, certificates of approval, or codes of ethics. A vertical refusal to deal can occur when companies at different levels in the distribution chain agree to eliminate price-cutters or prevent other companies from entering the market.

□ Competitor agreements to allocate product, markets, and customers are illegal. Product allocation results when rivals agree to manufacture products that do not compete with one another and determine which firm will produce the particular product.

□ Tie-in agreements can run afoul of the Sherman Act. For example, if a supplier refuses to sell a needed item unless the customer purchases a second, unwanted item, then the buyer is being coerced into an illegal tie-in agreement. Reciprocal dealing occurs when Company X will purchase from Company Y if the latter buys from X.

□ A monopoly position is not in itself illegal. The critical factor is how a company achieves, attempts to achieve, or maintains a monopoly position. What's more, company size may not have all that much to do with monopoly charges. A small firm dominant in a local market could be vulnerable to monopoly litigation. To prove monopolization, a plaintiff must show that the defendant possesses monopoly power in the relevant market and acquired and maintains such power with the intent of exercising it. Monopoly power is equated with the ability to exclude competitors and to control prices. The exercise of power could be demonstrated by tie-in sales, acquisition of competitors, exclusive dealing arrangements, control of raw materials, and below-cost pricing.

The Robinson-Patman Act

Basically, this law requires that sellers charge competing customers the same price. The problem has been that the law's ban on price discrimination was made overly complex by the nuances of various FTC and court rulings that seemed to emit conflicting signals and exemptions. For example, genuine cost savings to the seller because of the buyer's purchasing habits or quantities can be passed on to the buyer. The precise circumstances and conditions could vary from case to case. In addition, the law allows a company to meet but not beat a competitive price as long as it does not sell below cost. The law does not bar quantity discounts if based on actual savings to the seller that are directly derived from the quantity purchased.

The law does not permit geographical price discrimination. This occurs when a company sells its product at lower prices in one area than in another and if competitors in the lower-priced area may be damaged. The intention of the law is to prevent large and powerful companies from cutting their prices in a small area and hurting local competitors, while the reduced income can be made up from sales in another area. Generally, the FTC will not pursue geographic price discrimination cases if based on the limited introduction of a new product in a given area.

A key provision of the Robinson-Patman Act requires that a seller must offer advertising and promotional allowances to competing customers on a proportionally equal basis. The language of the law recognizes that a seller cannot give every competing customer exactly the same allowances because of differences in the way they advertise and promote. However, the seller cannot arbitrarily allow some customers more funds (or free goods, etc.) than smaller customers on a per-unit purchased basis.

The seller that grants advertising or promotional allowances should set down on paper the specifics of a compliance program so that he or she can later prove that the customer actually performed the promotional service for which he or she was paid.

The law also requires that brokerage payments be genuine; otherwise the buyer most likely receives a discriminatory price. The broker must be independent and perform an actual and useful service. Finally, the law addresses buyers by prohibiting them from inducing, compelling, or receiving an illegal pricing advantage not received by competitive companies that buy from the same seller.

The Clayton Act

While the Sherman Act uses general language to condemn practices that do, in fact, restrain competition, the Clayton Act bars specific practices that may substantially lessen competition or tend to create a monopoly.

□ The law addresses the same restrictive buying and selling practices as the Sherman Act—exclusive dealings, requirements contracts, and tie-in agreements—but in a different way. While the Sherman Act is directed against agreements that have materialized into unreasonable restraints of trade, under the Clayton Act, exclusive dealings, tie-in agreements, and requirement contracts need only exhibit a substantial probability of becoming unreasonable restraints. In other words, the law bans these agreements if their probable effect "may be to substantially lessen competition or tend to create a monopoly in any line of commerce."

□ Mergers and acquisitions can be challenged under the law on the grounds that they may lessen competition or tend to create a monopoly. Both FTC and Justice Department require prenotification of plans for certain mergers to allow government study of the possible consequences. The government has also issued merger guidelines that give companies an idea of what percentage of the market held by the two merger candidates may trigger a government investigation or court challenge. There are three types of mergers that have been challenged in the courts— horizontal, vertical, and conglomerate.

Horizontal mergers occur when two competitors propose to merge. The government might intervene if (1) one of the removed companies is likely to have developed into a strong competitor, (2) the merged firms will assume a dominant position in the market, (3) foreclosure of eventual deconcentration of a concentrated market, and (4) there are prospects that the market will become substantially more concentrated.

Vertical mergers occur when a company either acquires its distribution channels or merges with a supplier. Competitors of a merged supplier may be seen as foreclosed from competing with it for sales to the firm that acquired the supplier. In addition, the government may be concerned that the integration of the merged companies may constitute a substantial barrier to the entry of nonintegrated firms into either the acquired or acquiring firm's market.

In conglomerate mergers, the products of the two companies are either unrelated, complementary, or are the same, but are sold in different geographic areas. The government may consider competition eliminated because one of the merger parties might have entered the other's market as a competitor or might have acquired a substantially smaller firm to achieve a toehold in the market. The merger could be attacked on the grounds that it erected barriers to entry of other firms because of the vast resources of the acquiring firm.

The Federal Trade Commission Act

This law prohibits unfair methods of competition (including most of the conduct covered under the Sherman and Clayton Acts) and unfair or deceptive acts and practices against consumers. FTC trade regulations, which have the force of law, apply nationally or regionally to a particular industry, type of anticompetitive behavior, or product.

Note: Basic knowledge of antitrust principles plus a major dose of common sense can keep a company out of antitrust woes. Certainly, the fine points of the law will change with each new court decision. But when a major shift in legislative, judicial, or enforcement policy occurs, corporate attorneys should be brought in to review its impact on company marketing plans and operations.

The Ban on False Advertising and Other "Deceptive Acts and Practices"

For the most part, advertising represents a company's window to the public. The window will project a clear image of the company and its products if the advertising message communicates the benefits of the product in an accurate and fair way. But the window can become clouded if the advertisement is false or misleading. Consumers will eventually catch on that product claims are exaggerated and will stop buying the product.

Also, a company that misleads consumers through false advertising is likely to encounter problems with the Federal Trade Commission. Through the FTC Act, which prohibits "unfair or deceptive acts or practices in commerce," the Commission monitors advertising and fields complaints from consumers and businesses. Like so many federal agencies, a majority of the Commission's rules are not spelled out in any one form. While there are some guidelines, such as those addressing endorsements in ads and industry trade rules, companies must learn what is and is not permissible either through policy statements or cease and desist orders leveled against the other firms. In fact, under the 1975 FTC Improvement Act, FTC gained a major enforcement weapon. Since then, it can notify Company A of a cease and desist order against Company B and hold Company A responsible for complying with the restriction imposed by that order.

General Limitations on Advertising

The advertiser (and possibly its agency) bears primary responsibility for the contents of the ad. To gain a measure of control over its advertising and sales promotion tactics, a company should be sure not to engage in the following practices:

1. Advertise a product that is unsafe or has the potential of injuring consumers.

2. Make false claims that may lead an unsuspecting consumer to expect more from a product than he or she will actually get.

3. Generate sales by using ads that create false impressions, such as promoting the word "free," or testimonials, or reduced special prices which are all untrue.

4. Disparage a competitor's product through false comparative advertising.

5. Tout certain product attributes without having substantive proof that the product can live up to these claims.

6. Make promises that will not be honored.

7. Misrepresent the company's services or ability to deliver a service.

8. Inaccurately claim affiliation, sponsorship, or participation with another organization.

9. Claim to offer degrees, awards, licenses, or jobs that the company is not in a position to offer.

10. Send unsolicited products and then require payment.

11. Bait consumers by advertising items they want and then trying to sell them other merchandise instead—often at a higher price.

New Policy on Deceptive Acts and Practices

In late 1983, the FTC revised its policy on deceptive practices, which seemed to have eased advertising standards. Under the new policy, the Commission decides whether an advertisement or other promotion is deceptive based on whether a "reasonable" consumer would be injured by it. Previously, an ad was considered deceptive if it had the capacity or tendency to deceive a substantial number of consumers, regardless of their level of sophistication.

Some critics, both within and outside the FTC, charged that the new policy would make it more difficult for the FTC to make a case against deceptive advertising. But a Commission member said that the policy can apply to an advertisement that is likely to harm consumers and that the FTC would not have to prove actual injury. In addition, he noted that the policy was based on recent FTC cases in which the Commission held that an ad isn't misleading if it will be misinterpreted only by an insignificant and unrepresentative segment of the population that sees it. "The idea of reasonable isn't that a consumer has to be particularly sophisticated or especially careful. Ordinary people are reasonable and ordinary people in some circumstances won't read all the fine print."

Ad Substantiation

In 1972, the FTC adopted a policy of requiring companies to have reasonable proof or substantiation to back an affirmative product claim even before it is made. Despite the high costs to the advertiser, the Commission defended the rule by pointing out that it is much more efficient for the individual seller to test its product than it is for thousands of consumers.

Comparative Advertising

The FTC defines comparative advertising as "advertising that compares alternative brands on objectively measurable attributes or price and identifies the alternative brand by name, illustration, or other distinctive information." In the 1979 policy statement, the FTC voiced its approval of comparative advertising and went so far as to say, "disparaging language is permissible so long as it is truthful and not deceptive." The FTC also made the following points: brand comparisons can be used if the basis for comparison is clearly identified, and substantiation of comparative ad claims must be made on the basis of the same standard necessary for other advertising techniques. The rule is that the advertiser must have a reasonable basis for making an advertising claim before the ad is circulated.

Caution: Despite FTC policy, companies that utilize comparative advertising have been successfully sued by their competitors. Again, in deciding such cases the courts determine whether the ad is a deceptive practice in violation of federal or state law.

Corrective Advertising

In its simplest form, this action would require the advertiser to announce that previous claims had been found by the FTC to be false or misleading and then to state the truth about the product's performance capabilities or attributes.

The rationale for corrective advertising is that the effects of a false ad campaign lasts long in the marketplace. Even after the ad has run, the consumer will continue to make purchasing decisions based on these lasting false impressions. The routine cease-and-desist order, according to FTC, does not eliminate the misimpressions nor does it return to competitors any lost market share that resulted from the false advertising. The Commission, however, uses this remedial tool only in major false advertising cases.

Appendix C

Guide to Federal Warranty Law

The following is intended as a guide to the basic features of the **Magnuson-Moss Warranty Act**, the federal law governing warranties on consumer products. The text provides citations to specific sections of the law—the Warranty Act itself, the Rules the Federal Trade Commission (FTC) adopted under the Act, and the FTC's Warranty Advertising Guides. For reference purposes, a supplement to this material containing the Act, the Rules, and the Guides is available from the FTC's Public Reference Branch.

Also addressed are some basic points of state law that you need to know to understand the requirements and prohibitions of the Magnuson-Moss Act. However, because state law varies, you should contact a private attorney or the offices of the attorneys general in the states where you do business to get specific state law information. The information is intended as a tool for you to use in consultation with your attorney, not as a substitute for your attorney's advice.

The names of the companies in the examples in this document are fictitious; any resemblance between them and the names of actual companies is completely coincidental.

Understanding Warranties

Generally, a warranty is your promise, as a manufacturer or seller, to stand behind your product. It is a statement about the integrity of your product and about your commitment to correct problems when your product fails.

The law recognizes two basic kinds of warranties—implied warranties and express warranties.

Implied Warranties

Implied warranties are unspoken, unwritten promises created by state law that go from you, as a seller or merchant, to your customers. Implied warranties are based upon the common law principle of "fair value for money spent." There are two types of implied warranties that occur in consumer product transactions. They are the **implied warranty of merchantability** and the **implied warranty of fitness for a particular purpose**.

The implied warranty of merchantability is a merchant's basic promise that the goods sold will do what they are supposed to do and that there is nothing significantly wrong with them. In other words, it is an implied promise that the goods are fit to be sold. The law says that merchants make this promise automatically every time they sell a product they are in business to sell. For example, if you, as an appliance retailer, sell an oven, you are promising that the oven is in proper condition for sale because it will do what ovens are supposed to do—bake food at controlled temperatures selected by the buyer. If the oven does not heat, or if it heats without proper temperature control, then the oven is not fit for sale as an oven, and your implied warranty of merchantability would be breached. In such a case, the law requires you to provide a remedy so that the buyer gets a working oven.

The implied warranty of fitness for a particular purpose is a promise that the law says you, as a seller, make when your customer relies on your advice that a product can be used for some specific purpose. For example, suppose you are an appliance retailer and a customer asks for a clothes washer that can handle 15 pounds of laundry at a time. If you recommend a particular model and the customer buys that model on the strength of your recommendation, the law says that you have made a warranty of fitness for a particular purpose. If the model you recommended proves unable to handle 15-pound loads, even though it may effectively wash 10-pound loads, your warranty of fitness for a particular purpose is breached.

Implied warranties are promises about the condition of products at the time they are sold, but they do not assure that a product will last for any specific length of time. (The normal durability of a product is, of course, one aspect of a product's merchantability or its fitness for a particular purpose.) Nor does the law say that everything that can possibly go wrong with a product falls within the scope of implied warranties. For example, implied warranties do not cover problems such as those caused by abuse, misuse, ordinary wear, failure to follow directions, or improper maintenance.

Generally, there is no specified duration for implied warranties under state laws. However, the state statutes of limitations for breach of either an express or an implied warranty are generally four years from date of purchase. This means that buyers have four years in which to discover and seek a remedy for problems that were present in the product at the time it was sold. It does not mean that the product must last for four years. It means only that the product must be of normal durability, considering its nature and price.

A special note is in order regarding implied warranties on used merchandise. An implied warranty of merchantability on a used product is a promise that it can be used as expected, given its type and price range. As with new merchandise, there are implied warranties on deals in such goods, but not when a sale is made by a private individual.

If you do not offer a written warranty, the law in most states allows you to disclaim implied warranties. However, selling without implied warranties may well indicate to potential customers that the product is risky—low quality, damaged, or discontinued—and therefore should be available at a lower price.

In order to disclaim implied warranties, you must inform consumers in a conspicuous manner, and generally in writing, that you will not be responsible if the product malfunctions or is defective. It must be clear to consumers that the entire product risk falls on them. You must specifically indicate that you do not warrant "merchantability," or you must use a phrase such as "with all faults," or "as is." A few states have special laws on how you must phrase on "as is" disclosure. (For specific information on how your state treats "as is" disclosures, consult your attorney.)

Some states do not allow you to sell consumer products "as is." At this time, these states are Alabama, Connecticut, Kansas, Maine, Maryland, Massachusetts, Minnesota, Mississippi, New Hampshire, Vermont, Washington, West Virginia, and the District of Columbia. In those states, sellers have implied warranty obligations that cannot be avoided.

Federal law prohibits you from disclaiming implied warranties on any consumer product if you offer a written warranty for that product or sell a service contract on it.

You should be aware that even if you sell a product "as is" and it proves to be defective or dangerous and causes personal injury to someone, you still may be liable under the principles of product liability. Selling the product "as is" does not eliminate this liability.

Express Warranties

Express warranties, unlike implied warranties, are not "read into" your sales contracts by state law; rather, you explicitly offer these warranties to your customers in the course of a sales transaction. They are promises and statements that you voluntarily make about your product or about your commitment to remedy the defects and malfunctions that some customers may experience.

Express warranties can take a variety of forms, ranging from advertising claims to formal certificates. An express warranty can be made either orally or in writing. While oral warranties are important, only written warranties on consumer products are covered by the Magnuson-Moss Warranty Act.

Understanding the Magnuson-Moss Act

The Magnuson-Moss Warranty Act is the federal law that governs consumer product warranties. Passed by Congress in 1975, the Act requires manufacturers and sellers of consumer products to provide consumers with detailed information about warranty coverage. In addition, it affects both the rights of consumers and obligations of warrantors under written warranties.

To understand the Act, it is useful to be aware of Congress's intentions in passing it. First, Congress wanted to ensure that consumers could get complete information about warranty terms and conditions. By providing consumers with a way of learning what warranty coverage is offered on a product before they buy, the Act gives consumers a way to know what to expect if something goes wrong, and thus helps to increase customer satisfaction.

Second, Congress wanted to ensure that consumers could compare warranty coverage before buying. By comparing, consumers can choose a product with the best combination of price, features, and warranty coverage to meet their individual needs.

Third, Congress intended to promote competition on the basis of warranty coverage. By assuring that consumers can get warranty information, the Act encourages sales promotion on the basis of warranty coverage and competition among companies to meet consumer preferences through various levels of warranty coverage.

Finally, Congress wanted to strengthen existing incentives for companies to perform their warranty obligations in a timely and thorough manner and to resolve any disputes with a minimum of delay and expense to consumers. Thus, the Act makes it easier for consumers to pursue a remedy for breach of warranty in the courts, but it also creates a framework for companies to set up procedures for resolving disputes inexpensively and informally, without litigation.

Stating Terms and Conditions of Your Written Warranty

The FTC's Rule on Disclosure of Written Consumer Product Warranty Terms and Conditions (the Disclosure Rule) requires a written warranty on a consumer product that costs more than $15 to be clear, easy to read, and contain certain specified items of information about its coverage.

To help you comply with the law and make your warranty clear and easy to read, you may wish to refer to Writing Readable Warranties, an FTC manual that is available from the Government Printing Office.

The information you must disclose in your warranty is explained in the remainder of this chapter. This information includes basic information about aspects of warranty coverage common to all written warranties, and specific information that is required only when your warranty contains certain optional terms and conditions.

Base Information Required for All Warranties

Under the FTC's Disclosure Rule, there are five basic aspects of coverage that your warranty must describe. It is useful to think of these as five questions that your warranty must answer:

1. **What does the warranty cover/not cover?** Answering this question is quite simple when the warranty covers every type of malfunction or defect that may appear in all parts of the product. However, if not all parts or not all types of defects are covered, you should clearly describe the scope of coverage.

2. **What is the period of coverage?** If coverage begins at some point in time other than the purchase date, your warranty must state the time or event that begins the coverage. Also, you must make it clear when coverage ends if some particular event would terminate it.

3. **What will you do to correct problems?** This requires an explanation of the remedy you offer under the warranty. This could be repair or replacement of the product, a refund of the purchase price, or a credit toward subsequent purchases.

    If necessary for clarity, you must also explain what you will not do. This requires a description of the types of expenses, if any, that you will not cover. This might include, for example, labor charges, consequential damages (the cost of repairing or replacing other property that is damaged when the warranted product fails, such as food spoilage when a refrigerator breaks down), or incidental damages (the costs a consumer incurs in order to obtain warranty service, such as towing charges, telephone charges, time lost from work, transportation costs, and the cost of renting a product temporarily to replace the warranted product).

4. **How can the customer get warranty service?** Your warranty must tell customers who they can go to for warranty service and how to reach those persons or companies. This means that the warranty needs to include the name and address of your company, and any person or office customers should contact. If they can call you locally or toll-free, you can give the telephone number instead of the address. If you want customers to contact your local or regional service centers first, explain how this should be done.

5. **How will the state law affect your customer's rights under the warranty?** Your warranty must answer this question because implied warranty rights and certain other warranty rights vary from state to state. Rather than require a detailed explanation about this on a state-by-state basis, the FTC adopted the following "boilerplate" disclosure to address this issue, which must be included in every consumer product warranty: "This warranty gives you specific legal rights, and you may also have other rights which vary from state to state."

Specific Information Required When Your Warranty Contains Certain Optional Terms and Conditions

Generally, if you wish to impose on your customers any obligations other than notifying you that they need service, you must state these obligations in your warranty. Also, if you wish to establish any other conditions, limitations, or terms that you intend to enforce, you must state them in your warranty; you cannot have "hidden" requirements. An example of such a condition or limitation would be a provision voiding the warranty if the serial number on the product is defaced.

There are also a number of other disclosures you must make in your warranty if it contains certain optional terms and conditions. These requirements are explained in the following paragraphs.

If your warranty contains a provision that restricts the duration of implied warranties, the Disclosure Rule requires you to include a statement that state law may override such restrictions. This is required because some states prohibit any restrictions on implied warranties. The requirement applies only to limited warranties, because only in limited warranties can you restrict the duration of implied warranties. To tell consumers that state law may not permit such a restriction, the Disclosure Rule requires you to use the following language: "Some states do not allow limitations on how long an implied warranty lasts, so the above limitation may not apply to you."

If your warranty contains a provision intended to restrict or eliminate your potential liability for consequential or incidental damages, you must include a statement that state law may not allow such a provision. To inform consumers that state law may not permit such a restriction, the Disclosure Rule requires that you use the following sentence: "Some states do not allow the exclusion or limitation of incidental or consequential damages, so the above limitation or exclusion may not apply to you."

If your warranty contains a provision that restricts who has rights under the warranty, you must include a statement explaining specifically who is covered. For example, if your limited warranty is valid only for the first purchaser, your warranty must state that. Note that this applies only to limited warranties. A full warranty must cover anyone who owns the product during the period of coverage.

If your warranty contains a provision that requires your customers to use a dispute resolution mechanism before suing under the federal Magnuson-Moss Warranty Act for breach of warranty, you must include:

- □ A statement informing customers that they can sue under state law without first using the mechanism, but that before suing under the Magnuson-Moss Act, they must first try to resolve the dispute through the mechanism.

- □ Information and materials about the dispute mechanism, including the name and address or a toll-free telephone number, or a form for filing a claim.

Of course, if you include a dispute resolution requirement in your warranty, the informal dispute resolution mechanism must comply with the FTC's Dispute Resolution Rule.

Making Warranties Available Prior to Sale

The FTC's Rule on Pre-Sale Availability of Written Warranty Terms requires that written warranties on consumer products costing more that $15 be available to consumers before they buy. The Rule has provisions that specify what retailers, including mail order, catalog, and door-to-door sellers, must do to accomplish this. The Rule also specifies what manufacturers must do so that sellers can meet their obligations under the Rule. These provisions are explained in this section.

What the Retailer Must Do

If you sell directly to consumers who come to your place of business to buy, you must make written warranties available at the point of sale. You must do this with all written warranties on the products you sell—warranties from manufacturers, as well as any written warranties you extend.

The Pre-Sale Availability Rule requires that sellers make warranties readily available to prospective buyers either by displaying them in close proximity to the warranted products, or by furnishing them upon request prior to sale and posting prominent signs to let customers know that warranties can be examined upon request. The Rule does not specify any particular method for fulfilling its requirements. For example, an appliance retailer might post a refrigerator warranty on the front of the appliance or in the freezer compartment. A retailer of small products, such as watches or electric razors, might keep the warranties readily available behind the counter, or keep them indexed in a binder near the warranted products and post signs stating their availability. Any of these methods is acceptable.

What Mail Order Companies Must Do

If you accept orders for warranted consumer products through the mail or by telephone, your catalog or other advertising must include either the warranty or a statement telling consumers how to get a copy. This information should be near the product description or clearly noted on a separate page. If you choose the latter, you must provide a page reference to the warranty statement near the product description.

What Door-to-Door Sale Companies Must Do

If you sell warranted products to consumers in their homes, or in some place other than your place of business, you must offer the customer copies of the written warranties before the sale is completed.

What Manufacturers Must Do

If you are a manufacturer and offer written warranties, you must provide retailers of your product with the warranty materials they will need to meet their requirements as described above. There are any number of ways to do this: you may provide copies of the warranty to be placed in a binder; provide warranty stickers, tags, signs, or posters; or print the warranty on your product's packaging. As long as you have provided retailers with the warranty materials they need to comply with the rule, you are not legally responsible if they fail to make your warranties available.

Advertising Warranties

The Magnuson-Moss Warranty Act does not cover the advertising of warranties. However, warranty advertising falls within the scope of the FTC Act, which generally prohibits "unfair or deceptive acts or practices in or affecting commerce." Therefore, it is a violation of the FTC Act to advertise a warranty deceptively.

To help companies understand what the law requires, the FTC has issued guidelines called the *Guides for Advertising Warranties and Guarantees*. However, the Guides do not cover every aspect of warranty advertising, and cannot substitute for consultation with your attorney on warranty advertising matters. To obtain a copy, contact the FTC at the address included later in this appendix.

The Guides cover three principal topics: how to advertise a warranty that is covered by the Pre-Sale Availability Rule; how to advertise a satisfaction guarantee; and how to advertise a lifetime guarantee or warranty.

How to Advertise Warranties Covered by the Pre-Sale Availability Rule

In general, the Guides advise that if a print or broadcast ad for a consumer product mentions a warranty, and the advertised product is covered by the

Pre-Sale Availability Rule (that is, the product is sold in stores for more that $15), then the ad should inform consumers that a copy of the warranty is available to read prior to sale at the place where the product is sold. Print or broadcast advertisements that mention a warranty on any consumer product that can be purchased through the mail or by telephone should inform consumers how to get a copy of the warranty.

For advertisements of consumer products costing $15 or less, the Guides do not call for the pre-sale availability disclosure. Instead, the Guides advise that the FTC's legal decisions and policy statements are the sole sources of guidance on how to avoid unfairness or deception in advertising warranties. Consult your attorney for assistance in researching and applying the FTC's case decisions and policy statements.

How to Advertise a Satisfaction Guarantee

The Guides advise that, regardless of the price of the product, advertising terms such as "satisfaction guaranteed" or "money back guarantee" should be used only if the advertiser is willing to provide full refunds to customers when, for any reason, they return the merchandise.

The Guides further advise that an ad mentioning a satisfaction guarantee or similar offer should inform consumers of any material conditions or limitations on the offer. For example, a restriction on the offer to a specific time period, such as 30 days, is a material condition that should be disclosed.

How to Advertise a Lifetime Warranty or Guarantee

"Lifetime" warranties or guarantees can be a source of confusion for consumers. This is because it is often difficult to tell just whose life measures the period of coverage. "Lifetime" can be used in at least three ways. For example, a warrantor of an auto muffler may intend his "lifetime" warranty's duration to be for the life of the car on which the muffler is installed. In this case, the muffler warranty would be transferable to subsequent owners of the car and would remain in effect throughout the car's useful life.

Or the warrantor of the muffler might intend a "lifetime" warranty to last as long as the original purchaser of the muffler owns the car on which the muffler is installed. Although commonly used, this is an inaccurate application of the term "lifetime."

Finally, "lifetime" can be used to describe a warranty that lasts as long as the original purchaser of the product lives. This is probably the least common usage of the term.

The Guides advise that to avoid confusing consumers about the duration of the "lifetime" warranty or guarantee, ads should tell consumers which "life" measures the warranty's duration. In that way, consumers will know which meaning of the term "lifetime" you intend.

Offering Service Contracts

A service contract is an optional agreement for product service that customers sometimes buy. It provides additional protection beyond what the warranty offers on the product. Service contracts are similar to warranties in that both concern service for a product. However, there are differences between warranties and service contracts.

Warranties come with a product and are included in the purchase price. In the language of the Act, warranties are "part of the basis of the bargain." Service contracts, on the other hand, are agreements that are separate from the contract or sale of the product. They are separate either because they are made some time after the sale of the product, or because they cost the customer a fee beyond the purchase price of the product.

The Act includes very broad provisions governing service contracts that are explained in the following sections.

Statement of Terms and Conditions

If you offer a service contract, the Act requires you to list conspicuously all terms and conditions in simple and readily understood language. However, unlike warranties, service contracts are not required to be titled "full" or "limited," or to contain the special standard disclosures. In fact, using warranty disclosures in service contracts could confuse customers about whether the agreement is a warranty or a service contract.

The company that makes the service contract is responsible for ensuring that the terms and conditions are disclosed as required by the law. This is not the responsibility of the seller or the service contract, unless the seller and the maker are the same company.

Disclaimer or Limitation of Implied Warranties

Sellers of consumer products who make service contracts on their products are prohibited under the Act from disclaiming or limiting implied warranties. (Remember also that sellers who extend written warranties on consumer products cannot disclaim implied warranties, regardless of whether they make service contracts on their products.) However, sellers of consumer products that merely sell service contracts as agents of service contract companies and do not themselves extend written warranties can disclaim implied warranties on the products they sell.

Additional Sources of Information

For additional information regarding the text of the Magnuson-Moss Warranty Act, the related FTC Rules, and the FTC Warranty Advertising Guides, write:

> Federal Trade Commission
> Public Reference Branch
> Washington, D.C. 20580

For other FTC warranty-related business manuals, contact the U.S. Government Printing Sales Office at (202) 783-3238.

Appendix D

Market Research Data Sources

To gather the data necessary to back up your belief in your product or service, you must do market research. This means looking into and becoming aware and knowledgeable of both your potential customers and your potential competition. You can be sure that if your product or service is successful there will be competition.

The first and most logical place to start is with a listing of your company's competitors. If you don't know who they are, then visit a major public library, where you should be able to locate the pertinent information. For those who do not know how to use a business library, a book on this subject may help:

Johnson, H. Webster, and S.W. McFarland. *How to Use the Business Library, with Sources of Business Information.* 4th ed. Cincinnati: Southwestern Company, 1957. Write the publisher of this paperback at: 5101 Madison Road, Cincinnati, Ohio 45227.

The major part of this book covers specific publications (handbooks, periodicals, business services, government publications), but there are also brief sections on the mechanics of locating information in libraries, writing reports, and using audiovisual aids, as well as on data processing.

Directories

Business directories are usually available through library services that provide information on products, manufacturers, potential buyers, and trade associations. A good place to start is the reference book:

Guide to American Directories, 9th ed. Rye, N.Y.: B. Klein Publications, 1975. Contact the publisher at: 11 Third Street, Rye, N.Y. 10580).

Its information on directories, classified by industry, profession, and function, is useful for identifying specific directories to locating sources of supply (competitors) and new markets.

Library services can also provide manufacturers' directories, often by state and industry. One of these is:

United States Industrial Directory, published by the Cahners Publishing Company, 89 Franklyn Street, Boston, Mass. 02110.

This three-volume set lists manufacturers alphabetically and gives a description of each firm's product lines, the number of employees, the address, and telephone numbers. A classified section includes products with names and addresses of manufacturers (competitors). The directory also offers special sections with chemical and mechanical data and trademark and trade name identifications.

Another good directory is:

Thomas Register of American Manufacturers, published annually by the Thomas Publishing Company, One Penn Plaza, New York, N.Y. 10001.

This 11-volume set is a purchasing guide, listing names of manufacturers (competitors), producers, and similar sources of supply in all lines.

Financial directories are an invaluable source of information. The *Dun & Bradstreet Reference Book*, published six times a year, contains the names and ratings of nearly three million businesses of all types located throughout the United States and Canada.

An excellent financial reference source for the electronics industry is:

Electonic News Financial Fact Book and Directory, published annually by the Book Division of Fairchild Publications, 7 E. 12th Street, New York, N.Y. 10003.

An alphabetical listing of most publicly held electronics corporations, it includes company addresses, corporate officers, directors, areas of work, divisions, subsidiaries, and a five year financial history covering sales and earnings, revenues by line of business, common stock, common stock equity, income account, assets, liabilities, and a statistical summary.

A directory for studying competitive successes and failures is:

World's Who's Who in Finance and Industry, published by Who's Who, Inc., 200 East Ohio Street, Chicago, Ill. 60611.

It provides biographical information of men and women prominent in finance, industry, and trade.

Security Exchange Commission and Other Public Sources

A listing of your competitors and data on each can be compiled by researching privately published directories and other sources. If your competitor is a public corporation, the job is simplified. Extensive company data are found in the registration statements, prospectus, proxy statements, and other reports resulting from the full-disclosure requirements of:

Securities and Exchange Commission (SEC)
Interstate Commerce Commission (ICC)
Federal Power Commission (FPC)
Federal Communications Commission (FCC)
Civil Aeronautics Board (CAB)
New York Stock Exchange (NYSE)

A registration statement is the basic disclosure document for a public distribution of securities registered under the Securities Act. It is made up of two parts. The first section, the prospectus, is the only part that is generally distributed to the public. It contains a wealth of information on company history, investment risk factors, use of stock proceeds, and capitalization; a financial statement of operations (usually covering several years); and a description of the business. It includes a general description of the products and their market, the percentage of sales for each, and how the products are marketed. Competition, product development, manufacturing facilities, number of employees, officers, remuneration of officers, stock option plans, principal and selling shareholders, and balance sheets are also discussed. The prospectus, in other words, offers everything you always wanted to know about your competitor but were afraid to ask.

Part two of the registration statement contains information of a more technical nature dealing with such matters as marketing arrangements, the expenses of distribution, relationships between the registrant and certain experts, sales of securities to special parties, recent sales of unregistered securities to subsidiaries, and the treatment of proceeds being registered.

The Exchange Act has four types of disclosure requirements relating to registration, periodic reporting, proxy solicitation, and insider trading. Listed (New York and American exchanges) and OTC (over the counter exchange) registered companies are required to file certain periodic reports. The most important of these reports are Forms 8K, 10K, and 10Q, of which 10K is the most useful for obtaining competitive information.

Form 10K is an annual report due 90 days after the end of the fiscal year. It contains certified financial statements, including a balance sheet, a profit and loss statement for each fiscal year covered by the report, an analysis of surplus, and supporting schedules. It includes a breakdown of both sales and earnings for each major line of business, although a company with sales greater than $50 million does not have to carry an individual breakdown unless a product line contributes 10 percent or more to the total volume of pretax profits. Although smaller companies must break out such product line data on their annual 10K reports to the SEC, they need not disclose the information in the annual report to their shareholders.

The 10K report must reveal the amount spent on R&D in the preceding year, the size of order backlogs, the availability of essential raw materials, competitive conditions in the industry, and the financial statements of unconsolidated majority-owned subsidiaries. The 10K report must also disclose any leasing and rental commitments and their dollar impact on both present and future earnings. The 10K report is therefore an information bonanza for evaluating a competitor's business.

Since not all of the information in a 10K report finds its way into the company's annual report to the shareholders, competitive research should be done with the 10K supplementing the annual report.

Large public libraries, larger financial houses, and leading business school libraries have microfilm copies of 10K reports and up to ten other reporting documents that are required by law. A company's 10K report can usually be obtained by requesting a copy in writing from the company's financial officer or marketing vice-president.

If a competitor is a private corporation, then the data, though more difficult to obtain, are not out of reach for an aware and observant analyst. Data are often published in the newspapers, trade journals, and information bulletins reporting on new contract awards and their value (companies love to announce these), contract losers, personnel movements, litigation, new product announcements and prices, user-reported product problems and manufacturers' responsiveness in correcting them, and other pertinent data.

Information Sources Within Your Industry

Trade shows offer a wealth of information. Visit your competitors' product booths and examine their products for the latest features, strengths, and weaknesses. Listen to their salespeople's stories, especially what they are telling other prospects. Many trade shows have seminars where competitors often present papers on their products and/or developments. This can be a rich source of information.

Another less-glamorous technique includes interviewing your competitors' personnel for positions in your own company. Much can be learned through intelligent questioning about their operations without compromising an employee's position.

If a competitor is local, a periodic inspection of its parking lot during working hours will reveal if its employee count is up or down, which has a direct relationship to its business activity.

Keep a current file on your competitors' product brochures and specifications. Often, changes in these indicate trends in a company or in the industry itself. Competitive information is available, if only you have the imagination, alertness, and determination to uncover it.

Evaluating the collected data to determine why a competitor is a success or a failure is the more difficult side of information gathering. With a public corporation, first examine the bottom-line profit on their income statements for several years to determine if they are a success or a failure. Since one good year doesn't make a success and one bad year doesn't make a failure, look for trends. A consistent growth in net profit in actual dollars and percentages of sales over a period of years certainly indicates a successful operation. Conversely, a consistent decline would seem to indicate failure. If a business is sensitive to national economic expansion and recession, then national conditions figure into your calculation.

A further examination of a business's income statement will reveal how it has allocated its sales dollar among labor, material, overhead, engineering, marketing, and G&A. If its allocation has been a success, try to duplicate it. If not, compare the expenditures against those of a successful company and try to determine the cause of failure. Knowing why a company has failed is as valuable as knowing why it succeeded.

If labor costs are too high or low, question why. If labor costs are too high, perhaps the firm has priced itself out of the market. If too low, it may have caused high labor turnover and thus incurred increased training costs and inefficiencies. This liability may show up in other cost areas, such as increased overhead and scrap. If labor turnover is high, question why. Is it because of low wages, poor working conditions, poor management, or even a high turnover in management itself?

If overhead costs are too high, perhaps your competitor has a staff larger than is required to do the job. Or perhaps building rent and operating costs are more than they should be. If overhead costs are too low, it could mean there is inadequate supervision to maximize labor's efforts. The same logic holds true for engineering, marketing, and G&A. Not spending enough is just as bad, and sometimes worse, than spending too much. Striking the right balance is the key.

If it is possible, and it often times is, visit and tour your competitor's facility. Be observant. Are their offices and manufacturing areas neat, clean, and well organized for a smooth logical flow of raw materials to completed and shipped products? Or are they unkempt and helter-skelter? It is often stated that the cleanliness and physical organization of a company is a direct reflection of its managment's thinking and a yardstick for measuring a product's quality.

The behavior of a firm's personnel is very revealing. If they are neat about themselves, it usually means that they generally take pride in their work. This point should not be taken lightly because it is people, not things, that make a company succeed or fail.

Observe the offices, how they are decorated, and the type of factory equipment employed. If a facility's furniture, floor and wall trappings, and manufacturing equipment are more expensive than required, it is also a reflection of management's thinking. Its priorities indicate whether the company will succeed or fail.

If financial statements are not available and facility tours are not possible, much can still be learned about a competitor's success or failure by examining its product—in detail! Buy one and have a manufacturing, purchasing, and engineering team dissect and examine it objectively.

A manufacturing expert can determine how it was put together and how much it cost to do so. The engineers can evaluate its performance and estimate its design and manufacturing cost. The industrial engineers and purchasing department buyers can estimate piece parts and subassembly costs. Put all the pieces together, and the development and manufacturing costs will be known.

The marketing people will know its selling price, competitor's discount policies, facility size, manufacturing capability, sales force, and customer base. The marketing data provides the remaining puzzle pieces. Product costs, gross margins, expenses, and profits (or losses) can be estimated.

Knowing your competitor's customer base even reveals the likelihood of their (your competition) being paid on time and discloses something about their financial condition. Added finance charges must either be absorbed (subtracted from profits) or passed on to the customer (higher prices).

Executive and first-level management stability is also an indicator of a successful or failing company. If the financial reports are available for several years, examine the names filling the executive management posts. If the same names appear year after year, it indicates stability. If not, it may mean that the company is still trying to find the right combination to make it work.

The same holds true for the first-level managers. Trade journals regularly report their comings and goings. Management changes are expensive. They cause morale problems, which foster inefficiency. This in turn is reflected in lower productivity, lower quality, higher costs, and the bottom line: lower profits.

There are many ways to be an effective industrial management detective and to evaluate competitive reasons for success or failure. It just requires imagination and common sense.

Summary

In summary, valuable lessons can be learned about how to and, equally important, how not to manage your organization by studying competitors' successes and failures. The first step is to determine who they are, using the resources of local public libraries.

If your competition is a public corporation, a library that carries its 10K report can provide much of the financial data needed to evaluate its profit and loss situation and how it spends its revenue. Compare the same type expenses for a successful and a not-so-successful competitor to determine what was done right and what was done wrong.

If your competitor is a private corporation, the business section of newspapers, trade journals, and trade shows are valuable sources of competitive information. They can often provide insights into what the other guy is doing right, or wrong.

Facility tours will reveal clues as to how management thinks and spends money, which has a direct bearing on success and failure. Product dissection and examination also tell a story about a product's performance and costs, which will be reflected in your competitors' profit and loss statements.

Finally, an examination of your competition's management stability will provide additional clues to its success or failure. Being successful in evaluating competitors requires only imagination and common sense.

Other Market Research Sources

The following reference sources are available through most public libraries and yield valuable marketing and competitive information:

- □ U.S. Industrial Outlook
- □ Industry Surveys
- □ Annual Statement Studies—Robert Morris Associates
- □ Industry Norms and Key Ratios—Dun and Bradstreet
- □ *Standard Industrial Classification (SIC) Manual.* Gives the definitions of the classifications of industrial establishments by activity engaged in and by SIC codes, which the government and the business information industry use to classify and track all segments of industry. The SIC classifies firms by the type of activity they are engaged in, and it is used to promote the uniformity and comparability of statistical data relating to market research.

Other helpful sources of information include:

Census of Business for 1982. Retail—U.S. Summary. Final figures from the 1982 Census of Retail Trade, includes statistical totals for each region, state, city, and standard metropolitan area. Tabulated by type of establishment.

Census of Manufacturers for 1982. Five-volume report about manufacturing industries. Location of manufacturing plants tabulated by state and counties.

Census of Wholesale Trade of 1982. Two-volume report of wholesalers, including geographical breakdowns by states, cities over 5000 population, and standard metropolitan statistical areas.

Census of Selected Service Industries for 1982. Two-volume report of more than 150 kinds of service industries.

Census of Population for 1980. Most complete source of population data in the United States. Census is taken every ten years.

County Business Patterns, 1982. A series of publications presenting first quarter employment and payroll statistics by county and industry. Separate reports issued for each of the 50 states, the District of Columbia, Puerto Rico, and outlying areas of the United States.

County and City Data Book. Contains data for 50 states, 3141 counties or county equivalents, 840 cities of 25,000 inhabitants or more, among others.

Statistical Abstracts of the United States. A general review of statistical data collected by the United States government and other public and private organizations. A good source of secondary data.

Survey of Current Business. The most current monthly and quarterly statistics on a number of general business and economic topics.

Business Statistics. A historical record of the statistics presented monthly in the Survey of Current Business.

Federal Reserve Bulletin. Current economic indicators and analysis of changing financial conditions.

Survey of Consumer Expenditures. Includes comprehensive information about consumer expenditures.

Census of Manufacturers (U.S. Department of Commerce). Detailed information on manufacturers by industry (SIC), includes number of establishments, employment, wages, and sales by customer categories. Published every five years. Priced by publication series.

Annual Survey of Manufacturers (U.S. Department of Commerce). Not as detailed as census but more timely. Data obtained from estimates rather than actual count. Generally available in the spring of each year. Priced by publication series.

County Business Patterns (U.S. Department of Commerce). Statistics by state and county on number of businesses by type (SIC), employment, and payroll data. Published annually. Includes summary volume and one for each state. Each volume approximately $5.00.

U.S. Industrial Outlook (U.S. Department of Commerce). Profiles about 200 manufacturing and nonmanufacturing industries, provides shipment values and market projections. Published annually. Price approximately $9.00.

Census of Population (U.S. Department of Commerce). Detailed data on U.S. population by geographic regions including such demographic breakdowns as sex, marital status, age, education, race, ethnic background, family size, employment, and income levels. Published every ten years. Priced by publication series.

Current Population Reports (U.S. Department of Commerce). Regular series of publications that includes interim reports on population estimates, projections, and special analysis of population characteristics. Priced by subscription series.

Statistical Abstract of the United States (U.S. Department of Commerce). Compendium of historic statistical tables covering a wide range of subjects including a variety of demographic and business enterprise data, and producer and consumer price indexes. Published annually in December. Price approximately $19.00.

State and Metropolitan Area Data Book (U.S. Department of Commerce). Compendium of statistical information on population, households, income, employment, housing finance, and trade for each census region, division, and state. Annual. Price approximately $15.00.

Bureau of Census Catalog (U.S. Department of Commerce). Subject guide to Census Bureau publications. Aside from those above, includes publications on such topics as agriculture, housing, and foreign trade. Annual. Price approximately $6.50.

Note: U.S. Department of Commerce publications listed are available from the Superintendent of Documents, Government Printing Office, Washington, DC 20402.

American Statistics Index (Congressional Information Service, Washington, DC). Comprehensive, detailed subject guide to all statistical publications of the federal government including administrative agencies, congressional committees, and federally sponsored studies. Updated monthly. Annual subscription approximately $1,550.

Survey of U.S. Industrial and Commercial Buying Power (*Sales and Marketing Management Magazine*, New York, NY). Statistical presentation of value of shipments by industry classification (SIC) by state and county. Published annually in April. Price approximately $35.

Survey of Buying Power (*Sales and Marketing Management Magazine*, New York, NY). Latest data on population, income, and retail sales by state, county, SMSA, and city. Published annually in two parts. Price for two volumes approximately $100.

Moody's Manuals: IndustrCiales; Bank & Finance; Public Utilities; Transportation; Municipal and Government (Moody's Investors Service, New York, NY). Detailed reports on publicly held companies and publicly financed government obligations; includes historical, financial, and statistical data on each company and government unit. Published annually. Manuals range from $400 to $600.

Million Dollar Directory (Dun & Bradstreet, New York, NY). Information on companies with assets of $500,000 and over. Includes identification of corporate officers, sales volume, number of employees, and product lines. Published annually, three volumes. Available on lease basis for $600 per year.

Standard & Poor's Register of Corporations, Directors and Executives (Standard & Poor's Corporation, New York, NY). Lists over 30,000 corporations, identifies executives, and provides data on sales, number of employees, and product lines. Published annually. Available on lease basis for $270 per year.

Thomas Register of American Manufacturers (Thomas Publishing Company, New York, NY). Lists over 100,000 manufacturing companies by company and product categories. Selected product catalogs included. Published annually, 18 volumes. Price $160.

Directory of Industry Data Sources—U.S. and Canada (Ballinger/Harfax, Cambridge, MA). Identifies and describes published research reports, surveys, data bases, and reference materials on 60 industries. Published annually. Price $195.

Guide to the High Technology Industries—a companion volume that concentrates on these industries alone. Price $65.

Findex: Directory of Market Research Reports, Studies, and Surveys (FIND:SVP, New York, NY). Provides brief descriptions by subject categories of over 7,000 marketing reports available from major market research houses and other sources. Published annually with supplements. Price $165.

Directory of U.S. and Canadian Marketing Surveys and Services (C.H. Kline and Company, Fairfield, NJ). Brief descriptions of over 3,000 available multiclient market research reports and descriptions of services provided by research firms. Published biannually. Price $145.

Directory of Online Databases (Cuadra Associates, Inc., Santa Monica, CA). Brief descriptions of bibliographic, full text, and numeric computerized data bases, indexed by subject to enable users to locate appropriate sources by area of interest. Access to data bases is individually priced by producers, in most cases on a per-minute basis plus telecommunication charges, and in some instances per-print series or page. (**Note:** Most of the material listed in these pages is available on-line as well as in the print forms described here.)

The Encyclopedia of Associations (Gale Research, Detroit, MI). Directory of over 16,000 trade and professional organizations with brief schedules. Many of these organizations are sources of primary and secondary statistical and analytical reports on their respective industries. Published annually with supplemental updates. Price $170.

Ayer Directory of Publications (Ayer Press, Fort Washington, PA). Primarily intended as a public relations directory, it includes over 22,000 newspapers and magazines arranged geographically listing publishers, editors, advertising managers, and circulation figures. Published annually. Price $95.

Predicasts F&S Index United States (Predicasts, Cleveland, OH). Index to trade and business periodical articles arranged by industry codes and company names. Also publishes *F&S Index International*, and *F&S Index Europe*. Monthly with cumulative updates. Price $600 per year each.

Business Periodicals Index (H.W. Wilson Company, New York, NY). The standard subject index to articles in business and trade periodicals. Monthly with cumulative updates. Price based on periodical subscription holdings of subscriber institution.

Sources of Ratio Analyses from All Industries

To be able to compare your business with other businesses in your industry, it is necessary to obtain pertinent data on other businesses. The following are sources of this information:

1. Dun & Bradstreet, Inc., Business Information Systems, 99 Church Street, New York, NY 10007. This firm publishes ratios in 125 lines of business annually. Copies can be obtained free on request.

2. Accounting Corporation of America, 1929 First Avenue, San Diego, CA 92101. This organization publishes *Parameter of Small Businesses*, which classifies its operating ratios for various industry groups on the basis of gross volume.

3. National Cash Register Co., Marketing Services Department, Dayton, OH 45409. This firm publishes *Expenses in Retail Businesses*, which examines the cost of operations in over 50 kinds of businesses obtained from primary sources, most of which are trade associations.

4. Robert Morris Associates, Philadelphia National Bank Building, Philadelphia, PA 19107. This firm has developed and published ratio studies for over 225 lines of business.

5. The Small Business Administration. The SBA has a new series of reports that provide expenses as a percentage of sales for many industries. Although the reports do not provide strict ratio information, a comparison of percentage expenses will be very useful for your financial management. Contact your Regional office.

6. Trade Associations. National associations which have published ratio studies in the past include the following:

   American Association of Advertising Agencies, 666 Third Avenue, 13th Fl., New York, NY 10017

   American Camping Association, 5000 State Road, 67N, Martinsville, Indiana 46151

American Meat Institute, P.O. Box 3556, Washington, DC 20007

American Paper Institute, 260 Madison Avenue, New York, NY 10016

American Society of Association Executives, 1575 Eye Street, N.W., Washington, DC 20005

American Supply Association, 20 N. Wacker Drive, Suite 2260, Chicago, IL 60606

Bowling Proprietors Association of America, Box 5802, Arlington, TX 76011

Building Owners and Managers Association, International, 1250 Eye Street, N.W., Suite 200, Washington, DC 20005

Door and Hardware Institute, 7711 Old Springhouse Road, McLean, VA 22102

Florist's Transworld Delivery Association/Interflora, 29200 Northwestern Highway, Southfield, Michigan 48037

Foodservice Equipment Distributors Association, 332 South Michigan Avenue, Chicago, IL 60604

Food Market Institute, Inc., 1750 K Street, N.W., Suite 700, Washington, DC 20006

Laundry and Cleaners Allied Trades Association, 543 Valley Road, Montclair, NJ 07043

Material Handling Equipment Distributors Association, 201 Rt. 45, Vernon Hills, IL 60061

Mechanical Contractors Association of America, 540 Grosvenor Lane, Suite 120, Bethesda, MD 20814

Menswear Retailers of America, 2011 Eye Street, N.W., Washington, DC 20006

Motor and Equipment Manufacturer's Association of America, P.O. Box 1638, 300 Sylvan Avenue, Englewood Cliffs, NJ 07632

National American Wholesale Grocers' Association, 201 Park Washington Court, Falls Church, VA 22046

National Appliance and Radio-TV Dealers Association, 10 East 22nd Street, Lombard, IL 60148

National Arts Material Trade Association, 178 Lakeview Avenue, Clifton, NJ 07011

National Association of Accountants, P.O. Box 433, Ten Paragon Drive, Montvale, NJ 07645

National Association of Electrical Distributors, 28 Cross Street, Norwalk, CT 06581

National Association of Food Chains, 1750 K Street, N.W., Suite 700, Washington, DC 20006

National Association of Furniture Manufacturers, P.O. Box 497, High Point, NC 27261

National Association of Independent Insurance Agents of America, 100 Church Street, 14th Floor, New York, NY 10007

National Association of Music Merchants, Inc., 5140 Avenida Encinas, Carlsbad, CA 92008

National Association of Plastics Distributors, 5001 College Blvd., Suite 201, Leawood, Kansas 66211

National Grocers' Association, 1825 Samuel Morse Drive, Reston, VA 22090

National Association of Textile and Apparel Distributors, P.O. Box 1325, Melbourne, FL 32902

National Association of Tobacco Distributors, 1199 N. Fairfax Street, Suite 701, Alexandria, VA 22314

National Automatic Merchandising Association, 20 N. Wacker Drive, Chicago, IL 60606

National Beer Wholesaler Association, 5205 Leesburg Pike, Suite 505, Falls Church, VA 22041

National Confectioners Association of the United States, 645 N. Michigan Ave., Suite 1006, Chicago, IL 60611

National Financial Services Association, 1101 14th Street, N.W., Washington, DC 20005

National Decorating Products Association, 1050 N. Lindbergh Blvd., St. Louis, MO 63132

National Electrical Contractors Association, Inc., 7315 Wisconsin Avenue, Bethesda, MD 20037

National Farm and Power Equipment Dealers Association, 10877 Watson Road, P.O. Box 8517, St. Louis, MO 63126

National Home Furnishings Association, 220 West Gerry Lane, Wood Dale, IL 60191

National Kitchen Cabinet Association, P.O. Box 6830, Falls Church, VA 22314

National Lumber and Building Material Dealers Association, 40 Ivy Street, S.E., Washington, DC 20003

National Machine Tool Builders Association, 7901 Westpark Drive, McLean, VA 22102

National Office Products Association, 301 N. Fairfax Street, Alexandria, VA 22314

National Paint and Coatings Association, 1500 Rhode Island Avenue, N.W., Washington, DC 20005

National Paper Box and Packaging Association, 231 Kings Highway East, Haddonfield, NJ 08033

National Paper Trade Association, Inc., 111 Great Neck Road, Great Neck, NY 11021

National Parking Association, 1112 16th Street, N.W., Washington, DC 20001

National Retail Hardware Association, 770 N. High School Road, Indianapolis, IN 46214

National Retail Merchants Association, 100 West 31st St., New York, NY 10001

National Shoe Retailers Association, 9861 Broken Land Parkway, Columbia, MD 21046

National Soft Drinks Association, 1101 16th Street, N.W., Washington, DC 20036

National Sporting Goods Association, Lake Leveter Plaza, Building 1699, Wall Street, Chicago, IL 60051

National Tire Dealers and Retreaders Association, 1250 Eye Street, N.W., Suite 400, Washington, DC 20005

National Wholesale Druggist's Association, 105 Oronoco Street, P.O. Box 238, Alexandria, VA 22313

National Wholesale Hardware Association, 1900 Arch Street, Philadelphia, PA 19103

National Jewelry Marketing Association, 1900 Arch Street, Philadelphia, PA 19103

North American Heating and Airconditioning Wholesalers Association, P.O. Box 16790, 1389 Dublin Road, Columbus, OH 43216

North American Wholesale Lumber Association, Inc., 2340 S. Arlington Heights Road, Suite 680, Arlington Heights, IL 60005

Northeastern Retail Lumbermens Association, 339 East Avenue, Rochester, NY 14604

Optical Laboratories Association, P.O. Box 2000, Merrifield, VA 22116

Painting and Decorating Contractors of America, 7223 Lee Highway, Falls Church, VA 22046

Petroleum Equipment Institute, P.O. Box 2380, Tulsa, OK 74014

Petroleum Marketers Association, 420 Vermont Avenue, Suite 1130, Washington, DC 20005

Printing Industries of America, 1730 North Lynn Street, Arlington, VA 22209

Scientific Apparatus Makers Association, 1101 16th Street, N.W., Washington, DC 20006

Shoe Service Institute of America, 112 Calendar Mall, LaGrange, IL 60525

The Society of the Plastics Industry, Inc., 1275 K Street, N.W., Washington, DC 20006

United Fresh Fruit and Vegetable Association, 727 N. Washington Street, Alexandria, VA 22314

Urban Land Institute, 1090 Vermont Avenue, Washington, DC 20005

Wine and Spirit Wholesalers of America, Inc., 1023 15th Street, N.W., Washington, DC 20005

Index